£4·00
R

Robin Pearson
Beverley
March 1989

WALTER BOYD

WALTER BOYD

A Merchant Banker
in the
Age of Napoleon

S. R. Cope

ALAN SUTTON

London School of Economics
and Political Science

1983

Alan Sutton Publishing Limited
17a Brunswick Road
Gloucester GL1 1HG

First published 1983

British Library Cataloguing in Publication Data

Cope, S.R.
 Walter Boyd: a merchant banker in the age of
 Napoleon.
 1. Boyd, Walter   2. Capitalists and
 financiers—England—Biography
 I. Title
 332'.092'4   HG172.B/

 ISBN 0-86299-040-8

Typesetting and origination by
Alan Sutton Publishing Limited
Photoset Times Roman 10/12
Printed in Great Britain
by Redwood Burn Limited, Trowbridge

Contents

Preface

The last few years of the eighteenth century and the early years of the nineteenth saw great changes. The revolution which broke out in 1789 transformed not only France, but other countries as well, and the wars which followed redrew the map of Europe. Great Britain, although spared violent revolution and invasion, felt the impact of war in many ways. Nowhere was this clearer than in banking and currency affairs, seen most dramatically in the loss of gold abroad, the suspension of cash payments by the Bank of England, and the rise in prices. Committees of enquiry were appointed, reports were issued, pamphlets published, and lively controversy ensued, attention being directed mainly to the monetary system as a whole, rather than to the individual institutions which composed it, except, perhaps, for the Bank of England.

One of the reasons why this emphasis has continued is that little material for studies of individual firms of this period has been found. There is a great deal in the Baring and Rothschild archives which has hardly been used, but elsewhere, there appears to be only fragmentary material. It seemed worthwhile, nevertheless, to see what could be told of one merchant banker, Walter Boyd, who was prominent at this period.

Boyd started a banking firm, Boyd, Ker et Cie, in Paris in 1785. At first it was very successful, but after a few years the Revolution forced it to close and its partners to flee. In 1793, Boyd started afresh by forming the mercantile house of Boyd, Benfield & Co. in London, where he quickly became the leading loan contractor. His success was short-lived, for the firm failed in 1800, although it eventually repaid all its creditors in full.

The fate of the books and other records of the Paris firm is not clear. Some were impounded by the authorities and released later to facilitate the firm's liquidation and settlement of the partners' claims for compensation. Most of the material then disappeared. Fortunately, some of the papers of the Paris houses with whom Boyd dealt have survived and are in the Archives Nationales and other depositories. Nearly all of the records of the London firm have been lost. However, some of Boyd's correspondence with ministers, officials, merchants and bankers has found its way into various collections, one of the most useful being the Chatham papers. The evidence given before various committees of enquiry has also yielded much useful information.

Material thus comes from widely scattered sources, and I am indebted to the many people who have made it available to me. I have to thank the Keeper of Public Records for permission to use and quote from Crown copyright records of the Admiralty, Chancery, Court of Bankruptcy, Court of Common Pleas, Exchequer, Foreign Office, Paymaster-General, and War Office, and the Chatham Papers. I have been allowed to use copyright material as well as published works held by a number of libraries. I thank the Syndics of Cambridge University Library for permission to quote from the Pitt Correspondence; the British Library for the use of the Huskisson and Liverpool Papers and the Paul Benfield Papers in the India Office Library and Records Collection; and the National Library of Scotland, for the use of the Melville, Forbes of Fettercairn and Stuart Stevenson Papers, and the account books and papers of Alexander Houston & Co. The Signet Office gave me access to the Sessions Papers and the Scottish Record Office material relating to Boyd, Benfield & Co. and Alexander Houston & Co., including the McDowall of Garthland Papers, to which Dr. T.M. Devine kindly drew my attention.

I have had much help from institutions in the City of London. Guildhall provided London directories; the Bank of England, Court Books, Stock Ledgers and Drawing Accounts Ledgers; Baring Bros. & Co. Ltd, the Northbrook Papers; and Lloyds, extracts from the Shipping Register. Elsewhere, Mr L.J. McDonald, chief archivist of Pilkington Brothers Ltd, gave me information on the British Cast Plate Glass Company. On the Austrian negotiations, in addition to material in the Public Record Office, I drew on Professor Karl. F. Helleiner's work 'The Imperial Loans', and the Director of the Haus-Hof und Staatsarchiv, Vienna, provided copies of documents in his custody. Professor Dr. Marten Buist of the University of Groningen listed for me letters between Boyd and the Hopes held by the Gemeentelijke Archiefdienst, Amsterdam, who made copies for me. The National Archives in Washington, D.C. gave me access to the US Stock Ledgers.

Much of my work was done in the British Library, and in the libraries of the University of London, The London School of Economics and the Institute of Historical Research, and all of them gave me every facility. I remember with gratitude the guidance I received, many years ago, from Professor T.E. Gregory, Professor T.S. Ashton, and Mr P. Barrett Whale, on my original thesis, and more recently, from Professor Arthur John, in revising it. The present text was read by Professor Leslie S. Pressnell of the University of Kent at Canterbury, and I benefited greatly from his comments.

Publication of this book has been ably and sympathetically handled by the LSE Publications Committee under Professor Matthew Anderson, and aided by generous grants from the Isobel Thornley Bequest, the Twenty-Seven Foundation and Guinness, Mahon & Co. Ltd. The last-named gave me, in addition, the invaluable opportunity of learning at first hand, something of the art of merchant banking. Without it, I would never have ventured to write this book.

Introduction

'There is properly no history; only biography.'
Ralph Waldo Emerson, Essays.

The origins of banking in England can be traced to many other occupations, for the receipt of money on deposit and granting credit, essentially banking operations, arose naturally from everyday business life. Some bankers started as manufacturers – for example in the iron and steel, textile and brewing industries. Some came from service occupations, such as scriveners. Many were originally merchants: drapers, mercers, ironmongers, tea dealers, wine merchants, and so on. Sometimes financial and mercantile activities remained in the same firm; in others cases, there were separate firms, one for merchanting and the other for banking, perhaps linked by having one or more partners in common and operating from the same address. The combination did not always last; not infrequently the partners eventually decided to be either merchants or bankers, but not both.[1]

In London, the note-issuing bankers had usually been either goldsmiths or merchants. Their non-banking interests tended to become unimportant at a fairly early stage, although the trend was by no means uniform. They issued notes, accepted money on current accounts and on deposit, made loans, discounted bills and invested in government securities. There were also merchants, usually those in foreign trade, who took a somewhat different path. They did not issue notes, nor did they attempt to attract current and deposit accounts. Typically, they carried accounts for merchants and others whose foreign business they financed, for shipping people whose insurance they placed at Lloyds, and for foreign houses needing a London correspondent. Even when this kind of banking came to represent an important part of their activities, they generally preferred to call themselves merchants rather than bankers. Henry Thornton recorded in his diary in 1802 his mother's opinion that 'to cease being a Merchant in

---

1. For the development of country banking, see Leslie S. Pressnell, *Country Banking in the Industrial Revolution*, Oxford, Clarendon Press, 1956.

1

order to become a Banker was to descend in life'.[2] Nowadays they would be called merchant bankers, a term which did not become current until the end of the nineteenth century, although there are isolated examples of its use much earlier.[3] In a description of the London banking scene at the end of the eighteenth century the term is thus somewhat of an anachronism, but it provides a convenient way of referring to those London merchants who carried out banking activities, and it will be so used in the present study.

The activity most characteristic of a merchant banker was financing overseas trade. Merchants buying goods abroad through correspondents or agents, or receiving goods from abroad on consignment, were accustomed to having bills drawn on them in payment. Sometimes merchants of established credit would be drawn on for goods shipped from one country abroad to another, the beginning of a role for London merchant banks in financing goods which do not touch Great Britain. Exports from Great Britain were typically made on long-term credit (although the terms varied widely) and were paid for in due course by means of remittances, in bills (often in the bills drawn to pay for another British merchant's imports), or in the form of shipments of goods. Eventually bankers developed a technique whereby they undertook, for a commission, to accept drafts drawn to finance merchandise transactions. The merchant banks played a major role in this 'acceptance business', which became the means by which a great deal of the international trade of the second half of the nineteenth century was financed.

Whenever foreign trade developed beyond mere barter, one of the parties, buyer or seller, was involved in a foreign exchange transaction. Thus foreign exchange, the business of dealing in foreign means of payment, such as gold and silver coin and bullion and bills of exchange and similar instruments, originated with merchants, and it remained largely in their hands until well into the nineteenth century. They dealt in foreign currencies not only in payment for goods. When travellers needed money for their journeys in foreign countries, when investors bought securities abroad, or when governments had to subsidise their allies or pay for their own military adventures they usually turned to merchant bankers. The reason was that in the ordinary course of their business, merchants had close connections with others in foreign places, and were in a good position to make and receive payments abroad. Bankers in London and the country, it is true, also handled foreign drafts from time to time for their customers, and sometimes maintained accounts abroad for the purpose, but they did not reckon it to be part of a domestic banker's business to be regularly in the market for foreign exchange. Nor did the Bank of England have any role in the foreign exchange market, other than through its bullion dealings.

Inevitably, the 'funds', the British government stocks dealt in on the Stock Exchange, attracted merchant bankers. They formed groups, made

2. Quoted in F.A.v. Hayek's introduction to *Henry Thornton, an Enquiry into the Nature and Effects of the Paper Credit of Great Britain (1802),* London, George Allen & Unwin, 1939, p. 17.

3. No support has been found for the statement by Leland Hamilton Jenks,*Migration of British Capital to 1875,* New York, Alfred A Knopf, 1927, p. 18, that the term came into use early in the nineteeth century.

up of other bankers, brokers or dealers to contract for government loans. They also undertook 'money' operations, buying stock for immediate delivery and simultaneously selling it at a slightly higher price for delivery at the next six-weekly settlement. Not infrequently they speculated on their own account, sometimes with unfortunate results. In one section of the market they played a major role; thanks to their foreign connections, issuing foreign loans and dealing in foreign securities became their particular preserve.

These were the main activities of the merchant bankers of London from early in the nineteenth century. Individual houses were not equally involved in all of them. There was also some geographical specialisation, often reflecting the countries from which these merchant bankers had come. Nathan Meyer Rothschild, arriving in England in 1797, started in Manchester and moved to London in 1806, where he quickly became involved in remitting subsidies to Britain's continental allies. John Henry von Schröder started in London in 1804, importing wheat from Russia. Kleinworts, established in Cuba in 1792, came to London in 1830 and developed a central European business. Carl Joachim Hambro, originally from Copenhagen, opened in 1839 a house in London, where be built up close banking connections with Scandinavia. But there were no fixed demarcation lines, and over the years firms shifted the focus of their interests.

The wars and political convulsions of the Napoleonic age inevitably brought about many changes in the London scene. New firms sprang up to share in lucrative government contracts or to speculate in government loans on the Stock Exchange. Well-established and prudently-run firms could sustain war losses and adapt themselves to change. Some, starting in the eighteenth century, remained in business well into the nineteenth century. Gurnell, Hoare & Co., the Quakers, starting in 1753, became Harman, Hoare & Co. in 1786 and lasted as Harman & Co. for another sixty years. Reid, Irving & Co., founded by John Rae in 1769, lasted until 1847. John Baring, coming from Exeter, formed in 1763 a merchant firm which is today, as it has been for more than a century, the leading merchant banking house in the City. Others, less fortunate or less skilled, did not survive. Bird, Savage & Bird, Carolina merchants and bankers to the United States, failed in 1803; Smith & Atkinson in 1800 and Charles Herries & Co., much involved in the French Compagnie des Indes, in 1798.

There was also the Scot, Walter Boyd. He started a banking house in Paris in 1785, in the closing years of the monarchy. In the speculative environment of the late 1780s, he advanced rapidly, and soon his firm, Boyd, Ker et Cie, was counted among the leading banking houses in Paris. The Revolution put an end to his prosperous career in the French capital. Forced to flee for his life, he reached England, leaving behind his personal property and the assets of the firm. In London, he started life again within a few months of his arrival, forming in 1793 a mercantile house in partnership with Paul Benfield, an Indian nabob and former customer. With his partner's capital and his own skill and business connections, he rose quickly, and within four years he had become banker to the Austrian Government and the leading loan contractor in the market.

This was the peak. Within another four years the firm became insolvent and its partners bankrupt. In Paris, to recover the assets of Boyd, Ker et Cie after the peace of Amiens, he was detained when war broke out again in 1803, and spent long, frustrating years in internment. By 1821, thanks to Waterloo, he had recovered enough of the assets of the Paris firm to repay all his creditors, and was established in England in considerable comfort. At intervals in his crowded life he found opportunity to contribute to the currency controversies of the day, earning a permanent place in the economic literature of the period. Well might Sir John Clapham in his history of the Bank of England comment: 'A resilient man'.[4]

This is the story of Walter Boyd, the banker.

4.   Sir John Clapham, *The Bank of England, a History*, London, Cambridge University Press, 1944, vol II, p. 18.

CHAPTER I

Banker in Paris

M. Boyd est un homme courageux autant que clairvoyant. Il a d'ailleurs toujours
du bon papier en portfeuille.........
Barthélémy Huber to Jacques Necker, November 1789.

Practically nothing is known about Walter Boyd's family and early life. He was born on 18 November 1753,[1] possibly in the north of Scotland, but the names of his parents are unknown. He had a brother, Archibald, and there may have been other brothers, and sisters. He is said to have been educated in Amsterdam and Switzerland, and to have served an apprenticeship with a mercantile house in France,[2] but reliable information about his career dates only from 1774, when, twenty years of age, he became an agent to manage farm properties at Cressy and Heckington in Lincolnshire, owned by Patrick Heron of Heron in Kirkcudbright. In the late 1770s these properties fell on bad times, and Boyd, after recommending to Heron drastic cuts in rents, decided in 1781, at the age of twenty-eight, to seek better prospects elsewhere.[3]

Without influential sponsors, he soon discovered that he had slight chances of obtaining a suitable appointment. There was, however, a compatriot in London, who had extensive mercantile interests – Sir Robert Herries. In addition to a house in Barcelona, Herries had interests in two London firms. One was the merchant firm of Sir Robert Herries & Co. in Jeffery's Square, in the City, in which he, his two younger brothers, Charles and William, and his wife's brother, George Henderson had each a quarter share. The other was the firm founded in 1772 under the name of the London Exchange Banking Company to provide travellers with cheques they could cash in a number of European places, and which became known, like the City house, as Sir Robert Herries & Co. Its partners included the four who were partners of the City house, together with two partners of Coutts & Co., Edinburgh, and Sir William Maxwell

1. Richard Holworthy, *The Monumental Inscriptions in the Church and Churchyard of Bromley, Co. Kent*, London. Michel Hughes and Clarke, 1922, p. 16.
2. *Papers of Thomas Jefferson*, ed. Julian P. Boyd, Princetown, Princetown University Press, 1950, Jefferson to Boyd, April 16 1790, vol. 16, p. 311; [Joseph Lancaster], The Bank — The Stock Exchange — The Bankers . . . 1821, p. 25.
3. Boyd to Patrick Heron, 30 June 1781, Boyd to Andrew Stuart, 6 Aug 1781, Stuart Stevenson papers, ff 1–3, NLS, MS8281.

and William Johnson Pulteney. A year earlier, in 1780, war had broken out between England and Holland, and one of its consequences was to make the neutral Austrian Netherlands a most convenient base for international mercantile activities. To exploit this situation, Sir Robert Herries decided to set up a mercantile house in Ostend for his youngest brother, William, who would retire from the two London firms.[4]

Boyd, hearing of these developments, turned to the idea of Ostend as the field for his future activities. He did not know Sir Robert Herries personally, but obtained an introduction, apparently through a Mr. Irving. What transpired is not recorded, but the result was that within about a year, Boyd was in the Austrian Netherlands and in touch with William Herries. Through Herries he became associated with the old-established house in Brussels, Veuve Nettine et Fils, who had an active mercantile and financial business, and were bankers to the Austrian administration in the Netherlands. It was managed by Édouard Dominique Sebastian de Walckiers, son of Dieudonnée Louise Josèphe de Nettine, who had inherited it from her mother.

In February 1782, Walckiers, for Veuve Nettine at Fils, and William Herries, for his house at Ostend, took the bold and imaginative step of forming the Private Bank in the Austrian Netherlands (Banque particulière dans les Pays-Bas autrichiennes) with a capital of 500,000 florins (roughly £36,000). Seeking help in running this bank, Walckiers and Herries turned to Walter Boyd and a certain John William Ker, from Edinburgh, some three years Boyd's junior, and made them assistant managers (secrétaires de direction).[5] The bank was a success: in 1783 its capital was doubled to one million florins, and in the following year doubled again to two million, by which time it had opened offices in Brussels, Ostend, Bruges and Ghent. It provided banking services for private individuals as well as for businessmen; it accepted current and deposit accounts, made payments for customers in other towns, discounted bills and held customers' securities for them and managed their portfolios. Thanks to their position, Boyd and Ker gained valuable banking experience, and had the opportunity of getting to know important customers of the bank and the firms associated with Veuve Nettine et Fils. These connections were to be important in Boyd's future career.

It was not long before Boyd and Ker were looking beyond the confines of the Austrian Netherlands. There were several places which offered opportunities for young and ambitious men. Boyd once referred to 'The three great places of Exchange upon which the commercial circulation of Europe depends . . . London, Paris and Amsterdam.'[6] Each had its advantages and drawbacks. Paris had the advantage of being near Brussels, where Veuve Nettine were based, and communication between the two

4. Jacob Myron Price, *France and the Chesapeake* . . . Ann Arbor, University of Michigan Press, 1973, pp. 622–3. The Austrian Netherlands coresponded roughly to present-day Belgium, without the provinces of Liège and Limburg. Pulteney (1729–1805) later became Sir William Pulteney, Bt.
5. Herbert Lüthy, *La Banque protestante en France*. . . vol. II S.E.V.P.E.N., Paris, 1961, pp. 657, and 660.
6. *Third Report from the Committee of Secrecy on the Outstanding Demands of the Bank, 1797,* Evidence of Walter Boyd, Reports, Committees, 1826, vol. III.

cities would be easy. Boyd and Ker both spoke French, so that there would not be the language problem, which might arise if they established themselves in Amsterdam. There were many banks in Paris, and an active Bourse, giving plenty of scope for dealing in securities and foreign exchange. Foreign bankers were accepted readily in Paris, and the fact that there was no bank there with British partners would give Boyd and Ker an advantage in competing for British tourist and other business. At the time, the decision no doubt seemed sound, and none of those participating in it could have had any inkling of the dramatic events which were to take place in France in the ensuing decade.

In 1785, France was predominantly rural, and of the estimated population of twenty-six million, only two million lived in towns. Manufacturing was largely domestic, or at least small-scale, and the peasants followed agricultural practices little changed in centuries. Movement of produce within France was greatly hampered by local duties and tolls, and was not much helped by the network of good roads, radiating from Paris, which had been built in the middle of the century. Foreign trade was handled mainly in the great ports, cities in themselves, Marseilles, Bordeaux, Nantes, and Le Havre, which together had a population approaching that of Paris itself. There were some 800,000 people in Paris, many of them living in the narrow streets within the area formerly confined by the city walls. When Boyd arrived, builders were working on another ring of walls. This was the customs barrier of the Farmers-General, which was to encircle the city, embracing not only the old city, but wide areas outside, some not yet built on, including the wooded area known as the Champs Elisées. To the west, beyond the customs barrier, was the Bois de Boulogne.

Paris had few manufacturing industries, and its main business was trade in articles of consumption, and banking and finance. There were many merchants and bankers, providing links with the ports and places abroad, and playing an active role in the 'lively and dangerous' Bourse.[7] There was the Caisse d'Escompte, not quite a central bank, but an important source of credit for merchants, bankers, speculators and investors, and providing, indirectly, the means by which the chronic state deficits were covered. Above all, Paris was the capital of France, the Court was there and the royal treasury and other departments of government. It was also the intellectual centre of France, 'la ville où les passions prodigues sont le plus en fermentation.[8]

The Caisse d'Escompte played a major role in the money market. Inspired by the financier and speculator, Isaac Panchaud, and created by Turgot, Controller-General of Finance, under a decree (Arrêt du Conseil) of 24 March 1776, its basic purpose was to discount commercial paper at low rates, and generally to keep interest rates down. For bills with a currency of over thirty days, its maximum rate was four and a half per cent. To be eligible, bills had to carry two good names, and holders of

7. George V. Taylor, *The Paris Bourse on the Eve of the Revolution, 1781–1789*, American Historical Review, vol. 67 1961–2, p. 951.
8. H.G.V. Requeti, Comte de Mirabeau, *De La Caisse d'Escompte*, Paris, 1785, pp. 18–19.

current accounts had priority. A committee of three met every Monday, Wednesday and Friday to fix the amount of bills to be taken. Discounting had to be restricted if the cash in hand were less than one-third of liabilities, and had to stop if the proportion fell below one-quarter. Discounting bills was far from being the only activity of the Caisse. It accepted money on current account, made and received payments for its customers, free of charge, and held their securities. It dealt in gold and silver, but was not permitted to deal in merchandise, or engage in shipping, insurance, or commerce, or borrow at interest or at sight. Its notes, some forty million livres of which were outstanding in 1783, circulated freely, particularly in the Paris area, although they were not legal tender.[9]

While the Caisse had been intended for the mercantile community, it was soon used, indirectly, to help the ailing Treasury. The rates of return on annuities (rentes) issued to the public were high, and by 1785 it had become the practice for investors and speculators to take up loans issued by the Treasury, paying for them by drawing on their Paris bankers bills which were then discounted with the Caisse. The often substantial difference between the return yielded by the annuities and the discount rate of the Caisse was divided between the accepting bank and the subscriber. There might be a further profit to be divided: the annuities usually carried full interest from the date of issue, although payment for them was made in instalments spread over several months. Discount operations were not only for French residents: bankers and merchants abroad would operate similarly. Foreign business was facilitated by the fact that many of the Paris bankers who had come from abroad retained links with their native countries, their number including descendents of French refugees from Geneva. Over one-half of the thirteen directors (administrateurs) of the Caisse were members of, or connected with, banking firms, several of these being of foreign origin.

The Caisse, which, in part, had been modelled on the Bank of England, had many of the features of a central bank. Its major weakness was the rigid provision in its constitution governing its discount rate, which led it into financing at second hand the budget deficits of the state.[10]

The Bourse (Bourse pour Negociants) had been established under a decree (Arrêt du Conseil) of 1724, although the regulation of brokers (agents de change) started much earlier. Admission of brokers and supervision of dealing were the responsibility of the Lieutenant-General of Police of Paris, who had three officers to maintain order. The number of brokers was limited: in 1785 the maximum number was forty, but it was soon to be raised to sixty. A broker was not permitted to deal outside the Bourse, to enter into partnership with anyone not a broker, or to deal on his own account. In theory, brokers had a semi-public function; they carried a medal (jeton) which bore the device 'ad reipublicae utilitatem', and they were closely regulated, both by their own corporation, and by

9. Alph. Courtois, fils, *Histoire de la Banque de France*. . ., Paris, Librairie de Guillaumon et Cie, 1875, pp. 69–70. Up to 1789, the livre can be taken as roughly equivalent to ten pence sterling.
10. Robert Bigo, *La Caisse d'Escompte (1776–1793)*. . . Paris, Les Presses Universitaires de France, 1927.

public authority. A broker was required to record each deal in a journal, and render a contract note, and was not to disclose his principal's business. Only a few years earlier, in 1781, a regulation had been issued requiring a broker to put up real estate or cash as a guarantee that the contracts he negotiated would be duly settled. Commission was a quarter per cent., payable half by the buyer and half by the seller.

Merchants, bankers and others could deal between themselves for their own account, without employing a broker, but only a broker was allowed to act as intermediary. This rule was often disregarded, and there were many who slipped in and made clandestine deals. Dealing took place daily between ten o'clock in the morning and one o'clock in the afternoon in the courtyard of the Hotel de Nevers, which was occupied by the Compagnie des Indes. Under a decree of March 1774, an enclosure three feet high had been erected in the courtyard, and it was there that the brokers congregated.[11]

There was a great deal of speculation on the Bourse, commonly by a speculator and his banker working on joint account (compte à demi), and financed by bills discounted with the Caisse. Much of the dealing was for time (marché à terme), the time contracts for a particular security sometimes exceeding the total amount of the issue. An attempt to check speculation was made in August 1785, when a decree was made declaring deals for future settlement void, unless the securities were deposited at the time the contract was made. However, speculation continued, and was to reach a peak in 1788.

The securities dealt in consisted largely of state annuities (rentes), and in the preceding decade more than 1,100 million livres of them had been issued. They were mainly of two kinds. Annuities bearing a fixed rate of interest, but without a date for redemption of principal (rentes perpetuelles), amounted to about 600 million livres. Life annuities (rentes viagères) amounted to over 500 million livres. Some were based on the life of one person, at whose death payments ceased. Others were based on the lives of a number of persons (sometimes as many as 100), known as heads (têtes), and payments on them decreased as the heads died, ceasing altogether on the death of the last head. Life annuities were offered by the Treasury at rates which usually varied according to the number of heads. For example, an annuity of one head would be offered at ten per cent., on two heads at eight-and-a-half or nine per cent., and on three or four heads at eight per cent. These terms applied irrespective of the ages of the heads, and since subscribers could select the heads on which their annuities were to be based, they usually selected children at an age at which their expectation of life was reckoned to be greatest (five to seven years of age); girls were preferred to boys, and the Canton of Geneva was the favoured place from which to select them, as living conditions there were thought to be healthier than elsewhere.

These annuities were also popular because they could be held by foreigners, whether resident in France or not, even if they were nationals

11. François Olivier-Martin, *L'Organisation corporative de la France,* Librairie du Recueil Sirey, Paris, 1938, pp. 279–281; *Almanach Royal,* 1785, pp. 471–2.

of a country at war with France, and they were exempt from French taxation. Many were held by investors in Geneva. It was common for blocks of annuities to be divided into 'billets' of 1000 livres which, indorsed in blank, passed from hand to hand as bearer instruments. Annuities could also be held on an account (dépôt libre) with the Caisse d'Escompte (when they became transferable by book entry), at a charge of 0.0625 per cent. for six months. They were in the form of printed documents, which listed the names and birth dates of the heads. Each billet bore a distinctive number and carried a sheet of coupons, which were detached as annuity payments fell due. In form, they were much like a modern bond.[12]

Of the shares quoted on the Bourse, those most actively dealt in were those of the Caisse d'Escompte and of the Compagnie des Indes. The Compagnie des Indes was formed in 1785 with a capital of twenty million livres in shares (portions d'intérêt) of 1000 livres, 14,000 shares being offered to the public and 6,000 reserved for the directors (administrateurs). The 'Indes' soon attracted speculators and within a few months they were quoted at 1240 livres for settlement at the end of 1786. The shares of the Banco Nacional de San Carlos, which had been formed in Madrid in 1782, with an exclusive concession from Charles III to export silver dollars (piastres, sometimes called Spanish dollars, or pieces of eight), and shares of the Compagnie des Eaux de Paris, sponsored by Isaac Panchaud, were also dealt in actively.[13]

To hold their securities and collect payments on them, investors turned to the banks. Parisiens and foreigners would usually deposit their securities with a Paris bank: investors elsewhere would mostly use a local banker, who would send the securities to his Paris correspondent. This 'service des rentes', as it was called, although it included other securities as well, was an important and remunerative business, for the banks charged one per cent. for collecting annuity and other payments, and for handling purchases and sales. For the sake of convenience, shares and annuities were frequently registered in the name of a senior clerk of the custodian bank, and because payments on annuities were made in alphabetical order, according to the first name of the holder, it was usual to register them in the name of someone whose first name began with 'A'. For example, the banking house of Greffulhe, Montz et Cie had annuities in the name of Armand Pierre Marie Bévière,[14] who was chief of their service des rentes. It was the accepted practice of Paris banks to vote the shares they held for customers and corespondents as though they were their own, which sometimes gave them great influence at shareholders' meetings.

Dealing in foreign exchange, which also took place on the Bourse, was limited, in theory at least, to bankers authorised by the Controller-General of Finance to deal in drafts and remittances (banques pour les traites et remises de place en place). A list of authorised dealers was issued yearly, and to be admitted, a newcomer had to be proposed by ten bankers

12. For a further description of life annuities, see Lüthy, op. cit., vol. II, pp. 469–478.
13. Jean Bouchary, *Le Marché des Changes de Paris*. . . Paris, Paul Hartmann, 1937, p. 15.
14. Guy Antonetti, *Une Maison de Banque à Paris au XVIIIe siècle: Greffulhe, Montz et Cie (1789–1793)*, Editions Cujas, 1963, pp. 92–4, Lüthy, op.cit, vol. II, p. 683.

already authorised. In 1785 there were fifty-three names on the list. Exchange rates were fixed by the leading bankers in the light of the latest advices of rates abroad, the scarcity or abundance of bills in various currencies in the market, and political news. Acting as intermediaries between dealers were brokers (agents de change) and authorised clerks (commis-courtiers). The currency of France was the livre tournois, which was a unit of account, not a coin, and it was the écu, a silver coin equivalent to three livres, which was in general circulation. Some foreign exchange rates quoted on the Paris Bourse were expressed in livres, others in écus.

Several of the places with which Paris dealt had banks to provide merchants with money having a constant value in silver. This was known as banco money, and because the money in everyday use, known as current money, tended to be debased, banco money was at a premium, or agio, compared with current money. Amsterdam had such a bank and there, banco money carried an agio of about five per cent. There was also a bank at Hamburg, where banco money had an agio of twenty-four to twenty-five per cent. In Paris, Amsterdam was quoted in groots (pence Flemish) for an écu, there being forty pence to the florin. Hamburg was quoted in so many livres for 100 marcs banco. London was quoted in pence sterling for an écu. There was no official 'Course of the Exchange', but several news-papers published rates for Amsterdam, Hamburg, London, Cadiz, Madrid, Genoa, and Leghorn.

The period between the date a bill was drawn and the date on which it fell due had been fixed at thirty days by the French Commercial Code of 1673, the period being known as the 'usance'. Before the end of the eighteenth century, however, it had become common to draw for longer periods, and by 1790, exchange quotations were usually for bills at sixty days. There was, however, no uniform rule, and the currency of a bill was determined according to the purpose for which it was drawn, and the place at which it was payable.[15]

Banking and dealing in securities and foreign exchange would be the principal activities of Boyd and Ker over the next few years. For this purpose, they set up the firm of Boyd, Ker et Cie, in the middle of 1785, under a partnership agreement for the customary term of six years, Boyd and Ker being full partners. It has been suggested that there were also two limited partners (associés commanditaires), William Herries of Ostend and a Baron de Watemael Kessel of Brussels, but documentary evidence to support this suggestion has not been found[16] Although newly-established, the firm soon gained a leading position among Paris banking houses. By 1787, they had been authorised to deal in foreign exchange, their name apearing as 'Boyeker' in the list of authorised dealers published in the Almanach Royal. At first they were at 4 rue d'Amboise, a short street running between the rue Basse du Rempart and the rue de Richelieu. In

15.   A good account of the Paris foreign exchange market is in Bouchary, *Le Marché des Changes de Paris*, op. cit.
16.   The suggestion is in Jean Bouchary, *Les Manieurs d'Argent à Paris à la fin du XVIIIe siécle*, Librairie des Sciences Politiques et Social, Paris, 1940–3, vol. II, p. 123, and in Lüthy, op. cit., p. 660.

1788, Boyd bought for 200,000 livres 9 rue de Grammont, to the left of the house of the Compagnie des Indes, and after making extensive repairs and alterations, used it both as residence and counting house.[17]

To operate effectively, Boyd had to build up a network of correspondents, in France and abroad. He formed connections with merchants in Lyons, Nantes, Honfleur, Calais and Dunkirk. In the Austrian Netherlands, Boyd, Ker et Cie corresponded with J. Vercour et Cie and L'Arbalète et Eicke (both of Liège), as well as with Veuve Nettine et Fils. In Hamburg their correspondents were Parish & Co. and Martin Dorner: in London John and George Ward, Smith & Atkinson, Richard Buller & Co. and Harman, Hoare & Co. The Herries' Jeffery's Square business had been taken over by Sir Robert Herries' younger brother, Charles, in 1784, and had an active relationship with Boyd, Ker et Cie.

Boyd's connection with Hope & Co. was close, dating from the time he was in Brussels, if not earlier, and his letters to the firm and to Henry Hope, one of the partners, had somewhat the tone of those of a student to his tutor. Much of his correspondence merely retailed market gossip about the credit standing and troubles of individual firms, but he was clearly anxious to do business with Hope & Co. Not long after they had set up in Paris, for example, Boyd, Ker et Cie were offered at par 'several millions' of the rentes viagères of 1782 at ten per cent. These rentes had to be sold abroad and Boyd promptly offered participations to Hope & Co. and Veuve Nettine et Fils, describing the deal as 'an opportunity which may never return'. Hope nevertheless turned the offer down, saying that they did not want to increase their holdings in French funds. Nettine's said that they would take an amount described as 'considerable'. To Boyd's very great disappointment, however, the deal fell through.[18]

A few months later Boyd was able to engage in an important transaction with Hope & Co., although, significantly, he was not offered a major part in it. In August 1787 Henry Hope conceived the idea of gaining control of the highly volatile cochineal market by buying up stocks in Cadiz, Amsterdam and London. For this purpose he proposed to John and Francis Baring and to François Louis Joseph de Laborde-Méréville, son of the banker, Jean Joseph, Marquis de Laborde, to form a syndicate with them. Laborde was not interested, but the Barings were, and the deal went ahead, with Hopes taking three quarters and Barings one quarter. In Cadiz, the principal centre, Thomas Ryan & Co., merchants who were reputed to know the cochineal market, were to buy for cash for syndicate account. To finance these purchases, Henry Hope arranged two credits, one with Vandenyver Frères et Cie of Paris, the other with Boyd, Ker et Cie. As a speculation the operation was a disaster. Hope had seriously misjudged the size of the cochineal stocks in various markets, and Hopes and Barings lost heavily[19] Boyd was fortunate that his rôle in this deal was only that of a banker, not of a syndicate participant.

17. Claims on France, PRO, T78/9 award II.
18. Boyd, Ker et Cie to Hope & Co., 22 Dec. 1786 and 5 Jan., 1787, Hope Archives.
19. Marten G. Buist, *At Spes non Fracta, Hope & Co. 1770_1815*, Martinus Nijhof, The Hague, 1974, pp. 431–451, and p. 677.

Boyd was clearly anxious to show to the Hopes that he was able to act vigorously and independently. At the beginning of 1787, credit was tight, with two-and-a-half per cent. per month being paid for money. In this situation, the publication of a draft edict for creating a new Caisse d'Escompte unsettled the market, and caused the existing Caisse to lose specie and restrict its discounts. In a rather smug letter to Hope & Co. Boyd related his reaction to the crisis: 'For our own part our idea was that instead of taking out specie, everybody should have carried specie to the Bank (sic); but we pretend not to set up for Reformers and therefore contented ourselves with practising what it would have been in vain to preach. We will however confess that we considered it necessary to be prepared for whatever might have happened, and that we ordered very considerable sums to be sent to us in specie which we carried to the Caisse d'Escompte (where we keep the greatest part of our funds) and at same time made arrangements by which, on the supposition that the Notes had been no longer convertible into Cash, we could have done without them. All this we did quietly and of our own accord. . .'[20]

The crisis passed, but unfortunately the respite was only short, for after a troubled year in which the Treasury was intervening in its affairs, there was a further run on the Caisse in August 1788. The directors secretly solicited a decree suspending cash payments, and making the notes of the Caisse legal tender. At a meeting of bankers this action was generally approved. Only two objected: one was Jean Frederic Perregaux, and the other was Boyd. Later, Boyd wrote: 'On no occasion did I ever take so warm a part against any measure . . . I did so from the most intimate conviction that ruin must inevitably be the consequence.'[21] Ruinous it was.

Boyd's Paris customers included diplomats, such as Thomas Jefferson, United States Minister in 1788 and 1789,[22] and Count Mercy-Argenteau, Austrian Minister, whose account no doubt came through Veuve Nettine et Fils. The link with Herries still remained strong. Sir Robert Herries' business of supplying the Farmers-General with American tobacco brought him to Paris from time to time, and it was believed in the market, probably correctly, that Boyd, Ker et Cie acted as Herries' agent early in 1791, in bidding for a contract to supply the proposed tobacco regie.[23]

Boyd, Ker et Cie, like other Paris bankers, were in the profitable business of catering for the needs of well-to-do English tourists, even if they did not provide the service which Perregaux (le banquier de toutes les dames galantes de Paris) was said to supply for visiting Englishmen.[24] Sir Robert Herries had certainly considered that cashing circular notes and letters of credit was profitable enough to justify his opening in 1787 an office in Paris for this purpose, in association with the bankers Girardot, Haller et Cie, under the name of John Forbes & Co.[25]

20. Boyd to Hope & Co., 12 Feb, 1787, Hope Archives.
21. Walter Boyd, *A Letter to the Rt. Hon. W. Pitt. . .*,London, J. Wright, 1801, pp. 104–5.
22. Papers of Thomas Jefferson, op. cit., vol. 14, p. 11, vol. 15. p. 9.
23. Alexander Donald to William Short, 15 Mar. 1791, Papers of William Short, f. 2342, Library of Congress.
24. Lüthy op. cit., p. 324n, p. 626, and p. 720.
25. Bouchary, op. cit., vol. II, p. 125.

One of the English visitors Boyd was able to help was Lord Bolingbroke, who wrote to Boyd, Ker et Cie early in 1788 to ask whether they could arrange for him to hunt on a nobleman's estate. It so happened that one of their customers was the rich Joseph François Xavier de Pestre, Comte de Seneffe et de Tournout. Born in Brussels in 1757, he had settled in Paris in 1786, and to his hereditary estates in the Netherlands he had added extensive estates in France and several houses in Paris. Soon after arriving he had become heavily involved in speculating in shares of the Compagnie des Indes. When, therefore, Boyd told him about Bolingbroke's request, Seneffe felt it wise to co-operate, and wrote in fulsome terms to Boyd, Ker et Cie, expressing his readiness to place one of his properties, the Château de la Ferté, at his lordship's disposal.[26]

At this moment, Seneffe needed Boyd's help. At the end of 1787, he had subscribed for three million livres of an issue by the Treasury of 120 million livres of rentes, payable ten per cent. on subscription, and the balance in monthly instalments of fifteen per cent. He either lacked ready funds, or having them, did not want to lock them up to such a large extent. He therefore asked Boyd, Ker et Cie whether, if he deposited the annuities with them, they would grant him a credit to a like amount, which he would use by drawing drafts on them. He was willing to pay the usual commission of one-third of one per cent. on the drafts they accepted and the usual one per cent. on the annuity payments they collected. Accepted by Boyd, Ker et Cie, the bills could be readily discounted at the Caisse d'Escompte, and at maturity would be paid out of the proceeds of new bills drawn in similar fashion. To Boyd, this seemed to be good business, involving little risk, and he promptly agreed to it, but prudently reduced, banker-like, the amount of the credit to 900,000 livres to provide some margin for price fluctuations.[27] Seneffe, too, found this attractive, for money rates were rising, and did in fact go up to twenty per cent. in August 1788.

Boyd, Ker et Cie made loans to other members of the aristocracy. When in April 1788 the Marchaux des Entelles wanted to obtain a one-third share in the administration of the estates of Louis XVI, they advanced the 333,000 livres required.[28] A year later, they started to make to the Duc de Luxembourg a series of unsecured advances. Another customer was Louis Philippe Joseph, Duc d'Orléans. Dissolute, a spend-thrift, and lacking ability to put his estates on a profitable basis, he was heavily in debt. In March 1789, he created an obligation of two million florins at four-and-a-half per cent., secured on his hereditary estates at Avesnes, in favour of Christian van Osy en Zoon, merchant bankers of Rotterdam, with a view to their placing them with investors. A year later, they had not been sold, and Orléans used 200,000 florins of them as part of the security for advances from Greffulhe, Montz et Cie. This was not enough, and he applied to other Paris bankers, Le Couteulx et Cie and Tourton et Ravel,

26.   Bouchary, op. cit., vol. II, pp. 14–21, and p. 124, Comte de Seneffe to Boyd, Ker et Cie, 2 Feb, 1788; Taylor, op. cit., p. 970.
27.   Bouchary, op. cit., vol II, pp. 40–1.
28.   Commissioners for French Claims, Minute Book, 18 Oct 1814, PRO, T. 78/267, p. 545.

for loans secured on 700,000 florins of similar annuities, and to Boyd, Ker et Cie, who lent him 800,000 livres against 500,000 florins of annuities.

Shortly after this, Boyd decided that it would be better to acquire the florin annuities outright, instead of holding them as collateral, and in February 1791 he purchased from Orléans the 700,000 florins of annuity held by Le Couteulx and Tourton et Ravel and the 500,000 florins collateral held by his own firm, at a discount of fifteen per cent. payable in livres.[29] This transaction was made for account of Édouard de Walckiers, who had long been associated with Boyd, and who was soon to join the firm as a partner. In June, four months later, Boyd, Ker et Cie bought the annuities from Walckiers on the basis of two-and-two-thirds livres to a florin, crediting him with 3,200,000 livres. On its face, this appeared to be a bad deal for Boyd, Ker et Cie. Their object, however, according to Walckiers, was to obtain some protection against the depreciation of the livre.[30] The annuities were not only expressed in a sound currency, the Dutch florin, they also contained a clause specifying payment in gold or silver coin 'to the exclusion of paper money of any kind.'

Pressed by his creditors, Orléans tried to raise money on his other assets. One of these was the dowry, represented by a five per cent. obligation of the French treasury, amounting to 4,158,850 livres, which had originally been given by Louis XV to his aunt, Louise Elizabeth d'Orléans, and which he had inherited. In October 1790 he applied to Boyd, Ker et Cie, who bought from him a one-half share in the dowry for 2,079,425 livres under his guarantee. The purchase price was credited to his account in Boyd, Ker et Cie's books and in effect used to repay earlier advances. The other half of the dowry, which he transferred to Greffulhe, Montz et Cie in December 1790.[31], was no doubt applied in similar fashion. In the revolutionary atmosphere of the period, the transaction did nothing to improve Boyd's reputation in republican circles. On 9 January 1791, the journal, *Le Patriote Français,* attacked it vehemently, referring to the 'prodigalities and follies of Orléans, which had cost France inculculable amounts of gold, to which it was indecent to add another theft.[32] Two months later, Boyd, undeterred by newspaper attacks, made a further arrangement with Orléans. This was the purchase by Boyd, Ker et Cie for one million livres of an annuity of 200,000 livres paid by the French treasury on Orlean's life, which had cost 2,500,000 in 1783.[33] At that time, giving the forty-four-year-old Orléans a life expectancy of five years might have seemed conservative. In the end, it proved to be not conservative enough, for he was guillotined in 1793.

Not long after his intervention in the crisis of the Caisse d'Escompte, Boyd became involved in the complex manoeuvring for control of the Compagnie des Indes, which had been formed by the Minister of Finance, Calonne, in 1785 as a result of the efforts of Girardot, Haller et Cie and

29. Lüthy op.cit p. 632.
30. Declaration by Walckiers, 6 December, 1818, Claims on France, PRO, T. 78/9, award 148.
31. Lüthy, op. cit., p. 632.
32. Bouchary, op. cit., vol. II, p. 125.
33. Claims on France, PRO, T. 78/5, award 56.

the London merchant banking firm of Bourdieu, Chollet & Bourdieu. An important part of the business of the company was the payment in London of bills issued in India to Englishmen wanting to remit money to England and the insurance of ships in the India trade and their cargoes. For this purpose the company made an agreement with the English East India Company under which its London business would be handled by Bourdieu, Chollet & Bourdieu. This firm was not on particularly good terms with Thomas Simon Bérard, the company's president and director-general. He, supported by a number of directors, succeeded in March 1786 in having the London business transferred to Charles Herries & Co., merchants of Jeffery's Square.

Dissension on the company's board continued. In 1789 certain of the directors became restive at what they regarded as the autocratic ways of Bérard, and the annual general meeting in August decided to appoint 'commissaires' to supervise five of the company's departments. Bérard, however, was able to have some of his friends appointed. Among them was Boyd, who with another banker, Sabatier, was nominated to supervise the cash department, and who, with the bankers Abbema, Greffulhe and Sabatier, was to supervise purchasing. A few months later the board co-opted the commissaires to assist in drawing up accounts for submission to shareholders. This somewhat makeshift arrangement did not last very long, for in August the shareholders approved new statutes, which enabled them to appoint a new board. Bérard fell in the following November, Boyd and Greffulhe retired at the same time and the London agency business handled by Charles Herries & Co. went back to Bourdieu, Chollet & Bourdieu, who shared it with John Henry Cazenove & Co. What part Boyd played in these events the records do not reveal. He was close to Bérard, and no doubt supported, as far as he could, the interests of Charles Herries & Co.[34]

If, amidst all these pressing problems and preoccupations, Boyd looked back to his start in the French capital, he would have been justified in feeling well satisfied with the progress he had made. In 1785, when he arrived, he had little except some support from friends in Brussels. He now had one of the leading banking houses in Paris, with an active securities business, wealthy customers at home and a network of correspondents abroad. Currency stability was threatened by the over-issue of assignats, but this, so far, he had been able to turn to his own advantage. The future was uncertain, however, and his satisfaction might well have been tempered by a nagging fear of political developments he was powerless to influence.

34. For these events, see Holden Furber, *John Company at Work,* Harvard University Press, 1948, chapter II; Lüthy, op.cit., pp. 673–685.

CHAPTER II

Paris Becomes Untenable

'. . . il est imprudent d'avouer que l'on spécule sur le change, sur l'argent, sur l'or, et que sa fortune croît avec la dépréciation de l'assignat et la hausse du prix des denrées, quand la guillotine est installée en permanence'[1]

Jean Bouchary

The original partnership agreement constituting Boyd, Ker et Cie was to expire at the end of June 1791, a fateful time in the history of the Revolution. On June 20 there was the flight of the royal family to Varennes, and a few days later their humiliating return to the capital, virtually prisoners. These dramatic events provided a sombre background for the discussions between Boyd and his associates regarding the future structure of the firm. So far, their business had not been touched. The bourgeois elements in the National Assembly seemed to be in control, and there seemed reason to believe that business could continue much as before.

The new partnership agreement, made on 30 June 1791, ran, like the first agreement, for six years. In addition to Boyd and Ker, who were full partners, the agreement provided for the admission of three limited partners (commanditaires). One of the three was the Vicomte Édouard de Walckiers, whose association with Boyd and Ker, as already related, went back nearly a decade. He was born in 1758, the son of the Adrien Ange de Walckiers and Dieudonnée Louise Josèphe de Nettine, who inherited the family banking business of Veuve Nettine et Fils. On her death, the business passed to her husband, and came under the management of their son, Édouard. A handsome and flamboyant figure, he had taken full advantage of the wealth and social position of his family, and his grand style of living earned him the nick-name 'Édouard le Magnifique'. He and his wife, Barbe Marie Thérèse de Reul, maintained a splendid house in Brussels, facing the park, and at nearby Laken he built and furnished a pavilion in the Italian manner. Among his official positions was that of financial counsellor to the Austrian Emperor, Joseph II, and director of the royal treasury.[2]

In 1789, imbued with the spirit of the times, Walckiers saw himself as

---

1. Bouchary, op. cit., vol. I, p. 9.
2. *Biographie Nationale . . . de Belgique*, Brussels, Éstablissements Emile Bruylant, 1936–8, vol. 26, p. 38.

the Lafayette of the Netherlands, and took a leading role in the popular and democratic insurrection of de Vonck. He soon clashed with the clerical and reactionary elements in the movement, and in March 1790, with his father and William Herries, he took refuge in France.[3] In Paris, even in 1791, Boyd, Ker et Cie could make use of his family and social connections, as well as his capital contribution of one and a half million livres.[4]

The second limited partner admitted was François Louis Joseph de Laborde-Méréville. He was the eldest son of Jean Joseph, Marquis de Laborde, who had made a fortune as a banker in Bayonne, and of Rosalie Claire Josèphe de Nettine, the sister of Dieudonnée de Nettine, and he was thus Édouard de Walckiers' cousin. François, born in Paris in 1761, was brought into his father's banking business, and while still young reached a high position at Court. In the early days of the Revolution, his liberal ideas gave him some protection. In the National Assembly he opposed Necker's plan for an issue of legal-tender paper money, and in December 1789 presented a plan which he, and, it was said, Boyd, had worked out. The plan was to set up a private bank, which would pay off the liabilities of the state and increase revenues by reforming the tax collection system. In return, the bank would have the privilege of note issue. Laborde claimed that he could raise 200 million livres of capital for the bank by the issue of 50,000 shares. The idea, however, failed to gain support, and he retired from public life. Laborde was not only a wealthy aristocrat with a penchant for politics, he was familiar with mercantile and banking operations. On one occasion in 1790, he bought up all the sugar and coffee available in Bordeaux, in anticipation of trouble in the West Indies,[5] revealing an aptitude for speculative operations which accorded well with those of the firm's other partners.

The third partner to be admitted was Boyd's cousin, a namesake, twenty-seven years of age, who was called Walter Boyd, Junior. A bachelor, a volunteer grenadier in the Filles Saint Thomas battalion, in splendid uniform, he lost little time in conforming to the manner of life expected of a banker. In November 1791 he fell for the charms of twenty-three-year-old Marie Nicole Montréal, who soon became his mistress, installed in a sumptuous apartment, with appropriate staff, in the rue projectée Michaudière.[6]

One of the objectives of the reorganisation of the firm was the introduction of fresh capital. Capital was important, but Boyd also needed partners who could contribute banking ability and experience, good connections, sound judgement and political sensitivity, personal qualities which are always scarce, and especially so in the circumstances in which he found himself. The three new partners admitted in July were a disparate group, but this was not necessarily a disadvantage. Boyd had long been

3. Bouchary, op.cit., vol. I, pp. 190–5 and 205–7.
4. Contract dated August 21, 1797 between Boyd and Laborde. NLS, Forbes of Fettercairn papers.
5. Bouchary, op.cit., vol II. p. 61.
6. Albert Mathiez, *Robespierre Terroriste,* La Renaissance du Livre, Paris, 1921, p. 42, Bouchary, op.cit., vol. III, p. 251.

close to Walckiers, as is evidenced by the nearly 900 letters he had written him during the preceding five years.[7] Now that he had left the Netherlands, his energy and his connections with Veuve Nettine et Fils could be useful to Boyd, Ker et Cie. As his record showed, he was sympathetic to the ideas which inspired the revolution. On the other hand, Boyd might have had some question about his volatile character and his desire to play a political role, in a situation in which the cross-currents could be dangerous for him personally and for the firm. The Arch-duchess Marie Christine, sister of Leopold II of Austria, once judged him harshly, but perhaps not unjustly, as 'a light-weight and easy to influence'.[8]

Laborde, too, had some liberal ideas, but he could not shake off his aristocratic origins, and Boyd might have weighed the danger of having a partner so closely associated with the ancien régime, against the advantages which might stem from his wealth, connections and banking experience. About Boyd, Junior, no such questions would arise. Boyd needed one of his own family whom he could trust and who would support and assist him. Desparate they were, yet their addition to the firm strengthened it and represented continuity, which in troubled times was not a bad recipe.

On 4 September 1791, Boyd, Ker and Walckiers made an agreement with Baron de Watemael Kessel, under which he made a deposit of 200,000 livres, and became entitled to one-tenth share in the profits and losses of the firm in the six years from July 1791, without having the right to inspect the books.[9] No other information has been found relating to this rather strange arrangement, which might conceivably be an extension of the one, mentioned earlier, which was said to have been made in 1785.

Towards the end of the year, Boyd, having successfully concluded a new partnership agreement, bought for himself a large house in extensive grounds at Belin de Villeneuve, near Boulogne-sur-Seine, at a cost of 60,000 livres. The property included barns and stables, an orchard and vegetable gardens large enough to occupy regularly a head gardener, five under-gardeners, and two boys.[10] A purchase on this scale suggests not only that he had prospered during his first six years in Paris, but also that he was confident of being able to ride out the political storms which might lie ahead. Ker made a purchase of real estate of a different kind. William Herries, as has been seen, left the Austrian Netherlands with Walckiers in March 1790. Just over a year later, in July 1791, he sold his house, warehouse and garden in Ostend to Ker for 360,000 livres,[11] a deal which was probably for account of the firm, the proceeds being used in reduction of Herries' indebtedness.

In 1791, the effects of the Revolution on the economy, particularly on the banking and currency situation, were beginning to be felt. A law of 21 December 1789 had authorised the issue of 400 million livres of 'assig-

7. Bouchary, op.cit., vol. I, p. 206.
8. Bouchary, op.cit., vol. I, p. 193.
9. Claims on France. PRO, T. 78, vol. 16, item 126; Paul Benfield, *Case of Paul Benfield, Esq.,* Paris, January 1803, p. 1; Bouchary, op.cit., vol. II, pp. 125–6.
10. Bouchary, op.cit., vol II, pp. 126 and 129.
11. Claims on France, PRO, T. 78, vol. 16, item 126[II], T. 78/8, award 12.

nations sur le Trésor', bearing five per cent. interest and secured on confiscated property. They were not legal tender, but subsequent issues were: 400 millions in April 1790, carrying three per cent. interest, and 800 millions in October, without interest. These were the assignats, which have been described as 'the classical example of paper money made worthless by over-issue'.[12] Exchange rates reflected these issues, not that the amounts were very large, but because of fears for the future. By the end of 1790, the exchange on London was twenty-five-and-three-quarters compared with 'parity' of twenty-eight-and-five-eighths, a fall of ten per cent. Already those who owned securities were looking for ways to protect themselves, and speculators were looking for ways in which they could profit by a falling exchange.

It was not in Boyd's character to let these opportunities go by. Early in 1791, he joined with Hope & Co., Amsterdam, who headed the group, Parish & Co., Hamburg and Harman, Hoare & Co., London, to carry out bear operations.[13] Details of the procedures followed are lacking, but what probably happened was that Hope, Parish and Harman, Hoare & Co. drew on Boyd, Ker et Cie in livres, sold the bills in their respective markets, and with the proceeds bought bills payable in guilders, marcs and sterling, which matured just before the due date of the drafts on Boyd, Ker et Cie. At maturity these bills would be sold for livres, providing enough, if the operation had gone well, to cover Boyd, Ker et Cie's acceptances, and leave some profit to be divided among the participants. How profitable these operations were, it is difficult to judge. The exchange rate on London fell from twenty-five at the end of January 1791 to seventeen-and-a-half a year later. Ignoring costs, which were sometimes significant, the operation, if it had been repeated over a twelve-month period, could have yielded a gross profit of thirty per cent. on the amount of the original commitment.

Boyd's other bear operations in 1791 were apparently on a considerable scale. In June, James Bourdieu, of Bourdieu, Chollet & Bourdieu, were writing to Barthélémy Huber of Paris: '. . . . The house of B[oyd], K[er] et Cie is always working for a fall [of the French exchange], we understand that they have invited everybody to draw on them so as to profit by remittances at a higher rate (for sterling) of the large amounts falling due, and it is these goings-on which are so bad for your exchange.'[14]

There were other situations, which Boyd was quick to exploit. There was an active market in Paris in gold and silver bullion and coin, and it might have been expected that prices would reflect fairly closely the movement of exchange rates. This did not happen. So great was the distrust of the assignats, that people in France were prepared to pay more for gold and silver than was warranted by the exchange rate. It was illegal to deal in French coins at a premium, but there was no ban on dealing in foreign coin. Boyd, working with Charles Herries & Co., London, decided to take

12. Sir Ralph G. Hawtrey, *Currency and Credit*, 4th edition, Longmans, Green & Co., London, 1950, p. 245.
13. Richard Ehrenberg, *Grosse Vermögen, Ihre Entstehung und Ihre Bedeutung-Das Haus Parish in Hamburg*, Verlag von Gustav Fischer, Jena, 1925, vol. III, pp. 38–9.
14. Lüthy, op.cit., p. 661.

advantage of this situation. What they did was revealed in the letter from James Bourdieu to Barthélémy Huber, already mentioned. 'We understand that H[erries] have recently bought here considerable quantities of [silver] dollars which they have shipped to France, they did not buy écus or Louis d'ors, which convinces us that they have not bought for the government, as we do, for in that case they would not have refused your specie [i.e. coin]. What then is the purpose? is it for some expedition to China[15] or is it to exchange them at a high price for assignats, which perhaps could not be done with écus or Louis d'ors without exposing them to danger? . . P.S. We know that H[erries] dollars were sent to Boyd by diligence, some by night.' There was great rivalry between Bourdieu, Chollet & Bourdieu and Charles Herries & Co. in the affairs of the Compagnie des Indes, and this explains the slightly sarcastic tone of Bourdieu's letter.

Walckiers, long accustomed to handling speculative merchandise transactions for Veuve Nettine et Fils, was, like Boyd, prepared to use any opportunities which arose for making a profit. After coming to Paris from the Austrian Netherlands in March 1790, he seems to have continued to operate on his own account, no doubt using 9 rue de Grammont as a base. His credit was good, and Boyd thought he would be doing a favour to the Hamburg house of Parish & Co. by introducing him. Walckiers' first transaction with Parish came in January 1791, when he instructed them to buy 'at best' sugar and coffee to the value of 500,000 Dutch florins, and cover by drawing on Hope & Co., Amsterdam. It was not by chance that he chose sugar and coffee for this operation. There had recently been reports of unrest among the slaves in St. Domingo, which, if it became worse, would disrupt production, if not stop it altogether, and knowledgeable merchants in French ports were quietly buying. A secondary consideration in Walckiers' mind was the desirability of establishing a relationship with Parish for the future. These tactics were successful, and in the following two months Walckiers sent two ship-loads of the same products from Bordeaux to Hamburg, for Parish to sell.

Walckiers followed up this transaction with much larger ones, financed by Parish's drafts on Harman, Hoare & Co. in London. All seemed well until Parish received a letter from Harman, Hoare & Co., saying that they had refused to accept his drafts for £38,000 for Walckiers' account, but had accepted them for Parish's honour, in order to protect his credit as drawer. By the same post came an advice from Boyd, Ker et Cie, of their further drawings on Parish for Walckiers, totalling 450,000 marcs banco. Parish was shaken. If he now accepted Boyd, Ker et Cie's drafts, the total of his commitments for Walckiers would be £100,000. On the other hand, to refuse to accept would damage Walckiers' credit and Boyd's as well. In this dilemma he sent an express letter to Hope & Co, saying that he was willing to accept only under their guarantee. Fortunately, he soon received a stiff letter from Hope & Co., expressing astonishment that he had worried about trifles, and giving the guarantee asked for. Eventually, Boyd heard of the affair, and wrote to Parish indignantly, regretting that he had

15. The balance of trade with China was adverse, and had to be settled by exports of silver.

entrusted his credit to Parish's weak nerves, and announcing that he would close his account with Parish 'for ever'. The relationship between the two houses hung by a hair, but eventually, through friends, the incident was smoothed over.[16]

If operators like Boyd and Walckiers could regard the depreciation of the livre as an opportunity to make profits, for investors it posed the problem of how to safeguard their capital. Among them was Florimond Claude, Count Mercy-Argenteau, who was among the wealthiest of Boyd, Ker et Cie's customers. He had been appointed Austrian minister at the court of Louis XVI in 1770, and had cultivated close relations with the royal family. He owned extensive estates in France and in Liège and Brabant, and a plantation in St. Domingo, but much of his income, which for 1790 was estimated at 475,000 livres, came from his large holdings of securities, including 'rentes viagères sur les têtes génévoises', and the 125 million and eighty million loans, held for him partly by Boyd, Ker et Cie, partly by the Marquis de Laborde.

Mercy-Argenteau made no secret of his sympathies for the royal cause, and towards the end of 1790 his position in Paris was becoming untenable. He was accordingly instructed to move to Brussels, leaving Blumendorf as Austrian chargé d'affaires. He left Paris in October, and in December became minister plenipotentiary to the Government-General of the Netherlands in Brussels. Doubtful about the security of his communications, he arranged for his letters to Blumendorf to be sent through Boyd, Ker et Cie.[17]

His personal affairs were handled by one of his secretaries, Wolfgang Kruthoffer, who remained in Paris. He was greatly worried: income from his estates was falling because of the suppression of feudal rights, and fearing that assignats would fall further, he sought ways to protect his position. In March 1791, he and Kruthoffer discussed a plan to buy sugar and coffee, but they found that prices had already risen by a quarter. They therefore decided to take an exchange loss, and invest one million livres in three per cent. Consols through Harman, Hoare & Co., using for this purpose most of Mercy's balance of 871,000 livres with Boyd, Ker et Cie. In May, they considered a speculation in coffee, of about 35,000 livres, using funds to be drawn from Boyd, Ker et Cie. For some reason Mercy was dissatisfied with them, possibly because of the way they had treated remittances received for his account. This matter was certainly in dispute in August, when Dunkel, a financial secretary acting for Mercy in Paris, was insistent that amounts paid to Boyd, Ker et Cie for Mercy's account in specie should be repayable to him on the same basis, and not in assignats, which were then at twenty per cent. discount compared with specie. Boyd denied that these payments had been in specie, and explained that remittances to Paris were in the form of bills which were payable in assignats. In October, Mercy was still complaining about Boyd's intention to pay him in assignats, regardless of their value. For Mercy, the dispute only confirmed

16. Ehrenberg, op.cit., pp. 41–3.
17. Comte de Pimodan, *Le comte F-C. de Mercy-Argenteau*, Librairie Plon, Paris, 1911, pp. 261–4, and 287 n.

him in his intention of reducing still further his balance with Boyd, Ker et Cie, which, by November, represented only the proceeds of the sale of his sugar from St. Domingo.[18]

In December 1791, the French exchange rate against sterling was around nineteen, and opinion among French bankers was that it might fall further. Boyd was of this view, and together with Barthélémy Huber, decided to embark on a series of bear operations on joint account. Huber, originally from Lyon, had lived for several years in England, where he had been involved in a number of highly speculative deals, with varying success. In 1787 he had returned to France, where he could give his speculative talents full rein.[19] Their first exchange operation took the form of a purchase of £6244 of bills on London, which at twenty-and-a-quarter cost 222,000 livres. These bills were drawn at three and four months' sight on three of Boyd, Ker et Cie's correspondents, Turner, Gammell & Co., Tod & Co., and Charles Herries & Co. A similar purchase of £8229 of bills, mainly on John and George Ward, William Collow and Herries, was at nineteen-and-three-quarters, and cost 300,000 livres. Early in January there was a purchase of £5208 of bills at eighteen and three quarters, costing 200,000 livres. These purchases totalled 722,000 livres, which was probably financed by discounts with the Caisse d'Escompte. As Boyd and Huber foresaw, the exchange was falling, and touched a low point for the year of fifteen in March, which should have given them a satisfactory profit.

The market, however, was unpredictable. The declaration of war on Spain on March 7 and on Austria in April did not lead, as might be expected, to a further fall in the rate, and by the middle of June it had recovered to eighteen and three quarters. At this point Boyd started to work with Jean Louis Grenus et Cie. The technique adopted was for Grenus to draw bills for 300,000 livres on Boyd, Ker et Cie and discount them, when accepted, with the Caisse d'Escompte. With the funds so obtained, Grenus would buy bills in foreign currencies, payable shortly before the bills drawn on Boyd matured.[20] In the same month, there was a similar operation, when Philippe Gaillard Grenus of Lyon drew 150,000 livres on Boyd, Ker et Cie. The draft drawn by J.L. Grenus matured in August, when the livre was somewhat weaker, but instead of closing out the transaction, the participants renewed it by Grenus drawing 310,000 livres on Boyd, Ker et Cie.[21] But rates were nominal, and the massacre of prisoners in September closed the market altogether for two weeks.[22]

During the rest of the year the market was quiet, and bankers reduced their commitments, partly because of the difficulty of getting drafts discounted. As a result, the rate remained firm, and reached nineteen and a quarter in December. Just how profitable Boyd's operations in 1792 were

18. H.E.B., *Flight of Capital from Revolutionary France*, American Historical Review, vol. XLI, July, 1936, pp. 710–1.
19. Bouchary, op.cit., vol. III, pp. 73–89. AN, T. 250–2. Exchange rates were expressed in pence sterling for an ecu of 3 livres.
20. Bouchary, op.cit., vol. II, p. 166.
21. Idem, p. 172.
22. See G. Aust to Lord Grenville, Sept. 8, 1792, *Report on the Manuscripts of J. B. Fortescue, Esq., preserved at Dropmore,* Historical Manuscripts Commission (hereafter cited as *Dropmore Papers,* vol. II, Report 14, Appendix 5.

is impossible to judge, since complete information on them is not available. Those described above were relatively small, and probably did not yield large profits on balance. One operation discussed in this period promised great reward, but never came to fruition. The story, however, is worth telling, because it illustrates the high reputation which Boyd, Ker et Cie enjoyed in the French capital.

In 1792 the debt of the United States to France, which amounted to nearly forty million livres, was partly in arrears; and on both sides there was a desire to put it on a paying basis. The subject was not new. In 1798 the United States had had negotiations with the Dutch houses who acted as their bankers, and with a group headed by a Boston speculator, Daniel Parker, but none of these negotiations resulted in an agreement. Early in the year, with the exchange weak, the idea arose of paying off the debt in assignats.

At this point Boyd decided to make specific proposals, the general tenor of which can be gathered from the correspondence between William Short, American chargé d'affaires in Paris, and Alexander Hamilton, Secretary of the Treasury in Philadelphia. 'I have good reason to believe. . .,' Short wrote on 24 March 1792, 'that the debt to France might be immediately paid off by one stroke by a contract with the first banking house in Paris, Boyd & Kerr (*sic*), who would engage to pay into the public treasury the amount of the balance of the American debt to France as well due as to become due & receive in payment the obligations of the U.S. at four per cent. interest, either in London or Amsterdam, according to the rate of exchange at present. . . .The banking houses here wch. would make this contract having in their hands & at their disposition the funds of La Borde, the richest individual in France, & being connected closely in their operations with Hope of Amsterdam & his correspondent in London & becoming thus stockholders in the American funds to so great an amount would be powerful auxiliaries enlisted in support of their credit.'[23]

Although, based on the current exchange quotations, the deal appeared to offer the United States the prospect of repaying its debt at not much more than half its value, there were references to an amount, unspecified, which the United States would 'prefer to give' as an 'indemnity for the depreciation of the assignats,' a concession no doubt intended to win the support of the French. For Boyd, pessimistic about the future of the exchange, the deal offered the attraction that while the amount of the four per cent. American obligations to be received was to be fixed, the cost of the assignats to be given would depend on their market value when, some months later, they were paid over: hence, if assignats continued to depreciate, there would be a profit for the contractors.

Conclusion of the deal was delayed pending the arrival in Paris in May of Gouverneur Morris, newly appointed to Paris as minister plenipotentiary to replace Short. By this time, however, the exchange had recovered, and in June the rate was eighteen-and-a-half. Thus instead of a profit, the

---

23. William Short to Alexander Hamilton, 24 March 1792, *Papers of Alexander Hamilton*, ed. Harold C. Syrett, vol. XI, p. 181, Columbia University Press, 1966. The correspondent in London was doubtless John & Francis Baring & Co.

contractors would have incurred what Short termed a 'ruinous loss.' In these circumstances the whole operation was suspended, Short remarking a little caustically that the contractors 'will be more timorous now, the game being much less sure than they expected.'[24] For Boyd, it was a narrow escape.

Boyd was always ready to seize whatever opportunities presented themselves for profitable dealing in coin and bullion, and, as for other speculators, the ability to obtain silver dollars from the Banco de San Carlos was sometimes attractive. In February 1792 he participated with Barthélémy Huber in the purchase of piastres at eighty, which Huber succeeded in selling later for eighty-seven.[25] Later in the year, the situation changed radically. In September, dealing in coin contracted sharply. Whereas, a year earlier, hoarders had been buying foreign coin, and (illegally) écus and louis d'ors, this had now become too dangerous. Departing emigrés did not dare to carry gold or silver with them, and people remaining in France did not like to hoard for fear of house visits.[26] The result was that in the last quarter of the year there was only a slight premium on gold and silver in terms of assignats, sometimes none at all, in spite of the twenty-five per cent. depreciation of the livre on foreign exchange markets.

One influence which tended to support the exchange was the speculative interest in London and Amsterdam during 1792. Some of Boyd, Ker et Cie's English customers bought French securities. Between April and July, twenty, most of them in London, bought altogether six blocks of annuities, having a capital value of 2,800,000 livres. In November Boyd, Ker et Cie bought through their brokers 146,000 livres of the loan of 125 million for James Gage of London.[27] Speculation also took the form of purchases of assignats, which were blamed for what, in British eyes, was the weakness of sterling, and in January 1793, a law (33 Geo.III, c.1) made assignats void in Great Britain.

In 1792, there were signs that the political situation in France was becoming more sensitive. There were, for example, certain repercussions from a transaction carried out earlier by Boyd, Ker et Cie for the royal princes. In November 1791, Calonne, who was looking after their finances in Coblentz, had arranged for a draft for 150,000 livres on the Caisse d'Escompte to be sent to Boyd, Ker et Cie, with instructions to send 50,000 livres in assignats, and remit the balance in bills. This done, the money was duly paid in by Calonne to the Treasurer-General. Nothing more was heard for nearly a year, until, in fact, October 1792, when Bonnefond, a member of the Commission of twenty-four, made a denunciation, saying that he had learned 'from a certain source' that Boyd, Ker et Cie had arranged to pay much money to émigré refugees in Coblentz. For some reason the Commission took no action.

Boyd, however, had already sensed the way events were shaping, and had decided that it would be an advantage for him if he could have a base

24. Short to Hamilton, 4 May 1792, op. cit., pp. 298–403.
25. Bouchary, op.cit., vol. III, p. 88.
26. Jean Bouchary, *Le Marché des Changes,* op.cit., p. 67.
27. PRO, Claims on France, T. 78/16 and 78/10.

in London, from which he could work with the Paris house as far as conditions permitted, and to which, if the worst happened, he could transfer much of its business. He was able to get a passport through Bérard, the former director (administrateur) of the Compagnie des Indes, and left for London on September 23.[28]

During the ensuing few months the general political situation became increasingly tense and the outlook increasingly uncertain. The King, placed on trial in December, was condemned and executed in January. On February 1 came the French declaration of war on England and Holland. On March 10 a Revolutionary Tribunal was set up with wide powers, and eleven days later the National Assembly passed a decree ordering the establishment in each commune of watch committees (comités de surveillance). All foreigners had to report to their local watch committees, and enemy nationals could remain in France only if authorised to do so; failing this authorisation they had to leave the country within seven days. Ker decided to leave immediately: he obtained a passport without difficulty and reached England in April. His mistress was the thirty-five-year-old Baroness Catherine Denise Jeanne d'Estat, whose husband Tobie Gothereau Billens, was formerly an officer of the Swiss Guard. She, sadly, was left behind, with only a letter of credit on Boyd, Ker et Cie to console her.[29]

Boyd, Junior, was in as much danger as Ker, but he was in charge of the firm and decided to stay. Laborde, although not an enemy subject, was an aristocrat, and felt that he could not safely remain. Accordingly he left the family estate at Méréville at the end of March, and escaped to England. On April 8 he was denounced: two days later the Commune of Paris issued an order for his arrest to the local Commune, who soon discovered that he had fled. He was able to save a small part of his fortune, thanks to Walckiers, who bought French and Italian masters for him at a cost of 900,000 livres and sent them to Brussels, whence they were shipped to London.[30] Now, only two partners remained in Paris, Boyd, Junior, and Walckiers.

On April 6 a Committee of Public Safety had been set up, consisting of nine members of the National Convention, authorised to take measures to bring the deteriorating economy under control. In May a decree was issued requiring stocks of grain to be reported. On June 27 the Bourse was closed. In such conditions, banking became a precarious occupation: a number of banks closed and those that remained open did little business. Boyd, Junior, did not long remain immune from political pressures. Towards the end of June, without warning, he was denounced and arrested, suspected, the *Journal de Paris* reported, 'of being for long agent of the coalition against France and of being the channel through which the corrupter's gold had flowed', and 9 rue de Grammont was searched and

28. Boyd to St. Maures, 17 Nov. 1791, Calonne Papers, PRO, PC1/124/228; C. de Parrel, *Les Papiers de Calonne*, 1932, p. 34; Bouchary, op.cit., vol. III, p. 251.
29. Bouchary, op.cit., vol II, p. 155.
30. Bouchary, op.cit., vol. II, pp. 142–3; *Biographie Universelle (Michaud), vol. 22, pp. 291–2.* He sold the pictures to Jeremiah Harman, of Harman, Hoare & Co., for £40,000.

sealed. According to one story other banking houses came to their aid by paying their maturing acceptances and instructing their foreign correspondents to do the same. By bribing the commissioners investigating the matter, he obtained a written confirmation of what were described as 'his republican views', and he was released, and allowed to resume business. The *Chronique de Paris* of 27 June 1793 reported reassuringly that an examination of the papers and books of Boyd, Ker et Cie had proved that 'cette maison s'est toujours conduite avec autant de délicatesse que de civisme', although the next day *Le Moniteur* hinted darkly that 'on fait courir les bruits les plus extraordinaires sur cette arrestation'.[31]

Conditions became more strained. On August 23 a general mobilisation decree (levée en masse) was issued, making practically everyone liable for some kind of national service, and rendering property liable to be requisitioned for the war. It was probably no coincidence that, a few days earlier, Walckiers had thought it prudent to give to the district of Noyan two horses, hay and oats, and iron grills from his house sufficient to make 500 pikes, an act which earned him the commendation of the National Convention.[32] Political interference with business continued. On August 24 a decree was issued ordering the suppression of all companies with a share capital, which included the Caisse d'Escompte. Grenus, writing to Boyd, senior, in London at the end of the month, put the situation very succinctly: 'Il se fait peu d'affaires; tout le monde liquide'.[33]

On September 7 Boyd, Ker et Cie's premises were again sealed. However, by placing a carriage and horses at the disposal of the local revolutionary committee, and equipping a number of volunteers, Boyd, Junior, was able to have the seals removed on September 18, after convincing the committee that he had no foreign bills in his possession.[34] The story is related by John Parish of Hamburg that a night or so later, Boyd, Junior, was awakened by three agents of the National Convention, and dragged from his bed. His unwelcome visitors soon made it clear that all he had to do was to show his loyalty to the régime by drawing bills on his foreign correspondents in favour of the Convention, who wanted money to pay for imports of corn. They demanded £50,000 in bills on London, 500,000 florins on Amsterdam and 500,000 marcs banco on Hamburg. In vain he protested that such large sums were impossible, as the firm's credit had been seriously impaired by previous investigations. In the presence of his visitors he was forced not only to draw bills for the amounts demanded, but to write letters of advice, in French, to the drawees.

Fortunately, the general trend of events in Paris became known abroad. When, therefore, Parish received advice of these drawings he replied on October 14; 'The system which has been adopted [in Paris] destroys all confidence. A general resolution has been made here not to accept bills drawn from France. . '.[35] Hope & Co. also wrote a firm letter: 'We repeat

31. *Quoted by Bouchary, op.cit., vol. II, p. 127; Réimpression de l'ancien Moniteur,* Paris, Plon Frères, 1843–5, vol. XVI, p. 745.
32. *Réimpression de l'ancien Moniteur,* vol. XVII, p. 483.
33. Bouchary, op.cit., vol. II, p. 196.
34. Bouchary, op.cit., vol. II, pp. 128–9.
35. Ehrenberg, op.cit., pp. 39–40.

that we will neither accept nor pay these bills, nor any others drawn from France, until we have the positive certainty that all the drafts furnished by us or by others will be freely and punctually paid'.[36] Apparently Harman, Hoare & Co. in London took a similar position. This was not the only attempt made by the authorities to obtain foreign exchange through Boyd, Ker et Cie. The Treasury were said to have bought from them about this time ten million livres of bills on England. These reports seem to have been greatly exaggerated, for when the National Convention had the matter investigated a year later, the Treasury reported that between 1 July and 14 August 1793 they had bought bills amounting to only 2,175,000 livres, of which over a quarter had been returned, protested.[37]

With action of this sort being taken by revolutionary committees, and by the National Convention itself, Paris banking houses had for some time been considering what they might do if normal banking business became impossible. In August 1793, Louis Greffulhe, one of the partners of Greffulhe, Montz et Cie, who was then in London, suggested to his partner in Paris, Jacques-Marc Montz, that he should find a buyer for the firm's 'service des rentes'. Montz came up with a somewhat different solution, and on October 1 made an agreement for the transfer of the business of the whole firm to Bévière et Cie, Greffulhe, Montz et Cie having the right to take it back whenever they wished.[38]

Boyd knew Greffulhe from his dealings with Orléans, and it would be surprising if Boyd, senior, and Greffulhe had not discussed the matter in London. Be this as it may, two days after Montz had acted, Boyd, Junior, and Édouard de Walckiers entered into a basically similar agreement with the firm's cashier, Antoine Grégoire Geneste. For some years annuities had been registered in his name as the firm's nominee: now he was to take over the whole banking business, or what remained of it. The stated purpose of this arrangement was 'to conserve the assets of the business in these stormy times, inseparable from the establishment of the Republic, so that they could be returned, better than before, when tranquillity returned'. Geneste, therefore, was not to seek new business, but merely to collect payments on the annuities and handle other current business which involved no risk. According to the agreement, Geneste was the sole responsible partner, subscribing 100,000 livres, of which he paid only 15,000 livres. Boyd, Ker et Cie were limited partners and contributed 200,000 livres. Boyd, Junior, and Walckiers reserved the right to take back the business at any time, but if they did, they had to give Geneste a share of the profits of the new firm. The agreement was a rather transparent device to make Geneste the nominal owner, with the partners of Boyd, Ker et Cie retaining ownership in substance.[39]

Having done what he could to safeguard the firm, Boyd, Junior turned to his own safety. During the next few days he was in touch with various

36. Bouchary, op.cit., vol. II, pp. 126–7.
37. *Réimpression de l'ancien Moniteur,* Paris, Plon Fréres, 1847, vol. XXII, p. 691; Bouchary, op,cit., vol. II, p. 128.
38. Antonetti, op.cit., p.93.
39. The text of the agreement is in Bouchary, op.cit., vol. II, pp. 145–7.

people to obtain a passport. These efforts succeeded, at a cost, according to one report, of 400,000 livres. He then went into hiding, but only just in time, for on October 9 the National Convention voted a decree ordering the arrest of all British subjects and the confiscation of their property. On the following day representatives of the section searched 9 rue de Grammont, found that he had left, and had to content themselves with seizing his papers and sealing the premises. According to his own account, he remained in hiding in Paris for a month, eventually reaching Bâle, and from thence, England. The authorities expected that his mistress, Montréal, would try to follow him, so they arrested her on November 20. Interrogated, she claimed that she had not seen him since October 9, and that she did not know where he was. She was eventually released. [40]

Geneste expected that 9 rue de Grammont would be searched. Among the securities held there were 1277 shares of life annuities belonging to Paul Benfield, who was a customer of the firm and a friend of Boyd, senior, and who, as will be seen later, had by this time joined him in London. In order to conceal the true ownership of these shares, Geneste wrote to Boyd, Ker et Cie in September, saying that they were owned by C.R. Granmere of Brussels, Martin Dorner of Hamburg, Jean Grégoire of St. Petersberg and Édouard de Walckiers. He had also moved some of the firm's cash to his own home in the rue des Moineaux. While the firm's premises remained sealed, he was allowed to remove some books and papers to his home. From there he was able to keep in touch with the firm's customers and correspondents, but understandably there was little disposition on the part of foreign houses to do much business. On November 2, Heath & Co. of Genoa wrote: '. . .it is useless to deal in the exchange of France, which varies widely from week to week. . . .' Parish & Co. of Hamburg wrote on 6 January 1794: 'Please note that we are giving up all exchange business of any kind, having decided to limit ourselves entirely to business in merchandise.[41]

By this time, foreign exchange activities had been limited by a decree of 27 December 1793, which introduced exchange control. Anyone in France who held foreign assets had to declare them on oath, and draw bills immediately for sums owing to him from abroad, for which he would receive assignats at par of exchange. The decree was followed by a circular, warning bankers not to buy any foreign paper, or allow their correspondents abroad to draw on them, without having first obtained permission. The circular promised, optimistically, that the Government would take every measure possible to meet at par legitimate debts owed abroad, except to enemy countries.[42]

With foreign correspondents reluctant to do business and with exchange controls in force at home, even for quite small amounts, Geneste found foreign business virtually impossible. At the end of January, for example, Parish & Co. sent 410 livres in assignats to Boyd, Ker et Cie, requesting that paper on Hamburg be sent to them in exchange. Geneste referred the

40.   Bouchary, op.cit., vol. II, pp. 129–30; PRO, Claims on France, T. 78/11, award 428.
41.   Bouchary, op.cit., vol. II, p. 150, and pp. 152–3.
42.   Bouchary, op.cit., vol. III. p. 30.

matter to the Commission, who refused permission, but, 'always disposed to facilitate operations which may maintain links with friends of the Republic', decided that Parish could draw on Boyd, Ker et Cie for the amount they had sent. This was not very useful to Parish, for bills on France were paid in assignats and they might just as well have kept the notes in Hamburg. A month later, Geneste's request to the Commission for permission to pay drafts of L'Arbalète et Eicke of Liége was turned down flatly. 'It is absolutely prohibited to pay any draft drawn from countries with which the Republic is at war', said the Commission.[43] Geneste could hardly have expected any other answer.

The sealing of the firm's premises on October 9 warned Walckiers that he might be in danger, and at the end of the month he took the precaution of obtaining from the municipality of Carlepont a passport allowing him to travel within France. His large estates were an embarrassment; he talked of selling his property at Morlincourt, and in November he sold his library.[44] His sense of urgency increased when he heard that on November 17, the Committee of Public Safety and General Security had issued warrants for the arrest of Walter Boyd, Junior, and several other bankers.[45] In the next few days he was busy preparing to leave, giving instructions for the deer in his park to be slaughtered and given to the municipality, and for stocks of provisions to be taken from the house, for fear of being accused of hoarding. Having a passport, however, he felt fairly safe.

On 17 January 1794, the tribunal at Breteuil issued a warrant for his arrest, on grounds that he had circulated nine notes of an emigré, La Rochefoucault-Laincourt, but he remained at Carlepont, perhaps assured by friends that he would not be arrested. It was not until March 18 that the Committee of Public Safety ordered his arrest. A warning that this was coming had to be taken seriously. When, therefore, a week later, the citizens sent to arrest him arrived, they learned that he had left France for Hamburg.[46]

Walckiers' wife, Rose Françoise Renaut, remained at their town house in the rue Trudon, Chaussée d'Antin, and she was not molested. Realising, however, that the house might be searched at any time, she destroyed all documents that might be incriminating, including the shares in the Orléans mortgage that her husband had been so anxious to safeguard.[47]

One of those who called at 9 rue de Grammont in this period was Billens, who, needing money, presented the letter of credit Ker had given her. Twice Geneste gave her money, but before he could act on a third request she had been denounced as an aristocrat, and was under arrest. Accused of corresponding with Ker, she was sentenced to death and executed at the end of the year.[48]

43. Ibid.
44. Bouchary, op.cit., vol. I, pp. 201–2.
45. Bouchary, op.cit., vol. II, p. 130.
46. Bouchary, op.cit., vol. I, pp. 201–4.
47. Claims on France, PRO., T. 78/9, award 148. Walckiers' first wife had died in 1791.
48. Bouchary, op,cit., vol. II, pp. 130–1.

Geneste was not allowed to remain free for long. At the end of February 1794 or early in March he was denounced for intelligence and correspondence with the émigrés Boyd and Ker, and with Billens. Before the Revolutionary Tribunal, he was accused on April 18 of corresponding with London, Amsterdam, Hamburg and Brussels, and of causing his wife in Brussels to concert with bankers abroad. He was condemned to death and executed the same day, together with the Marquis de Laborde. Guilty of technical infringement of the decrees on exchange control he might have been, but it is impossible not to feel some sympathy for him and his wife. Married only eight months, she had been in Brussels on family affairs, when she heard about her husband's taking over Boyd, Ker et Cie, whereupon she wrote him a tender letter, expressing her joy at his being rewarded in this way: 'Voilà la récompense de tes travaux depuis tant d'années'.[49]

Thus, tragically, within eighteen months of Boyd, senior's leaving France, the last remains of the prosperous banking business he had built up so skilfully were swept away in a flood of revolutionary fervour. Nearly a quarter of a century would pass before it became possible to retrieve anything from the wreckage.

49.   Bouchary, op.cit., vol. II, p. 148 and pp. 153–6.

CHAPTER III

Boyd Moves to London

'. . . revolution destroying the great house of Messrs. Boyd, Ker & Co. in Paris, Mr. Boyd resorted to London where joining his talent and continental connections with the million brought by Mr. Paul Benfield from India they established the house of Boyd, Benfield & Co. . . .'

The Bank — The Stock Exchange — The Bankers . . . 1821.

Walter Boyd was no stranger to London, yet returning, he must have been struck by the contrasts it presented to Paris. London, including its suburbs, was somewhat larger, with a population of about one million, although the City proper, the heart of the metropolis, had only about 70,000 inhabitants. Unlike Paris, London was a seaport, and nearly two-thirds of the external trade of the Kingdom was handled on the quays that lined the Thames. It was shipping and insurance, overseas trade and finance, which gave the City its particular character.

At its centre was the Royal Exchange, built in 1669 to replace Sir Thomas Gresham's exchange, which perished in the Great Fire. Less important than in earlier times, it was still the place where merchants and brokers met to deal in commodities and foreign bills. Facing it was the Bank of England, noisy with the sound of workmen rebuilding the Stock Office under the Bank's architect, John Soane. To the East, a modest building housed the Stock Exchange. In Leadenhall Street was India House, built in 1724 and now inadequate for the greatly increased business of the East India Company, and it was soon to be rebuilt on a grand scale. Here and there were the halls of the City companies, forming focal points for merchants in particular trades. All around, in narrow streets and alleys, were the coffee houses, in which much of the City's business was transacted. Westwards was the City of Westminster. The royal palaces were there, and there in Downing Street and nearby, the King's ministers and their officials were busy with the multifarious affairs of state.

Every week-day, several hundred merchants and brokers met in the Royal Exchange to gather news and gossip, to trade in a varied range of goods and deal in foreign exchange. It was a rectangular building, consisting of an interior courtyard, paved and open to the sky, surrounded on all four sides by wide colonnades, so that in bad weather business could be done under cover. To the north was a gateway to Threadneedle Street, and to the south one to Cornhill. The Exchange was open from eight o'clock in the morning to six in the evening, and between these hours anyone could enter. By long-established custom, merchants dealing in the same commodities or trading in the same area formed little groups, each of which regularly occupied the same position, which was referred to as a 'walk'.

Intermediaries between merchants were brokers. By an Act of 1707 (6 Anne, c. 16), brokers had to obtain a licence from the City of London, furnish a bond of £500 for good behaviour and pay an annual fee of 40s. Each licensed broker had a silver medal, bearing his name, as evidence of his competency. There was no limit to the number of brokers who could be licensed, except that the number of Jewish brokers was limited to twelve. In 1792 there were 672 licensed brokers, but there were in addition many who were unlicensed.

A licensed broker did not have to limit himself to a particular trade and many, licensed and unlicensed, were active in several. Not every broker found his livelihood on the Royal Exchange. Stock-brokers had their own exchange, and ship and insurance brokers and underwriters met in Lloyd's subscription Coffee House on an upper floor of the Royal Exchange.

Dealing in foreign bills and arranging remittances were largely in the hands of merchants, who in the ordinary course of their business, were frequently drawing bills or being drawn on. Not always, however, was it possible to match the needs of importers for remittances with the supply of bills from exporters, and there had arisen 'a particular set of men', as a contemporary put it, merchants who were specialist exchange dealers. The bankers were little involved in the business of dealing in foreign bills; the Bank of England not at all. The Bank, however, was frequently buying and selling bullion and foreign coin, largely through its brokers, Mocatta and Goldsmid.[1]

The market in foreign drafts and remittances was held in the Royal Exchange on Tuesdays and Fridays, between noon and three o'clock in the afternoon, known as Exchange time, when brokers went from one merchant to another in search of business. 'To the broker everyone communicates his wants, so far as he finds it prudent; and by going about among all the merchants, the broker discovers the side upon which the greater demand lies, for money or for bills'.[2] Having done this, the broker was able to fix rates at what was described as 'a fair average'. Not all deals were arranged at these rates. Shrewd merchants sometimes dealt before the rate was fixed, and the principal houses could often negotiate their bills at a half per cent. or more better than the published rate, which merely 'formed the standard' on the basis of which deals were made. Rates were published immediately after the close of business in a list called 'The Course of the Exchange', published by a stockbroker, Edward Wetenhall. They were also in Lloyd's List, in various prices current, and sometimes in newspapers.

The period for which bills were drawn varied according to the place of payment. For Amsterdam, quotations were for bills at sight and at 'usance', which meant one month; for Paris, for bills at one day's date and two usances; and for Hamburg, for bills at two and a half usances. Rates

1. Clapham, op.cit., vol. I, p. 220.
2. *Encyclopaedia Britannica*, 3rd. ed., vol. VII, 'Exchange', Edinburgh, A. Bell and C. MacFarquhar, 1797.

were also quoted for towns in Spain, Portugal and Italy. Altogether, there were seventeen rates, including one for Dublin. Remittances to other places in Europe would be negotiated through Amsterdam or Hamburg; those for distant places like the West Indies had to be negotiated with merchants trading in those areas.

A transaction concluded, the broker noted the particulars on a slip of paper for the seller or drawer, and in his book, to serve as evidence in the event of dispute. Brokerage was one-eighth per cent. A merchant arranging a deal for someone else, such as a foreign correspondent, would usually charge one-half per cent. commission in addition to the brokerage, although it was sometimes cut to one-third per cent.

The market in securities in England goes back to the seventeenth century, when there was dealing on the Royal Exchange and in the neighbouring coffee houses in stocks and bonds of a few companies and in Exchequer orders and navy bills. In time, brokers took to meeting in Jonathan's Coffee House in Exchange Alley, and when this became overcrowded and noisy they built their own exchange at the north end of Sweetings Alley, facing west to Threadneedle Street and the northern portico of the Royal Exchange. A rather simple three-storied brick structure, it contained on the ground floor a dealing room lighted by five high-silled, round-headed windows, and on the floor above, a coffee room. Its façade bore the inscription, in bold characters, 'The Stock Exchange'.[3] Not all of the dealing in securities took place here. For many years there had been an active market in government stocks in the Rotunda of the Bank of England and adjoining transfer offices, and dealing in East India Company stock took place in India House and in South Sea Company stock in South Sea House.

Unlike the Paris Bourse, The Stock Exchange was not subject to official regulation, and although stock-brokers, like other brokers, were required by law to obtain a licence from the City, only one-third of the three to four hundred of them did so. By law, brokers were allowed to act only as agents. In practice they seem to have acted often as principals, buying and selling for their own account, and often charging brokerage for dealing in their own stock. By 1792, however, there were dealers who 'made a market' in the more actively traded stocks, quoting prices and supplying brokers with stock their clients wanted to buy, and taking from them stock their clients wanted to sell. Most of the dealing was in government stocks, the nominal amount of which was about £259 million. One stock, three per cent. Consols, accounted for forty per cent. of this amount. The stocks of the Bank of England and the East India Company were dealt in less freely and stocks of the insurance companies rarely.

Dealing was either for 'money' (settlement within two days) or for 'time' (settlement on the next six-weekly account day). In a bull market, the

---

3. S.R. Cope, *The Stock-Brokers find a home: How The Stock Exchange came to be established in Sweetings Alley in 1773,* Guildhall Studies in London History, April, 1977.

price for time was higher than the price for money, which meant that bulls had to pay, sometimes heavily, for carrying over their purchases from one settlement to the next. It also meant that bankers and other 'monied men' could invest profitably, without risk, by buying for money and selling for time. From time to time, particularly when the market was falling, there were complaints about speculation, or 'jobbing', as it was called. Under 'An Act to prevent the infamous Practice of Stock-Jobbing' (7 & 8 Geo. II, c. 8), of 1734, contracts for the sale of purchase of stocks for future settlement which were not to be delivered or taken up were void, no one was to sell a stock he did not own, and option contracts were illegal. Nevertheless, jobbing continued. To whet the speculator's appetite and to guide the investor, prices of about 20 stocks appeared in most London newspapers, twice weekly in the 'Course of the Exchange &c', in Lloyd's List, and also in various prices current.

Much of the speculation took place in newly-issued government loans. When the government needed to borrow, the Chancellor of the Exchequer would either negotiate the terms with a group of bankers or merchants, or invite them to bid for the issue, stating how much of a particular stock or stocks they would accept for every £100 they advanced. An issue in April 1783, for example, was negotiated with a group of eleven bankers. Subscriptions for loans were payable by instalments, spread over several months, and until a loan was fully paid it was in the form of scrip (subscription receipts), which, when signed, passed as a bearer security. If, as was usual, the loan was made up of more than one stock, scrip of the several stocks was known collectively as 'omnium'. Because scrip was only partly paid in the first few months after issue, buying it did not require a great investment of cash, and it was therefore popular with speculators. It was usual for the Bank of England to make advances to subscribers who had made the first one or two payments, to help them make subsequent payments. This was not always done, however. In May 1783, for example, the Bank refused requests for the usual advance on the £12 million loan, issued in April, but relented three months later.[4]

Towards the end of the eighteenth century, the Bank of England, founded in 1694, was gradually assuming the functions and duties of a central bank, although with some reluctance. It had long managed the government debt and held the government's accounts. Its capital, however, was privately owned: its directors, elected by the proprietors, came from merchant houses in the City. Notes of the Bank, although not legal tender, circulated throughout the London area, to such an extent that the notes issued by London bankers had virtually disappeared. The Bank's note circulation was about £11.4 million. Against its notes, it held reserves in bullion, foreign coin and guineas, which were a constant preoccupation whenever there was an unusual demand for guineas or gold for export.

4. For dealing and loan contracting practices see S.R. Cope, *The Stock Exchange Revisited* . . ., Economica, February, 1978, and *The Goldsmids and the . . . London Money market* . . . . Economica, May, 1942.

Deposits with the Bank on drawing accounts, amounting in February 1792 to £2.8 million, consisted mainly of balances on a few government accounts. By comparison, private deposits were small and were held on many accounts. There were in fact over 2000 of them, mostly accounts of merchants, traders and brokers, virtually all of them in London. Only a handful of London banking houses, perhaps not more than twenty, had accounts. There were a few corporate customers, prominent among whom were the East India Company, the South Sea Company and the Hudson's Bay Company. Four insurance companies had accounts; three banks (the Royal Bank of Scotland, the Bank of Scotland and the Bank of Ireland) and there were some local authorities and charities. The total amount on these many accounts could not have been more than £500,000. Although most of the considerable merchants had accounts with the Bank, many preferred to do much, if not most, of their banking with one or more of the London banks.

These banks numbered close to seventy. They no longer issued notes, but kept the current accounts of the increasing number of people, both private individuals and those in trade, who drew cheques. Bank of England notes, however, were still widely used, even for quite substantial payments. Most of the London banks were in the City. Their business was mainly with the mercantile community in or close to London, although they acted as correspondents for country banks. Since 1773, a number of City banks had participated in a clearing arrangement under which their clerks met daily in Lombard Street to exchange drafts on each other, settling differences in Bank notes. The West-End banks were not much concerned with trade, and they held mainly accounts of well-to-do and titled people.

In London, as in Paris, discounts were the life-blood of the business community. Unless his bills were acceptable to his bankers, no merchant could carry on a substantial business, and unless he had a discount account with the Bank he had little chance of surviving when money was tight. The Bank, wrote Sir John Clapham, 'remained the greatest and most accessible haven of refuge for storm-tossed traders.'[5] Its rule was that only a London resident in trade, recommended by a director, could have a discount account, which meant that it would not discount for private bankers. To be eligible, bills had to have a currency of not more than sixty-five days and carry at least two London names. The Bank's discount rate was uniformly five per cent., and when money was easy, as it was from 1790 to 1792, merchants preferred, whenever possible, to discount at the lower rates prevailing in the market. In February 1790 the Bank's discounts were only £650,000.

There were some 280 country banks in England and Wales, most of them quite small. None had more than six partners, because a clause in an Act of 1707 prohibited partnerships of more than six from issuing notes. Each of these banks found its customers and circulated its notes within its own locality. They were linked to the London market, not through the

5. Sir John Clapham, *The Private Business of the Bank of England, 1744–1800*, Economic History Review, vol. XI, 1941, p. 82.

Bank of England, but through the London banks who acted as their agents and correspondents.

Already, the beginnings of a money market could be seen. As early as 1788, Benjamin and Abraham Goldsmid were taking call money, and a few years later they were dealing in bills. If there were others, they have left no records. Bills were drawn for various purposes: for financing imports into Great Britain or the Continent; for financing inland trade; or for purely financial transactions. What contemporaries called the 'money market' was concerned mainly with short-term government paper, such as Exchequer Bills, and bills issued by public offices, such as the Navy and Victualling Offices and the Boards of Ordnance and Transport.

This was the City, with its hundreds of merchants, bankers and brokers, engaged daily in a myriad of trading and financial transactions, to which Boyd returned in the autumn of 1792. The time was not altogether propitious. Although at the beginning of 1792 the economy seemed to be sound, there were underlying weaknesses, which had not yet appeared. Credit throughout the country had been greatly over-extended, and by the time the autumn came the number of bankruptcies was abnormally high. There was anxiety, too, about developments in France. In January 1793 came the shock of the execution of Louis XVI, and in February, France's unexpected declaration of war on Great Britain. When, therefore, in March there was a run on banks in Newcastle, bank failures quickly spread throughout the country. By mid-April a hundred banks had stopped payment. In London a hastily-formed committee of eleven City men, including four Bank of England directors, met under the chairmanship of the Lord Mayor, Sir James Sanderson, whose Southwark banking house had been saved a month earlier by the Bank. The committee quickly recommended the issue of Exchequer Bills, which was authorised in May (33 Geo. III, c 29). Once anxiety about cash balances had been relieved, the demand for guineas slackened, and it proved necessary to issue only just over £2.2 million of bills, to 238 applicants.[6]

It is uncertain whether, when he left Paris, Boyd had decided what he would do in London. However, there are grounds for supposing that he was already thinking about founding a merchant banking house and had even made proposals in this sense to the man who would become his partner – Paul Benfield.

Paul Benfield was the son of John Benfield, carpenter and joiner, of Cheltenham, Gloucestershire, by Anne, daughter of the Rev. Stephen Cull of nearby Cranham, and was baptised in January 1741. In 1764 he went out to India as a civil architect at Madras, with the rank of lieutenant in the East India Company's army. Five years later he resigned his commission, and became a contractor for building ramparts at Black Town, Madras. Next, he began making fictitious loans, was twice dismissed the East India Company service for disobedience, and twice reinstated. By 1774 he had become chief creditor of Muhammad Ali Khan Walajah, the Nawab of the Carnatic, and was on the way to accumulating

6. David Macpherson, *Annals of Commerce* . . . London, Nichols & Son, and Edinburgh, Mundell & Son, 1805, vol. IV, p. 301.

a large fortune. The Nawab, after his invasion of the territories of the Rajah of Tanjore, borrowed large sums from Benfield on the security of lands in Tanjore. The Rajah, however, was reinstated in 1776 by the new governor of Madras, Lord Pigot, and refused to pay these debts. Benfield reacted stongly, not only threatening Pigot with charges of corruption, but becoming party to a plot to kidnap and imprison him. A year later, Pigot died in captivity. Hearing of these events, the Court of Directors in London ordered Benfield home.

Back in England, Benfield's first step was to procure a seat in Parliament. In 1780 he bought the Cricklade estate in Wilts, and, with another nabob, John Macpherson, stood in the general election of 1780. By wholesale bribery, both were elected, although Macpherson was unseated two years later. Benfield now made his peace with the Administration, and, still a member of Parliament, was able to engineer his return to India. Travelling overland, he reached India in October 1781, and was soon on the worst of terms with the new governor of Madras, Lord Macartney. After Macartney had resigned in 1785, Benfield was able to continue his activities undisturbed, but the arrival of Lord Cornwallis as Governor-General in 1786 ended his career in India. 'His conduct', wrote Cornwallis in November 1788, 'has been far more officious and exceptionable than that of any other of the Nawab's creditors', and he was suspended and once more ordered home.[7]

Returning home, however, was plainly inadvisable, for by this time he had incurred debts which he could not pay because of the Nawab's default to his creditors. In these circumstances, his two close friends, Nathaniel William Wraxall and John Call, urged him to remain out of the country while they worked to clear up his tangled finances and find him a seat in Parliament which would protect him from his creditors. Both were nabobs, and were still in close touch with East India Company affairs. Both, too, were members of Parliament, Wraxall representing Ludgershall, and Call, Callington, and Call had just become a partner in the Bond Street banking house of Pybus, Call, Grant & Co.[8] Even with such sponsors, 'moving heaven and earth', as they claimed they were,[9] it was not easy to find him a safe seat. Eventually, in 1790, with support from Pitt and Rose,[10] Secretary to the Treasury, they were able to buy him the seat for Malmesbury, Wilts, which he represented until February 1792. Meantime, he remained on the Continent, restlessly visiting a half-dozen countries.

It is all but certain that it was in this period that he first met Boyd. By 1789, if no earlier, some of his remittances from India were being passed through Boyd, Ker et Cie, and he had his correspondence sent to him there.[11] As has been seen, Boyd, Ker et Cie were reorganised in the middle of 1791 under a new six-year partnership agreement, and Boyd evidently meant to remain in Paris. Over the succeeding twelve months,

7. Sir Lewis Namier and John Brooke, *The House of Commons, 1754–1790*, H.M.S.O., vol. II, London, 1964, pp. 81–2.
8. Namier and Brooke, op.cit., vol. II, p. 176, vol. III, pp. 662–3.
9. Wraxall to Benfield, 13 Oct., 1789, Paul Benfield Papers, IO, Eur. c., 307/4.
10. Wraxall to Benfield, 27 Oct., 1789, idem.
11. Wraxall to Benfield 16 Nov., 1789, idem.

however, conditions in France deteriorated, and by the autumn of 1792 he felt it would be wise to leave and start afresh in London. Raising the capital which would be required, however, posed a serious problem. Boyd had a substantial stake in the Paris firm, but it was not readily realisable, and he had few assets elsewhere. If, however, he could obtain a part of Benfield's considerable, if somewhat uncertain, fortune, the problem might be solved.

Boyd could not have been under any illusions about Benfield's character. Nabobs were not highly regarded, and among them, Benfield was notorious. In the Commons, he was bitterly attacked by Edmund Burke, who referred to his conduct in India as 'the enchanted chalice of the fornication of usury and rapine which was tendered to Ministers by the gorgeous Eastern harlot.' Even his friend Wraxall called him 'exacting, dissatisfied and ambitious'.[12] Boyd, however, needed capital for a new firm in London; Benfield, according to Burke, had an income of nearly £150,000, and, in the end, financial considerations outweighed all the others.

It would not have suited Boyd if all, or substantially all, of the capital of the firm appeared to be coming directly from Benfield, for Boyd had no intention of being a junior partner, entitled only to a small share in the profits. The solution was for Benfield to buy French securities from Boyd, Ker et Cie, giving them funds which they could put into the new firm and thereby acquire the right to participate in its profits, the whole arrangement, however, being in the name of Boyd, who in any case had a major participation in Boyd, Ker et Cie. Accordingly, between June 1792 and May 1793, Benfield bought from Boyd, Ker et Cie three blocks of life annuities at a total cost of nearly £80,000. In a letter to Boyd, Ker et Cie Boyd wrote, presumably just for the record, 'I hope you will have reason to be satisfied with the operation, not only because it will ultimately be advantageous to you, but also because it must show that our friend Benfield thinks well of French stocks.'[13] Strangely, both Boyd and Benfield seem to have been oblivious to the fact that France and England were at war.

These somewhat tortuous arrangements having been agreed, it was possible to launch the new firm, Boyd, Benfield & Co., on 15 March 1793, with its counting house at 2 New Broad Street, in the heart of the City. The firm's capital was £100,000, of which Benfield subscribed £25,000 and Boyd £60,000, allocation of the balance of £15,000 being reserved to Boyd. The partnership deed provided that Benfield was to have twenty-five per cent. of the profits and Boyd, seventy-five. It was an apparently straight-forward arrangement which gave no hint that Boyd's capital contribution had really come from Benfield through Boyd, Ker et Cie, and it gave the

12. James Talboys Wheeler, *A Short History of India,* Macmillan & Co., 1880, p. 369; *The Historical and the Posthumous Memoirs of Sir Nathaniel William Wraxall, 1772–1784,* ed. Henry B. Wheatley, London, Bickers & Son, 1884, vol. IV, pp. 87–93.
13. Boyd to Boyd, Ker et Cie, 31 May, 1793, Claims on France, PRO, T. 78/5, award 176. The whole arrangement was later challenged by Benfield. See P. Benfield and M.F. Benfield to Treasury, 23 April, 1801, PRO., T. 1/884.

impression, certainly not a false one, that the firm was going to be run by Boyd.

Benfield soon found a place in London society. In September 1793 he married Mary Frances, daughter of Henry Swinburne of Hamsterly, Durham. The wedding was at fashionable St. George's, Hanover Square, and newspapers carried reports of his wife's diamond wedding ring, worth three thousand guineas, and of the settlement on her of an income of £3,500 a year.[14] Shortly after his marriage he bought from the executors of the nabob, Sir Thomas Rumbold, a large estate in Hertfordshire for £125,000, of which £60,000 was left on mortgage. The estate included Watton Wood Hall, which he enlarged by adding north and south wings. He also spent large sums on the park and on farms on the estate. For his town house, he bought 18 Grosvenor Square from the Earl of Thanet for £16,000,[15] in an area much favoured by nabobs. In London they lived in magnificent style, and the cerulean blue coach in which his wife drove through the parks was the talk of the town.[16]

All he needed to complete the setting for a life as a wealthy and influential City merchant was a seat in Parliament. This was no great problem. Shortly after his return from India, he had bought a two-thirds share in an estate costing £35,000, which included 300 of the 400 houses forming the Dorset town of Shaftesbury, the other third being bought by William Bryant. Scarcely more than a village, Shaftesbury returned two members, and ownership of the estate gave control of the representation. Hence, when William Grant, one of the members, resigned in June 1793, Benfield was returned in his place. In Parliament, he was a supporter of Pitt, but this apart, there is little to indicate his political views, or his role in political affairs, and no speech of his is to be found in the official record of debates.

Boyd's style of living was less ostentatious than that of his partner. He had married Harriet Anne Hooke Goddard five years or so earlier,[17] and they had at least two children. Where they lived during their first two years in London is not certain. Directories show Boyd, Benfield & Co., at 38 Dover Street in 1794 and at 14 Albermarle Street in 1795, although, from the start, the firm's counting house was at 2 New Broad Street in the City.[18] The West End addresses would have been convenient for the Austrian negotiations, which then occupied much of Boyd's time, and they no doubt provided living quarters for the family as well. By January 1795, Boyd had moved to 28 Sackville Street, which was to remain his residence for the next five years, although for a time he still used the Albermarle address. As a week-end retreat he acquired in 1793 or 1794 a house in Putney Hill Lane, Surrey, which was within easy reach of the City and

14. St. George's Hanover Square Register of Marriages. *The Times*, 7 Oct., 1793; *Gentleman's Magazine*, 1793, p. 955.
15. Walter Boyd, *Letter to the Creditors of the house of Boyd, Benfield & Co.* London, Henry Reynell, 1800, p. 12.; John Edwin Cussans, *History of Hertfordshire*, London, Chatto and Windus, 1877, pp. 171–2.
16. Wheeler, op. cit., p. 381.
17. Claims on France, PRO, T. 78/16.
18. *London Directory*, W. Lowndes, 1794 and 1795.

West End. He seems to have found his friends and business associates largely among his fellow countrymen, many of whom, like him, were members of the Scottish Corporation in London. He became Vice-President of the Corporation, which enabled him to meet easily political figures such as Henry Dundas, Sir William Pulteney and John Fordyce, and prominent merchants such as Sir Robert Herries and Alexander Houston.[19]

The business of Boyd, Benfield & Co. was intended to be a continuation, in some measure at least, of that of the Paris firm. It was obviously a sound policy to try to maintain the connections and goodwill built up in Paris. In a circular letter in French sent to foreign correspondents in March 1793, Boyd explained, tactfully, if not wholly truthfully, that some months previously, while in London on the business of the firm, he had thought it would serve their interests if an establishment could be formed in London, which, while working in close contact with them, could take advantage of business which offered itself in London. He had found in his friend Benfield, he continued, a partner whose fortune and abilities left nothing to be desired. This letter was accompanied by another from Boyd, Benfield & Co., announcing the firm's formation at the beginning of the year, and stating that their long experience, capital and respectable connections were at their correspondents' disposal for all mercantile and banking operations which did not involve risk. In spite of these brave words, it soon became obvious that it was not realistic to think of working in close contact with Boyd, Ker et Cie. France and Great Britain were at war, and although for a time some communication with Paris was still possible, a close working relationship between the two firms could hardly be maintained. Boyd therefore turned with characteristic energy to building up the business of the London house.

One of his early operations was in foreign exchange. In the spring of 1793, following the commercial crisis, the exchanges turned sharply in favour of London. The exchange on Hamburg rose from 35s. 3d. in January to 38s. 6d. in April, a rise of nine per cent. which brought sterling well above the parity, which was reckoned to be 35s. 1½d. The rate for bills on Lisbon fell from 72d. to 66½d., showing a similar rise in the value of the pound. At these rates, bullion shipments from Hamburg and Lisbon were profitable, even allowing for freight, insurance and commission, and Boyd, Benfield & Co. imported considerable quantities of bullion, both on their own account and on behalf of their correspondents abroad.[20]

In the summer of 1793 Boyd decided to enter into relations with the Glasgow firm of West India merchants, Alexander Houston & Co. This firm, long-established and having partners of considerable wealth, had extended credit on a great scale to its agents in Grenada, and found themselves in difficulties when the commercial crisis came in 1793. They received aid in the form of £180,000 of Exchequer bills, under the Act of

19. *A List of the Officers, Governors and Patronesses of the Scots Corporation in London*, ... 1807.
20. Boyd, *Letter to Pitt*, op.cit., pp. 29–30; Commons Committee of Secrecy, 1797, Evidence of Boyd. The Hamburg exchange was quoted in schillings and pence Flemish to the pound sterling.

27 June 1793 (33 Geo. III, c. 29), but the most active partner, William McDowall, realised that this was only a temporary expedient. 'I likewise forsaw', he wrote later to Dundas, 'that the only mode of saving the credit and honor of Alex. Houston & Co. was to establish a correspondence with a great house in London, which knowing the extent of our commerce & the large fortunes of the individuals comprising the Co., might step forward to assist me from the lucrative business which would naturally fall to their share – After several unsuccessful attempts. . . . I applied to a confidential friend completely acquainted with the London houses who told me at once that there was only one person, who could answer my expectations, a Mr. Boyd, who was about to establish a very great house supported with all the wealth of Mr. Benfield. . . . I accordingly made an appointment with him, settled the whole business in a very short time, since which period he has behaved with an unbounded confidence and liberality. . . . He began business with me by paying above 40,000 from confidence alone.[21]

The relationship developed with astonishing speed. The account was opened in September 1793, and by the end of the year Boyd, Benfield & Co. had advanced no less than £255,000, of which £117,000 had been repaid, making the amount due by Houston & Co. £138,000. At first, Boyd, Benfield & Co. passed the almost daily transactions for Houston & Co. over their account with Smith, Payne & Smiths. At the beginning of 1794, they opened a drawing account with the Bank of England, and for six months most of their Houston business went through this account.[22] This practice suddenly ceased, and their continuing business with Houston & Co. must have been done once more through Smith, Payne & Smiths.

The start in 1793 of an active banking relationship with Houston and the possibility of other, even larger transactions, convinced Boyd that he needed another partner. His eye lighted on a fellow countryman, James Drummond, who, since 1784, had been a partner in Charles Herries & Co. It was accordingly arranged for Drummond to leave Herries in November 1793. With a notional capital allocation of £5,000. he was not to bear any losses, but was to receive a fixed annual salary and, in addition, a small participation in profits, against which he was to be charged interest on his share of the capital.[23] He did not sign any deed of partnership, but he was held out to the firm's correspondents as a partner, and his name, along with those of Boyd and Benfield, was at the head of the firm's drawing account with the Bank of England.

The internal organisation of the firm was simple. There was a correspondence department, run by Drummond, under Boyd's direction. Securities, bills and other marketable paper were kept in a drawer, to which Boyd and Drummond each had a key, and were taken out when required by whichever of them was available at the time. Significantly,

21. McDowall to Henry Dundas, 6 July 1794, Chatham Papers, vol. 154; Houston & Co., ledger K, NLS. The name is sometimes spelled 'Houstoun'.
22. Bank of England Drawing Accounts Ledger.
23. Benfield, op.cit., p. 1; Drummond to Boyd, Benfield & Co., 8 Nov., 1798, Boyd, *Letter to the Creditors . . . of Boyd, Benfield & Co.*, op. cit, p. 8, and Appendix, p. 64.

Benfield did not have a key. In charge of the cash department was Henry Libotton, who might have been the lawyer, referred to as Lebotton, who was associated with Walckiers in Brussels.[24] It was under Boyd's supervision, and Libotton had to balance his books daily and report to Boyd. Benfield, who in one way or another had provided most of the firm's capital, was little involved in its affairs. Drummond said later that in the whole course of the partnership he seldom had any communication with Benfield on any subject of business whatever. As Benfield himself admitted, Boyd 'had the entire management of the concerns of the House'. Ker had left Paris in the spring of 1793, and it would have been natural for him to talk to Boyd about joining the firm. If he did, nothing came of it, although he received small amounts of money from the firm in 1794, and remained on friendly terms with Boyd.

In addition to seeking new business in London, Boyd had to attend to awkward legal problems originating in Paris. Towards the end of September 1793, Andrew French & Co., merchants of Copthall Court, Threadneedle Street, presented to Boyd, Benfield & Co. for acceptance, a bill for £600, apparently drawn by Boyd, Ker et Cie on August 16. Even if he had not heard of the closing of the Paris firm on September 7, he would have had reason to be suspicious, because of the incident of the previous June. In order to facilitate their extensive business in remittances, Boyd, Ker et Cie, like other Paris banks, were in the habit of drawing bills payable to one of their clerks, and keeping them ready for use. When they were required, all that had to be done was for the clerk to endorse the bills in favour of the remitter. This practice, no doubt justifiable in normal times, had its dangers in the disturbed conditions prevailing in Paris in the summer of 1793, and it was difficult for Boyd, in London, to be sure that the bills represented bona fide transactions.

The bill was drawn in favour of one of Boyd, Ker et Cie's clerks, who endorsed it to Chambaud, a Paris merchant, who in turn endorsed it to Andrew French. Boyd, after taking advice, refused to accept or pay. Andrew French. had the bill protested, and demanded the reason for nonpayment. This evoked a stiff reply from Boyd. 'I thought nobody', he wrote on November 23, 'could be at a loss to discover the reasons which have determined me to refuse acceptance and payment of the bills drawn on my house . . . by Boyd, Ker et Cie, of Paris that have been presented to me since the late decree of the National Convention [confiscation of British property and imprisonment of British subjects] . . . .I can hardly suppose that the bearer of the Bill for £600 . . . to be ignorant of the Decree, and if he prefers a suit in England to the natural and obvious recourse against the Endorsement, I must in that case defend myself'. French & Co. accepted the challenge, sued the partners of Boyd, Ker et Cie and obtained a verdict for £614.13.0.

Another similar case came before the courts. In October, Baril & Daubuz, merchants of Winchester Street, London, presented to Boyd,

24. Henri Pirenne, *Histoire de Belgique*, Brussels, Maurice Lamertin, 1926, vol. V, p. 464; Claims on France, PRO, T. 78/16; Report from the Select Committee on the Tenth Naval Report, 1805, Evidence of Drummond, pp. 69 and 75.

Benfield & Co. for acceptance, bills totalling £1,090. They had been made payable to one of Boyd, Ker et Cie's clerks, had been endorsed by him to Artaud Larabre et Cie, who had negotiated them through Texier, Angely & Massac of Amsterdam, who in turn sent them to Baril & Daubuz, their London correspondents. When the bills were presented Boyd refused to accept or pay them, and tried to find out from Baril & Daubuz whether the bills had been remitted for account of the National Convention. He offered to pay the bills if Baril & Daubuz were 'fair and bona fide holders' on their own account, and had been unable to obtain payment or satisfaction out of Boyd, Ker et Cie's assets in France. Baril & Daubuz refused, sued Boyd, Ker et Cie and obtained a verdict for £1,014.2.2.[25]

Reports of the exchange controls introduced in France at the end of December, 1793 reached London by the middle of January. Pitt, Chancellor of the Exchequer and prime minister, realising the implications, needed details with a view to countermeasures. Because England and France were at war, official channels were not open, and he enquired of Boyd. Whether this was his first contact with Boyd does not appear, but he apparently thought that Boyd was sufficiently close to the Paris scene to have the information required. As it turned out, he was wrong. Geneste, in Paris, had had his own problems, and had evidently not thought of sending to Boyd in London a copy of the decree. Boyd, in returning on January 19 a questionnaire Pitt had asked him to complete, had to admit that he had not been able to obtain a copy of the decree, or a newspaper giving an account of it. As a practical step, he thought that a declaration of 'a few Merchants of Eminence' would justify an order of council prohibiting the acceptance of any bill drawn from France, or for French account, or the transfer of any stock or the delivery of any property held for French account, pending legislation.[26]

Copies of the decrees reached London by the end of the month and, on February 1, Pitt, in the Commons, promised legislation. The *London Chronicle* published a translation, and commented on February 3: 'Several of the first merchants of London will be very deeply affected by the . . . arbitrary decree if some law is not passed . . . to counteract the effect of it and prohibit any money being remitted out of the nation under such circumstances. . . .'

On March 1 came the promised legislation, when an Act (34 Geo. III, c. 9) was passed making it treasonable for anyone in Great Britain to pay or remit money for the French government, or for anyone who was in France after 1 January 1794, or to accept, pay or endorse any bill for them. No one holding money or goods for anyone in France was to part with them, although goods could be sold if the proceeds were retained. No one was to be subject to a penalty or damages for conforming to the Act. This was obviously a stop-gap measure, and it was several months before a further Act (34 Geo. III, c. 79) provided for the appointment of five commissioners (a favourite eighteenth-century device), to whom those owing money or holding property for persons in France had to report. The

25. Boyd v. French, Chancery, Judicial (Equity Side), PRO, C. 12/650/11.
26. Boyd to Pitt, 19 Jan, 1794, Chatham Papers, PRO, ͻU/8/115.

Commissioners would order money to be paid to the Bank of England, who could invest it in certain government stocks. Alternatively, with the agreement of the commissioners, money could be paid to a British bank. Bills drawn before 1st January or accepted before 1st February 1794 were not covered by the Act.

Unfortunately, this legislation did not give Boyd the protection he needed, for the bills had been drawn earlier. He therefore entered a complaint in Chancery, pointing out that creditors of Boyd, Ker et Cie had the right to claim on the firm's assets which had been confiscated, and stating that Boyd, Ker et Cie received no consideration for the bills, that their clerk might have been compelled to endorse them, and that Baril & Daubuz merely held the bills in trust for persons in France. To this Baril & Daubuz answered that proceeding against Artaud, Larabre et Cie would be useless, since the firm had failed, that if the bills were paid no part of the proceeds would be remitted to France, and that they intended to apply the money in reduction of the amount due to them. Andrew French & Co. pointed out that payment could not be received from France, so that in practice the right to claim against the French government was useless. Furthermore, they said, the bills had been presented for acceptance before the October decrees were passed. After dragging on for a year, Boyd's complaint was dismissed in May, 1795.[27]

If the legislation did not give Boyd the protection he wanted, there is some evidence that it was effective in its avowed purpose of preventing the French from obtaining much foreign exchange as a result of the December decree. In a report of 19 March 1794 the Commission on Materials (Commission des Substances) informed the Committee of Public Safety that the requisition produced practically nothing, and that since the English legislation [of 1 March, 1794] and a similar ordinance passed in Holland, the small amount of paper obtained had been returned unpaid.[28]

Since Boyd left France in the autumn of 1792, there had been great changes in his world. War had broken out, first with Spain, then with Austria and then with England, and it was to be a bitter struggle, which would last longer and spread more widely that he, or any one else at that time, foresaw. The partners of the Paris house had scattered, never to come together again. Ker and Laborde were in England, but no longer in partnership with Boyd. Walckiers was in Hamburg. Only Walter Boyd, Junior, had joined Boyd, Benfield & Co., and he was not a partner, although he became a close associate of his cousin, Boyd, senior. The device for ensuring the Paris firm's survival had been rendered useless by the death of Geneste, and its assets were being liquidated by an official administrator. Their recovery, if possible at all, would be long and difficult, but it was a prospect which was never far from Boyd's tenacious mind.

27. Boyd v. Baril, Chancery, Judicial (Equity Side) PRO, C. 12/612/650.
28. Bouchary, *Le Marché des Changes*, op.cit., p. 78.

CHAPTER IV

Negotiations with Austria

'So great a Facility has never yet been given by this Country to an Ally'.
Lord Grenville to Sir Morton Eden, 14th April 1795.

'L'on est en verité à plaindre, lorsqu'on a à faire avec ces diables d'Anglais'.
Baron Thugut to Count Colleredo, 5th May 1795.

When Boyd, Benfield & Co. opened their doors in March 1793, France had been at war with Spain, Austria and Prussia for a year, and with Great Britain for a month. The French secured initial successes, and by November 1792 they had occupied Antwerp, Ghent and Brussels. The tide turned in 1793, and by the spring most of the invading forces had withdrawn. A British force under the Duke of York landed in May, and in the same month came the appointment of Count Starhemberg[1] as Austrian envoy extraordinary and minister plenipotentiary at the Court of St. James. His first task was to negotiate a treaty of alliance. In this he was successful, and an 'Agreement between Austria and Great Britain regarding Military Operations against France' was signed in London on 30 August, 1793.[2]

The Netherlands treasury was in no position to stand the strain of a war, and in November 1793 the Treasurer-General, Viscount de Sandrouin, was charged with the negotiation of a loan in England.[3] Early in 1794, Starhemberg was instructed to ask the British government for permission to raise a loan of £1 million.[4] The first step was to open negotiations through the Ghent firm of de Loose with Brook Watson,

---

1. Ludwig Graf (later Fürst) Starhemberg (1762–1833).
2. The succeeding negotiations between the British and Austrian Governments in connection with the loans to Austria have been described in some detail by Professor Karl Ferdinand Helleiner in *'The Imperial Loans',* Clarendon Press, Oxford, 1965. The present work touches on these negotiations only as background to a description of the activities of Boyd, Benfield & Co. as the Austrian Government's bankers. See also John M. Sherwig, *Guineas and Gunpowder: British Foreign Aid in the Wars with France 1793–1815,* Harvard University Press, Cambridge, Mass., [1969].
3. Mercy-Argenteau to Starhemberg, 5 Nov., 1793, A. Graf Thürheim, *Briefe des Grafen Mercy-Argenteau . . . an den . . . Grafen Louis Starhemberg . . .* Innsbruck, Verlag der Wagner'schen Universitäts-Buchhandlung, 1884, p. 154.
4. Starhemberg to Pergen, 13 April, 1795, Alfred von Vivenot, *Quellen zur Geschichte der Politik Oesterreichs während der französischen Revolutionskriege,* vol. V, Vienna, Wilhelm Braumüller, 1890, p. 168.

Commissary-General to the British army in the Netherlands, who was acting on behalf of certain English houses. Brook Watson had negotiated his bills for army supplies through de Loose,[5] but the firm were not well known, and it soon became evident that they had insufficient backing to carry through a major transaction.[6] Veuve Nettine et Fils then became involved in the discussions as bankers to the Austrian administration, and early in 1794 Rosalie Pauline de Walckiers, sister of Édouard de Walckiers and a manager of Veuve Nettine et Fils, came to London for discussions with Starhemberg and someone, referred to as a 'correspondent', who was probably Boyd.[7] De Loose, hearing of these moves, felt aggrieved, and indulged in what Starhemberg called 'mean and underhand intrigues which have ruined Austria's credit.'[8]

A new start was clearly necessary, and at the end of March de Sandrouin was sent to London bearing a letter from Mercy-Argenteau to Pitt, his main objective being to clear up the confusion resulting from Walckier's visit and to open negotiations with Boyd, Benfield & Co., who had been recommended strongly to the Government-General by Veuve Nettine et Fils.[9] In writing to Starhemberg, Mercy emphasised the importance of the loan for the forthcoming campaign, reminding him that Great Britain, no less than Austria, was interested in its success. The mere consent of Pitt to the issue, he continued, would be useless, or at best inadequate, unless it could be accompanied by more tangible assistance to the lenders.[10]

In London, de Sandrouin told Starhemberg that he had been instructed to increase the amount of the loan from £1 million to £3 millions. Starhemberg advised him to approach leading banking houses, rather than deal with Boyd, Benfield & Co. 'Le succès des affaires dépend essentiellement des personnes auxquelles on s'adresse.' De Sandrouin replied that he had orders to employ Boyd, Benfield & Co. Boyd, he explained, although relatively unknown in England, had great ability, and had a partner of considerable wealth in Benfield.[11] Whether convinced or not, Starhemberg accepted the situation, and the next few weeks were occupied in conferences and negotiations.

There were many obstacles to overcome. Boyd did not find it easy to obtain subscribers. The issue in London of a loan for a foreign power was unusual, and past experience in foreign lending was hardly reassuring. Merchants recalled the loan, secured on Silesian revenues, raised by the Emperor Charles VI in 1734, which went into default as a result of the conquest of Silesia by Frederick II of Prussia.[12] As an inducement to sub-

5. Thugut to the Emperor, 12 Aug., 1794, A. von Vivenot, op.cit., vol. IV, pp. 384–6; Treasury to Brook Watson, 7 May, 1793, Commissariat Out-Letters, PRO, W.O., 58/167; Bill Book of Brook Watson, PRO, T. 64/122.
6. Starhemberg to Pergen, 13 April, 1795, A. von Vivenot, op.cit., vol. V, p. 168.
7. Mercy to Starhemberg, 14 Jan, 1794, Thürheim, op.cit., p. 193; Metternich to Trautmannsdorf, 23 March, 1794, A.von Vivenot, op.cit., vol. IV, p. 159.
8. Starhemberg to Thugut, 6 May, 1794, A.von Vivenot, op.cit., vol. IV, 1885, p. 211.
9. Starhemberg's dispatches of 27 June and 22 July 1794, cited by Helleiner, op.cit., p. 5.
10. Mercy-Argenteau to Starhemberg, 23 Mar., 1794, Thürheim, op.cit., pp. 212–3.
11. Starhemberg to Pergen, 13 April, 1795, A. von Vivenot, op.cit., vol. V, p. 168.
12. T. Baty, ed., *Prize Law and Continuous Voyage*, London, Stevens & Haynes, [1915], p. 116.

scribe, Boyd had to promise a commission to some of those on his list – a payment which came out of his own profit.[13] He also had to contend with open opposition. On April 28 Godschall Johnson, John Julius Angerstein and James Morgan, contractors for the £11 million loan for Great Britain arranged some two months earlier, posted a notice in the Stock Exchange saying that they had expressly agreed with Pitt that there would be no further loan or funding during the year, apart from an issue of £2 million of Exchequer Bills.[14] Two days later *The Times* came out with a statement that the Austrian loan was not made with the sanction of government, 'nor has the Minister at all committed himself in this business'.

These difficulties did not discourage Boyd, who wrote to de Sandrouin at the end of the month to say that arrangements for the loan could be regarded as complete, promising a list of subscribers in the near future. He asked de Sandrouin to make a formal request for permission to raise the loan, adding that he (de Sandrouin) had assured him he could count on getting permission and that his friends had subscribed on this basis.[15] On May 5 Boyd, Starhemberg and de Sandrouin obtained an interview with Pitt, who assured them that the loan was legal and that the Government was pleased with its success.[16]

Opposition in the City, however, was still being voiced. On May 8 *The Times* wrote disparagingly: 'The Emperors Loan, we rejoice to hear does not fill; and no one can wonder at it for although . . . the Court of Vienna is justly esteemed, yet there is something which carries misfortune with it, to see large sums of money sent out of a nation to a foreign Power'. Boyd felt that such views should be countered, and wrote immediately to Pitt. He admitted that holders of the funds protested that it would cause a fall in market prices, and that leading merchants said that it would put pressure on the exchanges and cause an outflow of gold and silver. This, said Boyd, was in direct contradiction 'to mercantile experience'. He pointed out optimistically that Austrian credit was better known on the Continent that it was in England, and that a considerable part of the loan would be remitted to London from foreign countries. It was being issued in London rather than abroad because no other place had such important connections with every other country, and because remittance of the proceeds would be easier from London than from elsewhere. 'Why should she forego the advantages of being as it were the Banker of Europe?' he asked.[17] He pointed out that the exchange was at a premium, and that it did not matter if it fell nearer 'its natural level', as a high exchange hampered exports. In any case, he had his own ideas of the way remittances could be made. 'I have formed my plan of remittance', he wrote, 'in such a manner as that *produce* and *manufactures* may make the principal part of it, and instead of purchasing Bills of Exchange I intend to draw the greatest part of the Loan upon my Correspondents in Holland, Hamburg

13. Boyd to Pitt, 31 May, 1795, CUL, Pitt Correspondence, Add. 6958/10.
14. *The Times*, 29 April, 1794.
15. Boyd to de Sandrouin, 28 April, 1794, Chatham Papers, PRO, 30/8/180.
16. Boyd to Pitt, 5 May, 1794, *The Times*, 19 May, 1794.
17. An active foreign exchange market in London was an important factor in Great Britain's development as a lender overseas.

and other Countries and to send Manufactures and produce from this Country to pay my Bills'.[18]

In spite of these arguments, Pitt still hesitated. Boyd, anxious to press ahead while his subscribers were still interested, decided to release the terms of the loan to the press, which he did in a letter which was published on May 14 in the *Oracle* and *General Advertiser*, a journal generally sympathetic to Pitt. Signed rather inappropriately, 'No Loanist', it gave full particulars of the loan. Opposition to the loan was apparently voiced, for two days later, another letter from 'No Loanist' appeared. 'Why, Sir', he wrote, 'would you think it, they even carried their *boldness* and *imagery* so far as to assert, that the Imperial Loan does not fill, although it was been completely filled near three weeks ago?' He concluded with the jingle:

'Why all the rout about the Loan,
When all who want it — know its gone'.[19]

This publicity seems to have provoked Pitt to reply to Boyd's letter asking for Government approval of the loan, for on May 17 he wrote Boyd a carefully worded letter saying that he was 'not aware of any law to prohibit a loan to a foreign state at amity with this country and that in the present case Government by no means wish to object to a measure for the accommodation of his Imperial Majesty with whom his Majesty is engaged in the closest union and consort'.[20] Pitt's letter had a dramatic effect. A few days later *The Times* reported: 'The loan seems now to be generally approved of, and fills very rapidly . . . Very large orders from abroad have been received for this subscription, more than one-half of which is likely to go among foreigners'.[21]

While Boyd was thus preparing the ground for an issue, the Austrian representatives in London were sending optimistic reports to Vienna. Even though no contract had been signed, Starhemberg wrote on May 6 saying that the first payment had been made and remitted to Brussels, and a week later de Sandrouin reported that Boyd, Benfield & Co. were unable to satisfy the requests for shares in the loan which came to them from banking houses in Holland, Italy, Germany and elsewhere on the Continent.[22] The *Oracle* reported that the Emperor had written to the Chancellor of Brabant 'expressing, in high terms, the pleasing sense he entertains of the liberality and honour with which the Loan for 3,000,000L has been subscribed, . . . which, the commentator added, must be an agreeable and flattering circumstance to the very respectable Commercial House that undertook the negotiation'.[23]

The loan contract (octroi) was signed by the Emperor at Tournai in the Austrian Netherlands on May 18, no doubt much to Boyd's relief. It pro-

18. Boyd to Pitt, 9 May, 1794, Chatham Papers, PRO, 30/8/115.
19. A prospectus was published, probably about this time. A copy in English is in Chatham Papers, PRO, 30/8/61 and a copy in French in PRO, F.O. 7/40. Neither is signed or dated.
20. *The Times*, 19 May, 1794.
21. *The Times*, 22 May, 1794.
22. Starhemberg to Thugut, 6 May, 1794, Vivenot, op.cit., vol. IV, p. 211; de Sandrouin to Starhemberg, 14 May, 1794, Chatham Papers, PRO, 30/8/180.
23. *Oracle*, 19 May, 1794.

vided that 'A loan of three millions of pounds sterling, payable in ready money, shall be opened in the City of London, at the House of Walter Boyd, Paul Benfield and James Drummond, merchants in London, in the firm of Boyd, Benfield & Co., bankers to his Majesty, appointed for that purpose'. In consideration of their advancing £3,000,000 in cash, the lenders were to receive bonds for £5,000,000 three per cent. annuities, valued at sixty per cent., and annuity bonds for £150,000 a year for twenty-five years, payable half-yearly, valued at ten years' purchase. The three per cent. annuities had no fixed redemption date, but the borrower could redeem them at par at any time. There was to be a sinking fund of £60,000 a year, which, together with the interest on annuities previously redeemed, was to be applied by Boyd, Benfield & Co. in buying bonds in the market.

The borrower reserved the right to remit the amount required for interest, sinking fund and annuities, either to Veuve Nettine et Fils, Brussels, or to Boyd, Benfield & Co., London. Interest and half-yearly annuities were payable at the counting house of Boyd, Benfield & Co., or at an office designated by them. The anomaly of issuing a sterling loan payable in London, the service monies for which, could, at the option of the borrower, be provided either in London or Brussels, admits of no obvious explanation. Boyd does not seem to have envisaged the possibility of Veuve Nettine et Fils being unable to remit funds to London.

To secure the loan, the Emperor was to pledge 'the clear surplus, free from all charge, of all our royal revenues . . . and especially the revenues of our provinces in the Low Countries'. As collateral security, five per cent. debentures (referred to as 'mortgage actions') of the Bank of Vienna (Wiener Stadtbanco) in an amount equivalent to four million pounds sterling, were to be deposited with Boyd, Benfield & Co., and held at the Bank of England. The Bank of Vienna, although originally purely a municipal institution, had become to all intents and purposes a government department whose main function was to service public debt.[24]

Payment for the loan was to be made by instalments, the first, of five per cent., on the 20 May 1794, and the ninth and last in March 1795; those who paid in advance were allowed a discount. The twenty-five-year annuities showed a yield equivalent to 8.88 per cent. per annum. The three per cent. annuities gave a current yield of five per cent.: what they would yield to redemption could not be determined, since it would depend on the prices at which they were purchased for the sinking fund. Contemporaries usually avoided this difficulty by saying (quite misleadingly) that the yield on the whole loan was seven-and-one-half per cent., which they computed by adding the interest on the three per cent. annuities in the first year to the amount of twenty-five-year annuity which was payable each year.

In May, when the agreement was signed, there was much support for the loan, *The Times* maintaining that opinion on the Stock Exchange was that

24. An English translation of the octroi is in *Parliamentary History*, vol. 31, cols. 1561–4. Helleiner, op.cit., p. 10–11, criticises Boyd for making the Austrian government 'go through the motions' of putting up these debentures as security. In fact, it was not uncommon for them to be used to secure borrowings abroad. James C. Riley, *International Government Finance and the Amsterdam Capital Market 1740–1815*, Cambridge University Press, 1980, p. 127.

there was every prospect of the loan being fully subscribed and quoted at a considerable premium before the end of the month.[25] The advance of the French into the Netherlands in the summer of 1794 completely changed the situation. Boyd and his subscribers, seeing that the chief security for their loan – the revenues of the Austrian Netherlands – had disappeared, refused unanimously to advance a shilling unless the loan were guaranteed by the British government.[26] Some subscribers tried to withdraw altogether. Others, including the well-known merchant banker, Peter Thellusson, sold out at four per cent. discount.[27] This attitude, although embarrassing to the Austrian Government, was natural, having regard to the circumstances, and it must be admitted that the actions of the Austrians did not inspire confidence. For example, they allowed debentures of the Bank of Vienna, which formed the collateral security for the loan, to fall into arrears.

Boyd was left in no doubt about the view which the Austrian Government took of his refusal to fulfil his commitments. In June, Starhemberg, making no progress with Boyd, suggested to Baron Thugut, Austrian foreign minister,[28] that Veuve, Nettine et Fils should be pressed to meet Boyd's obligations, since it was at their particular recommendation that he had been brought in. He pointed out that the fact that Boyd, Benfield & Co. were not in the front rank of mercantile houses was not calculated to facilitate the operation, especially as many of the most wealthy and influential dealers in the funds had shown a marked jealousy that Boyd, a newcomer, had been given such a big contract.[29] The suggestion that Nettine should be approached was not very practical, for this firm's position had been undermined by the war, and it was common knowledge in London that a substantial proportion of their funds were invested in French bills and trading operations.[30] Not much help could be expected from Brussels.

The obvious course was to ask for a British guarantee. Austria was engaged with Great Britain in a struggle against a common enemy. What could be more appropriate than for the financially strong partner to aid the weaker partner? In fact there were several objections which could be raised. A British guarantee would require the consent of Parliament, and the opposition, strengthened by public opinion against foreign loans and subsidies, would doubtless try to ensure that consent was withheld. Secondly, since the terms of the Imperial loan had been fixed originally on the basis of Austrian credit, a retrospective guarantee would be for a loan raised on more onerous terms than could have been obtained had it carried a British guarantee from the start. The Treasury, it was said, would hardly guarantee the loan unless its terms were made less favourable to the lenders – a prospect which, for Boyd at least, held no attractions. For

25. *The Times*, 21 May, 1794.
26. Starhemberg to Pergen, 13 April, 1795, Vivenot, op.cit., vol. V, p. 168.
27. Starhemberg to Thugut, 27 June, 1794, Vivenot, op.cit., vol. IV, p. 306.
28. Johannes Amadeus Franz de Paula, Baron von Thugut (1736–1818) became foreign minister in 1793.
29. Starhemberg to Thugut, 27 June, 1794, Vivenot, op.cit., vol.IV, p. 306.
30. Thugut to the Emperor, 12 Aug., 1794, Vivenot, op.cit., vol. IV, p. 385.

Austria, there was the disadvantage that Britain would probably exact a price in terms of military commitments for any assistance she gave, and the Imperial Court would prefer to avoid conditions of this sort. Boyd accordingly sought another way out, and early in July he drew up a scheme which he forwarded to Petrie,[31] for submission to Pitt.

The scheme was simple. The Commissioners for the National Debt would be authorised to transfer three per cent. Consols valued at sixty-eight per cent. (the current market price) to holders of Imperial scrip wishing to make the exchange. Thus a holder of Imperial loan would never be worse off, and might be better off, as far as capital was concerned, than someone who had bought three per cent. Consols at sixty-eight, for if the price of Imperial loan fell relatively to Consols, it would pay him to exchange. Meantime, so long as he held Imperial loan, he would draw a substantially higher income.

The scheme was cleverly framed to avoid the objections which might be raised to a guarantee. The sanction of Parliament would be required, it is true, but the 'back door' method of using the sinking fund would attract less opposition than a direct guarantee. Secondly, it met the difficulty which arose from the disparity between Austrian and British credit. 'Great Britain would not in this case appear to guarantee a loan made on terms so much less favourable than those on which she is accustomed to borrow herself. On the contrary, the scheme would result in a most important advantage for the Sinking-fund, because every such exchange would, for an annuity of somewhat less than four and a half per cent., transfer an annuity of seven and a half per cent. to the Sinking-fund . . . were one to admit the possibility of the whole being availed of, there would be a gain to the British Sinking-fund of clear £90,000 a year'.

But, said Boyd, it was inconceivable that the whole loan would be exchanged. 'The moment that the Holders of Imperial Scrip should know that they could transfer it into three per cent. Consolidated Annuities, their desire to make the exchange would cease, because the bare knowledge of Government being thus ready to interpose its Credit in support of the Imperial Loan would give to this latter a degree of credit and currency little short of those which the British funds enjoy.'

Finally, the scheme would not offend Austrian susceptibilities, and would obviate further Anglo-Austrian negotiations. 'The Emperor's Loan would thus, so far as the Court of Vienna is concerned, be still a Loan made to him by Individuals in England and not by the Court of London'. As an alternative, 'in case there should be any strong objection to the offering of a funded Security,' Boyd suggested that an unfunded security, such as Exchequer Bills might be offered instead of Consols.[32] The scheme was ingenious — perhaps a little too ingenious for it to have much chance of success. Petrie sent it to Pitt on July 7, but Pitt was reluctant to intervene, and nothing was done.

31. John Petrie (1748–1816) was a brother of William Petrie: he had been in the Bengal Civil Service from 1773 to 1788, and had long been a customer of Boyd, Ker et Cie. He became member for Gatton, Surrey in 1796. He and his brother were partners in J. Petrie Campbell & Co., and in Walwyn, Petrie & Co.
32. Memorandum in Boyd's handwriting, undated, Chatham Papers, PRO, 30/8/166.

Two weeks later, de Sandrouin raised the subject at a conference with Pitt. He could not paint a bright picture. Austria's war expenses were equivalent to over £8 millions sterling, and the budget showed a deficit of £1 million. To cover this, and to provide in addition £2 millions towards the expenses of the next campaign, £3 millions had to be raised. Of the £3 millions loan arranged with Boyd, Benfield and Co., only the first instalment of £300,000 had been paid in full. The second instalment of a like amount had fallen due on July 20, but towards this only the trifling sum of £2,500 had been paid, and unless fresh steps were taken the loan would have to be considered a failure. Boyd, Benfield & Co. would make advances as far as they were able, but these could only be small in relation to the amount contracted for.

De Sandrouin then mentioned Boyd's idea of the option of exchanging into three per cent. Consols, a plan which, said de Sandrouin, seemed to give all that was desired. He admitted, however, that it would have to await the reassembly of Parliament, which made it necessary to consider other means. He therefore suggested that if £500,000 were applied secretly in the purchase of Imperial loan, it would have the double effect of placing money in the hands of Boyd, Benfield & Co. as Imperial agents,[33] and of raising Austrian credit. Even making secret purchases on a smaller scale to the extent of £10,000 to £20,000 a week, pending the result of further negotiations in Vienna, would inspire a new confidence in the loan. As an additional measure, he thought of issuing a pamphlet which would explain to the public the resources and credit of the house of Austria. If, by means such as these, the subscribers could be induced to make good their engagements to the extent of £1 million, this would be sufficient for immediate needs, and would allow time for new arrangements to be made to secure the balance of £2 millions.

Pitt did not seem to have been taken aback by these proposals, unorthodox, to say the least. While he would not give de Sandrouin any assurance, he 'thought it well worth Consideration whether . . . Measures might not be devised for advancing a moderate sum to induce the Subscribers to the present Loan to make good their Payments to the Extent of 1,000,000l (the Court of Vienna releasing them from their Obligation for the Remainder)'[34]

The arrival in London of the debentures of the Bank of Vienna in July raised Boyd's hopes that Austrian credit would improve, and that he would be able to find sufficient new subscribers to replace those who had withdrawn. But he seemed to have little confidence that this would be possible, and pressed Starhemberg to ask for a British guarantee. Starhemberg demurred; the credit of Austria, he thought, was sufficiently well established in Europe to make the guarantee of a foreign power unnecessary; moreover, an application would most certainly be refused, as

33. Presumably the money would be held by Boyd, Benfield & Co. only temporarily, pending its disbursement for purchases of Imperial loan in the market.
34. Memorandum by Pitt, 25 July 1794; Note by de Sandrouin to Pitt, received 27 July 1794, PRO, F.O. 7/38.

the terms of the last loan precluded the raising of any foreign loan.[35]

Meantime, Mercy-Argenteau was becoming anxious about these long-drawn-out negotiations, and was urging Starhemberg to lose no opportunity to bring about a favourable outcome.[36] In Vienna, too, there was much concern, and the Emperor decided to send Mercy himself on a special mission to London with the object of bringing the loan negotiations to a successful conclusion.[37] He was also to endeavour to obtain subsidies, but as their negotiation would take time, he was instructed to press for temporary advances, secured by a special mortgage on the Austrian Netherlands.[38] But Thugut's hopes were not to be fulfilled. The seventy-two-year-old Mercy fell ill soon after he arrived in England, and he died on August 25, without being able to fulfil his mission.[39]

At the same time as Mercy-Argenteau was being sent to London, Lord Spencer and Thomas Grenville were on their way to Vienna, their main object being to stimulate Austria to further military efforts.[40] On the subject of the loan, they were told that no guarantee was possible while Parliament was in recess, but they were not to reject any other suggestions which would facilitate receipt of part of the loan at once.[41] The Austrians lost no time in impressing on the British envoys the urgent need for financial aid, if Austria was to make any military contribution. Not only did Thugut urge the need for a loan; a subsidy was also necessary, and he suggested that the Prussian subsidy, which was due to stop at the end of the year, should be transferred to Austria.[42] Thomas Grenville was frankly cynical. 'They will, I fear,' he wrote to London, 'again play with us by giving orders to move when they get money only, and they will probably get none till the places are lost which they ought to recover.'[43]

Starhemberg, in London, had now come round to Boyd's idea of a guarantee.[44] At a meeting with Pitt and Grenville, the Foreign Secretary,[45]

35. Starhemberg to Thugut, 11 July, 1794, Vivenot, op.cit., vol. IV, p. 332. The terms appear to have precluded a loan for Great Britain as well; passim, p. 48.
36. Mercy-Argenteau to Starhemberg, 17 and 27 June and 7 and 12 July, 1794. Thürheim, op.cit., pp. 236, 244, 247, 251.
37. Thugut to Colloredo, 12 July 1794. Alfred von Vivenot, *Vertrauliche Briefe des Freiherrn von Thugut*, Willhelm Braumüller, Vienna, 1872, vol. I, p. 113. His terms of reference are in Emperor to Mercy, 15 July, 1794, Vivenot, *Thugut, Clerfayt und Wurmser, Original Documente*, Wilhelm Braumüller, Vienna, 1896, pp. 601–9.
38. Thugut to Mercy-Argenteau, (20–31?) July, 1794, Vivenot, op.cit., pp. 606–9.
39. *Biographie Nationale de Belgique* (1894–1895), vol. 13, pp. 462–495.
40. Foreign Office to Straton, 19 July, 1794, PRO, F.O. 7/37, Lord Spencer, George John, second Earl Spencer (1758–1834). Thomas Grenville (1755–1846) was Lord Grenville's brother.
41. Lord Grenville to Lord Spencer and Thos. Grenville, 26 Aug., 1794, PRO, F.O. 7/38; Thugut to Mercy-Argenteau, 21 Aug., 1794, Vivenot, *Quellen*, op.cit., vol. IV, p. 392.
42. Lord Spencer and Thos. Grenville to Lord Grenville, 12 Aug. 1794, PRO, F.O. 7/38.
43. Thomas Grenville to Lord Grenville, 12 Aug. 1794, *Dropmore Papers* vol. II, 1894, p. 614.
44. '. . . perhaps the rapidity of Count Starhemberg may carry it on more expeditiously than all the diplomatic buckram of the old Court', George III to Lord Grenville, 25 Aug., 1794, *Dropmore Papers,* vol. II, p. 625.
45. William Wyndham, Baron Grenville (1759–1834) was Foreign Secretary from June 1791 to February 1801.

towards the end of August, he reminded Pitt of his promise to support the loan and asked outright for a guarantee. Pitt immediately raised objections: a guarantee was impossible without the consent of Parliament, and it would be extremely inconvenient to call Parliament together at that time. Starhemberg said that he would be content for the present with a private undertaking from Pitt to obtain a guarantee as soon as Parliament reassembled, as this would at least inspire Boyd, Benfield & Co. with some confidence, and enable them to make further advances on account of the loan.

During the next few days, British policy, so long fluid, crystallised. Pitt decided that Austria had to be assisted — on terms. On August 26, Grenville informed Starhemberg that on his urgent recommendation the British Government would advance £150,000 immediately, independently of the loan, on an assurance that the Austrian armies would not retire except on direct orders from the Austrian Court: the Government would also consider further advances. On the important question of the loan, Grenville assured Starhemberg that the British Government desired sincerely to assist, although a formal undertaking to give a guarantee at some future date was as impossible as an immediate guarantee.[46]

At the same time as this decision was communicated to them, Spencer and Thomas Grenville in Vienna were told that if the question of the command of the two armies could be settled satisfactorily, 'His Majesty would then be disposed to listen to the idea of proposing to His Parliament to give an eventual Guaranty of the Austrian Loan'. Further assistance, as a subsidy, could provide for a proportional increase in the Austrian forces. The Government clearly had misgivings about the whole matter, but, as Lord Grenville put it, 'His Majesty's Servants . . . are on the whole induced to think that the Experiment ought to be hazarded.'[47] The decision did much to reassure Boyd, and he was soon able to show Starhemberg a long list of those ready to subscribe as soon as the guarantee was passed by Parliament. Starhemberg, greatly encouraged, reported confidently to Vienna that the list of subscribers would soon be complete, and that most of the instalments would be paid before the end of the year – two months earlier than had been expected originally. With prospects thus improved, Boyd, Benfield & Co. now found themselves having sufficient funds in hand on account of the Loan to enable them to remit £50,000 to Veuve Nettine et Fils, which they did in Spanish dollars.[48]

No time was lost in dealing with the advance of £150,000, the first £50,000 of which was to be made available early in September. It was agreed that the money should be paid to Starhemberg in London, who would hand it over to de Sandrouin as Treasurer-General, he in turn paying it to Boyd, Benfield & Co., who were responsible for remitting it to the Continent.[49] To provide the British government with some security for these advances, Boyd, Benfield & Co. deposited with the Bank of England

46. Starhemberg to Thugut, 26 Aug. 1794, Vivenot, op.cit., vol. IV, pp. 406 and 408.
47. Lord Grenville to Lord Spencer and Thos. Grenville, 29 Aug., 1794, PRO., F.O. 7/38.
48. Helleiner, op.cit., p. 20.
49. Starhemberg to Thugut, 29 Aug., 1794, Vivenot, op.cit., vol. IV, pp. 412–3.

the collateral security, consisting of 40 million florins of debentures of the Bank of Vienna.[50]

In Vienna, further discussions took place on the means to be adopted to relieve the acute position of the Austrian treasury, and Thugut raised his price, now demanding a British-guaranteed loan of £6 millions. This was to consist of the £3 millions contracted in the previous May, together with a further £3 millions to meet the expenses of the current campaign. By merging the two loans, Thugut hoped to obtain some compensation for what he regarded as the onerous terms on which the first loan had been arranged. These ideas were not encouraged by the British representatives, both of whom declared that £6 millions was an impossibly large sum.[51]

The amount was not the only difficulty; the question of security gave rise to some concern on the British side. The loan, in the Austrian view, was primarily secured on the surplus revenues of the Austrian Netherlands. The Austrian Government, however, showed no great concern at the fate of this part of their empire, being apparently content to rely on the territory being returned after the war, without their having to make great efforts to win it back themselves. If the sole or principal security for the loan were the revenues from the Netherlands, the Austrian resolve to recover the territory might be weakened. Furthermore, if eventually Austria did not recover the Netherlands, the security behind the loan would largely disappear. Thomas Grenville felt that this was a real danger, and suggested that the loan should be secured by a general charge on the Imperial revenues. The Austrian Government apparently acquiesced, although Grenville still had doubts as to their intentions.[52] In October, Spencer and Thomas Grenville returned to London,[53] and further negotiations were suspended, pending the arrival in Vienna of Sir Morton Eden, who had been appointed envoy-extraordinary to the Imperial Court.[54]

To Boyd, this was not altogether displeasing. It hardly suited him to have the main negotiations carried on so far away, where his influence could be so little felt. The interruption of negotiations in Vienna was therefore an opportunity rather than a setback. He and de Sandrouin redoubled their efforts in London, and pressed for a further £3 millions on the same terms as the first £3 millions, the whole to carry a British guarantee. Fortunately for him, he was on good terms with Starhemberg, who, after being at first somewhat critical, now had a very high opinion of his abilities. At the end of October, Starhemberg put his case for a guaranteed loan before Lord Grenville. He said that Austria would not insist on a subsidy, but would ask that the British Government, in ensuring the success of the £3 millions loan by a guarantee or other means, should also include a second £3 millions to cover the forthcoming campaign.[55]

50. Accounts and Papers, 1797–8, vol. 103.
51. Thugut to Colloredo, 20 Sept., 1794, Vivenot, *Vertrauliche Briefe,* op.cit., vol. I, p. 135.
52. Thomas Grenville to Lord Grenville (private), 22 Sept., 1794, Dropmore Papers, vol. II, p. 635.
53. Straton to Lord Grenville, 11 Oct. 1794, F.O. 7/37.
54. Sir Morton Eden, first Baron Henley (1752–1830).
55. Starhemberg to Grenville, 31 Oct. 1794, PRO., F.O. 7/37.

Pitt's reluctance to promise a guarantee was not primarily due to a desire to use the guarantee in bargaining to obtain the maximum military contribution from Austria, or the most advantageous terms for the loan itself. There was a very real doubt about the possibility of raising as large a sum as £6 millions, in addition to the £18 millions required to cover Great Britain's estimated budget deficit for 1795.

The problem was explained in Grenville's instruction to Eden. 'The difficulty', he wrote, 'does not depend so much on the Possibility that this Government might ultimately become liable to the Payment of the Interest and Capital of the proposed Loan, as on the Inconvenience which would arise from the Demand for so large a Sum to be taken from the floating Capital of this Country at a time when the Sum to be borrowed for the Service of this Government . . . will . . . exceed all former Example'. After pointing out the adverse effect of such an 'immense Demand for Money' on the price of the funds, he suggested that part might be raised abroad'. . . . . if the Opportunity should occur', he wrote, 'of raising a Loan, to some limited Amount, either in Holland or Italy, so that the Money lent should not be a Drain upon the Capital of the Country, the King would be disposed to recommend to Parliament to facilitate such an Operation by the Guaranty of the British Government . . . the Republic [of the United Netherlands] might unquestionably raise a contribution to a very large Amount. . . .'[56]

The idea of raising a loan on the Continent, however, was quite impracticable, and, in fact, the money required could be found only in London. During the second half of November there was much discussion involving Boyd, Pitt, Sir William Pulteney and others, about arrangements under which Great Britain's need for £18 million, together with £6 million for Austria, could be covered at a time when the scale of Austria's war effort was still being negotiated. Sentiment in the City was certainly not favourable to a foreign loan, even one with a guarantee. While Boyd was involved in these discussions, Benfield was not, and was aware only of their general course. Early in December, feeling somewhat isolated and depressed, he wrote to Boyd, coming out, as he said, with 'all that occurs to my Mind'. His two main suggestions were not very practical: one was an Austrian loan convertible into three per cent. Consols, an idea which Boyd had put forward, without success, in the previous July. The other was the inclusion of Austria's needs in the loan for Great Britain, which would have immediately put the whole burden on British shoulders, and would hardly be acceptable to the Treasury. There was also a third proposal, if all else failed, the 'liquidation in full in some proper time', of that part of the original £3 million loan that had already been disbursed.[57]

So far from being hopeless, prospects were in fact looking much better. Boyd had succeeded in winning to his side, some of the old-established houses who had previously contracted for loans, and he had just started to negotiate with them on the basis of linking the two loans together. Certainly, there were still problems. On the same day that Benfield wrote

---

56. Grenville to Eden, 26 Nov. 1794, PRO, F.O. 7/39.
57. P[aul] B[enfield] to [Boyd] 3 Dec. 1794, Paul Benfield Papers, IO. Eur. C. 307/5.

his rather defeatist letter, Boyd was reporting to Pitt that he had run into 'unexpected and ill-founded difficulties', with his friends.[58] These probably arose, not from any basic obstacles, but from the technical complication of having to bid for two loans, the terms of which differed, at a time when one of them (the Austrian loan) might never materialise, if Parliament refused its guarantee. Boyd's answer was to ask his friends to prepare two offers, one for the two loans together, the other for a loan for Great Britain only,[59] and on December 6 Boyd was able to say that his friends were ready. The cabinet then authorised Pitt to ascertain the terms that might be obtained and the standing of the parties proposing to contract.[60]

They formed quite an impressive group. Headed by Boyd, Benfield & Co., it consisted of Benjamin and Abraham Goldsmid, dealers and brokers in bills of exchange and stocks; the merchant bankers, Thelluson Brothers & Co., who had contracted for the loan for 1793; Abraham Robarts, principal partner in the banking firm of Robarts, Curtis & Co.;[61] John and George Ward, merchants; and Rawson Aislabie, Eleazer Philip Salomons, and Soloman Salomons, dealers in the funds.

The contractors proposed proved acceptable, and it remained only for Boyd to agree with Pitt, the amount of Long Annuity to be given, in addition to three per cent. and four per cent. Consols, under each of the two alternatives. On December 9 everything seemed ready, when at the eleventh hour, came the suggestion, almost certainly from Pitt, that there should be competition. The situation was delicate. After consulting 'the leading man' in his group (probably Robarts), Boyd wrote on December 9 to Pitt: '. . . I feel a peculiar repugnance to this new proposal, particularly as it seems to threaten disagreeable effects in the opinion of the Austrian Minister of finance'. He added, as if to clinch the matter: 'My friends are so convinced that the offer they will make is a fair and liberal one that they will surely decline a competition'. Faced with such determined opposition, Pitt gave way, and dropped the idea. On the same day, according to a report by Starhemberg to Thugut, Boyd told Pitt that his group would be willing to contract for a loan to Great Britain of £24 million, in addition to £6 million for Austria, to which Pitt apparently replied that £18 million would be sufficient. Considering that only the previous day Boyd had confirmed to Pitt, in writing, that his group would offer £18 millions for Great Britain, Starhemberg's story seems improbable.[62]

Two days later, on December 12, Boyd, accompanied by the other members of his group, met at the Chancellor's house to make their offer. Boyd considered it wise, in view of the large size and unusual character of the deal, to include in his list several banking houses, among them Smith, Payne & Smiths (the firm's principal bankers), Boldero & Co., Pybus &

58. Boyd to Pitt, 3 Dec. 1794, Chatham Papers, PRO, 30/8/115.
59. Boyd to Pitt, 8 Dec. 1794, Chatham Papers, PRO, 30/8/115.
60. Geo III to Grenville, 7 Dec. 1794, *Dropmore Papers*, vol. II p. 650. Robarts had been an East India Company director since 1786, and was soon to become member of Parliament for Worcester City.
61. Boyd to Pitt, 10 Dec. 1794, Chatham Papers, PRO, 30/8/115.
62. Starhemberg's dispatches of 12 and 16 Dec. 1795, A.von Vivenot, *Quellen,* op.cit., vol. V, pp. 55 & 60; Boyd to Pitt, 9 Dec. 1794.

Co., and Walwyn & Co., and also William Lushington. The agreement signed the same day was for £24 million, of which £18 million was for Great Britain and £6 million for Austria. Subscribers to the British loan would receive for each £100 advanced, £100 of three per cent. Consols, £33 6s. 8d. of four per cent. Consols, and 8s. 6d. of Long Annuity: if eventually the Austrian loan were not guaranteed, the amount of Long Annuity would be increased by 4s. 0d. to 12s. 6d.[63] The terms of the Austrian loan would be those agreed in the previous May. They gave a higher yield than that on the British loan: hence the need to compensate subscribers by giving them more Long Annuity if the Austrian loan never materialised. Although this uncertainty remained, and was not resolved quickly, there was justification for the triumphant claim in *The Times* that 'The Loan contracted . . . . by Mr. Boyd and his friends is the greatest money negotiation that ever took place in this or in any other country at one time'.[64]

63. *Commons Journals*, vol. 51, pp. 358–9.
64. *The Times*, 13 Dec. 1794.

CHAPTER V

The Imperial Loan of 1794

'My house was the only house employed by the Court of Vienna for remitting the Imperial Loan and for advances made to his Imperial Majesty.' Walter Boyd, giving evidence before the Lords' Committee of Secrecy relating to the Bank, 1797.

While Starhemberg and de Sandrouin in London shared the satisfaction expressed by *The Times* at the successful conclusion of the negotiation, there was little enthusiasm in Vienna. The day after the octroi was signed. Trauttmansdorff, Court Chancellor for the Netherlands, referred to the 'ruinous' loan which had been raised in England, commenting that it would provide only the bare minimum required to meet expenditures during 1794, and would deal a mortal blow to Austria's credit. The transaction, he wrote, was 'une véritable opération de fils de famille qui se ruine.'[1] In Vienna, in the same month, Thugut denounced it as usurious, and said that its extravagance was unprecedented in history.[2] When, therefore, Eden and Thugut set to work out in Vienna the political and military conditions for the British guarantee, the ensuing negotiations were frustrating and time-consuming.

In the City, the loan had few supporters. The Bank of England had long been opposed to it. As early as the previous June, Starhemberg had reported to Vienna 'La Banque d'Angleterre, jalouse des premiers succès de notre emprunt, s'efforce de les arrêter et de traverser les opérations de M. Boyd.'[3] Pitt did not venture to say anything about it to the Bank of England for six months, when he made a casual reference to it in conversation with the Governor. The subject came up more formally a few days later, when on December 11, Benjamin Winthrop, a director and future governor, proposed a resolution in the Bank's Committee of Treasury inviting the Directors 'to take the earliest Opportunity of Expressing their disapprobation of the said Loan & to Endeavour to prevent the measure being adopted, under the Sanction or Authority of Parliament.' This was going too far, and the motion was negatived by all except Winthrop.

---

1. Trauttmansdorff to [Kaunitz] 19 May, 1794, Vivenot, op. cit., vol. IV, p. 233.
2. Thugut to Colloredo 17 May, 1794, Vivenot. *Vertrauliche Briefe,* op.cit., vol. I, p. 99.
3. Starhemberg, dispatch of 13 June, 1794, quoted by Helleiner, op. cit., p. 12.

When, however, the Governor saw Pitt a day or so later, he told him that the directors 'had desired him to express their apprehension that such a measure may be attended with very serious unpleasant Consequences, to the Bank.' Pitt answered blandly 'that it was a public measure of necessity', and would the Bank receive payments for the Imperial Loan and pay the dividends on it? Winthrop was not abashed, and a month later proposed a motion that if the loan were made, the Bank would be unable to give its help to the government and trade of the country 'as it would be their Pride, their Happiness and their Interest at all times to afford.' Like his earlier motion, it was too direct a challenge, and it was negatived, although three directors ventured to vote for it.[4]

In Parliament, criticism could be open. In a debate in the House of Lords in January, the Marquis of Lansdowne attacked the policy of subsidising allies, on the grounds that the aid so obtained could not be relied on, and that it was unpracticable to pay by means of bills 'We must send our subsidy and the money to pay our troops in bullion, a comfortable consideration for this country. It would amount to one-fourth of all the specie in the Kingdom.'[5] In the City, too, there were merchants protesting against the loan. The day after the debate in the Lords, a paper appeared, signed 'A British Merchant', asserting that merchants were agreed 'that if this loan should unhappily take place, it must go, necessarily must go, in hard money . . . That if attempts were made to remit this money. . . by purchasing Bills on the different cities of commerce in Europe, the immediate consequence would be, that such an extraordinary demand for Bills, over and above the natural demand in the way of trade, would necessarily turn all the exchanges so much the more against us . . . and that finally the whole sum must go sooner or later in gold or silver.'[6]

On the same day that the British Merchant made his attack, Boyd, by a curious coincidence, was preparing a defence of the loan, which was probably intended for Pitt's use in the forthcoming debate on the King's message. His first point was to emphasise the adequacy of the security, the honourable way in which the Emperor had acted, and the fact that it had been usual for Austria to borrow at five, four-and-one-half or even three-and-one-half per cent. and that she had met her obligations 'with the same scrupulous exactness, that Merchants and Bankers observe.' There was therefore, in Boyd's view, little likelihood of this country having to pay out anything, except possibly the temporary advance of a half-year's interest. Even admitting that the loan might become a charge on the public purse, it was still worthwhile, in that it enabled Austria to keep an army in the field, and to continue to fight the common enemy. If aid to Austria were withheld, the Emperor might be forced to listen to French proposals for a separate peace.

Boyd was next at pains to deal with the argument that carried weight with most people, namely that the loan would cause a loss of bullion. His answer was to point to the exchanges. The exchange with Hamburg was

4. Bank of England, Committee of Treasury Minutes, 7 Dec, 1794 and 15 Jan., 1795.
5. *Parliamentary History*, vol. 31, col. 1271.
6. Guildhall Library, *Broadside* 6161, 21 Feb., 1795.

favourable; the Spanish exchange was twenty-five per cent. in favour of England, even allowing for the discount of between eight and ten per cent. on the paper currency. '. . . not a single Guinea or Shilling', he wrote, 'can be exported without a considerable loss to the remitter.' To meet the point that silver in the form of Spanish dollars would be exported, he added: 'Spanish Dollars are not the circulating coin of this Country – and where is the difference between a remittance in them and a remittance in Indigo, Cochineal or any other article of Merchandise?'

But remittances, however indirect, might turn the exchanges adversely. To this Boyd had two answers. First, not all the money remitted would be English in origin. 'England indeed will have all the advantages attending the original Negotiation of the Loan, as well as the various commissions to which the future Sales & purchases of it, must give rise, but in all other respects, England is merely the Market for the Commodity which will find Consumers in every Country of Europe.' This was a sound argument as far as it went, but even Boyd could scarely argue that more than a small part of the loan would be taken up on the Continent. Secondly, and here Boyd was on more debatable ground, he suggested that it did not matter if the exchanges did depreciate. 'All our Exports might be sold so much dearer to foreign Countries . . . and if we should not raise the prices we might at least expect an augmentation of Demand . . . an Exchange much above Par induces Foreigners to sell out of the Publick Funds of this Country, and to withdraw their Capitals; but an Exchange at Par of or below Par induces them, not only to reinvest their Dividends, but to remit future Sums to this Country for the purpose of new Investments . . .'[7]

While Boyd, in London, was endeavouring to allay the concern felt by many at the balance of payments effects of the Austrian loan, Eden, in Vienna, was engaged, as he had been for several months, in pressing Austria to make an adequate contribution to the war effort, and in countering Thugut's complaints that the loan terms were onerous. The Vienna negotations made little progress, and early in January Pitt had to admit that it might be necessary to accept a less extensive engagement on the part of Austria, which would involve a reduction in the amount of the loan to £4 million. On January 8 he sent a memorandum to the contractors to this effect, proposing that they received as compensation 8d. more of Long Annuity for each £1 million reduction in the loan.[8] This the contractors had to accept.

On 4 February 1795, two days after Boyd completed his memorandum, Pitt delivered to the Commons a message from the King stating that negotiations were in progress with the Emperor for a loan of £4 millions to enable Austria to put 200,000 men in the field, and that when these negotiations were concluded an appropriate measure would be introduced. The Commons were critical. William Hussey, member for Salisbury city, said that the loan, when added to the sums already sent abroad for payment of British and foreign troops, would have a considerable effect

7. Mr. Boyd's Paper on the Austrian Loan, 1795, with Supplement dated 2 Feb., 1975, Liverpool papers, vol. 165, BL. Add. MS 38354, ff. 12–25.
8. *Commons Journals*, vol. 51, p. 359.

upon the credit and paper currency of the country and that 'the diminution of cash might be an evil of the most serious and alarming nature.' He concluded by moving: 'That the Governor and Deputy Governor of the Bank do attend at the Bar of the House tomorrow, to give such information to the House on that subject as their experience and ability enabled them to do.'

The prospect of a public cross-examination of representatives of the Bank was little to Pitt's liking, and he spoke at once against Hussey's proposal. The motion, he said, 'tended to expose to public view all the transactions and speculations of that company to which these Gentlemen belonged, which, notwithstanding its great credit and influence, . . . was a private trading company, who could not but regard such a motion as highly unjust and violent.' He then turned to the possible effect of the loan, and here Boyd's brief was useful. He said that 'the prosperity of commerce depended on regarding cash like every other article of trade, and when occasion occurred, on using it in the same way,' that a very large sum would have to be exported before any effect would be felt on the circulation of cash or the credit and paper currency founded on it, and that 'no danger could therefore be apprehended from any export of cash, which it was probable could be proposed, much less the one in contemplation.' He denied that the whole amount of the loan would be exported. 'With this country for a guarantee, many of the Emperor's own subjects will be glad to invest their money in the loan, and whatever we advance, will probably be remitted in credit by Bills of Exchange, and many other ways.' Hussey's motion was eventually negatived.[9]

In spite of the fact that Pitt had won the day, Boyd was not satisfied that the distinction between bullion and specie had been made sufficiently clearly. There was still the danger that the Commons, anxious to prevent a contraction in the circulation of Bank notes and coin, might place an embargo on the export of bullion, a move which would hamper Boyd in making his remittances. He therefore wrote a long note to Pitt on February 5, so that in the debate which was to take place that day, the Chancellor should have the points clearly before him.

In this note, Boyd admitted that 'the Bank of England necessarily regulates the extent of its paper-Circulation by the quantity of Coin which they have for paying it. But 'while our Trade is constantly bringing into this Country property of all descriptions, such as Goods, Bullion, etc . . . why should any constraint be laid upon the exportation of that part of such property which may happen to consist of Bullion, seeing that has no sort of connection whatever with the quantity of *Coin*, and in fact is to all intents and purposes *Merchandise*?' He agreed that bullion was the material out of which coin was made, but asserted that 'when the Coin of the Country requires to be reinforced, the price of Bullion will rise and consequently no longer answer as an article of exportation.'[10] What Boyd ignored (no doubt deliberately) was that a high price for bullion would lead to a loss of

9. *Oracle* 5 Feb., 1795. The discussion was not reported in *Parliamentary History*.
10. Note by Boyd, 5 Feb., 1795, Chatham Papers, PRO, 30/8/115.

specie by encouraging the illicit melting down of guineas to be sworn off as foreign bullion.

On the same day, Pitt moved a reply to the King's message, approving the project of a loan.[11] In the debate which followed, speakers relied mainly on political, rather than economic arguments. Fox delivered a bitter attack on the loan, describing it as 'a profligate waste of the money of the people . . . It signified nothing', he continued, 'to make panegyrics upon the good faith of the Emperor, and upon the solvency of the Bank of Vienna . . . Let the Minister go into the City and hear the opinion of monied men . . . The answer of the monied men to the Emperor would be "I will not lend you my money upon your own security"'.

In spite of criticism of this kind, much of it to the point, Pitt's address in reply to the King's message was carried with a substantial majority.[12] Some three weeks later these attacks were repeated when the budget resolutions, which included provision for a loan to the Emperor, were under discussion. Fox again spoke against the loan, calling it 'an extravagant bargain', and Hussey, after describing it as 'a bankrupt transaction', suggested 'a plan, by which for an annuity of 450,000l. the sum of six millions may be raised in twentyfour hours, and upon a plan by which the whole would be liquidated in five and twenty years.'[13] Pitt contested these points and eventually the budget resolutions were carried.

Confident of being able to get a guarantee through Parliament, Pitt was not inclined to make a hasty agreement, and seemed determined to obtain from Austria the maximum military contribution, in consideration of a British guarantee. He refused to agree to any modification of the loan in Austria's favour, but promised that the guarantee would be raised from £4 millions to £6 millions, if Austria increased her military contribution from 200,000 to 300,000 men. As to the rate of interest, Pitt pointed out to Starhemberg that a reduction was out of the question, as the interest was less than that paid by Ireland, whose loan for the current year yielded seven per cent., whereas the Austrian loan cost only six per cent., as the one-and-a-half per cent. sinking fund went to reduce the capital, and could not properly be included in the annual cost of the loan.

What Starhemberg thought of this ingenuous argument is not recorded: all he could do was to report to Vienna that it was impossible to adjust the price for the additional loan, as although conditions had changed since the first loan of £3 millions was negotiated, the two had to be issued on identical terms. He took the opportunity of pointing out that Boyd, Benfield & Co. had been proposed as loan contractors by Mercy himself, who considered that the terms were very good, considering that it was the first time that Austria had borrowed in London, where foreign loans were not regarded with much favour. The only way of reducing the cost would be to ask Great Britain to bear some of it herself – a course unlikely to succeed, and in any event one which was beneath the dignity of the Austrian Court.[14]

11. Parliamentary History, vol. 31, col. 1304.
12. Parliamentary History, vol. 31, col. 1307.
13. Parliamentary History, vol. 31, col. 1316.
14. Starhemberg to Thugut 24 Feb., 1795, Vivenot, op.cit., vol. V, p. 108.

These long-drawn-out negotiations were very embarrassing to Boyd. Talk against the loan reached such a pitch that he complained to Pitt 'that it was industriously propagated by the Enemies of the War that there would be no Imperial Loan.' He continued: 'If it were possible that you could announce the certainty of the Austrian Loan taking place to a given Amount, this would be highly useful and acceptable to my fellow-contractors. Anything that could raise their spirits would be highly gratifying to me.'[15] The contractors were in fact getting very impatient, for it was most inconvenient for them to have to hold money idle so as to be ready to pay the first instalment, and when there was talk of an Irish loan, Boyd had difficulty in persuading the members of his group not to withdraw altogether from the Austrian loan, so as to be free to subscribe for the Irish one. In the end, he decided that the best way of keeping his group together was to give them 'the chance of a douceur' by bidding on their behalf for the Irish loan,[16] which in any case was for only £1,500,000, and would be out of the way before the Austrian loan arrangements were complete. This he did, and was successful in getting the English portion (£1,100,000) and the lottery.[17]

From the Austrian side there were also difficulties. The outcome of the negotiations with Vienna was still uncertain, and there was the possibility that Thugut would refuse to ratify the loan on the terms agreed by Starhemberg. Fortunately for Boyd, Pitt made it clear that the Government would not guarantee any loan for Austria, other than the one negotiated with Boyd, Benfield & Co., and would not consent either to an alteration in the terms, or to a transfer of the contract to another house.[18]

Thugut, in Vienna, was becoming impatient, for, despite an active exchange of dispatches between London and Vienna, no progress was being made. In March, therefore, he decided to send Count Joseph Pergen to London, as the representative of the Imperial Treasury. He felt, probably rightly, that Boyd and de Sandrouin would continue to oppose any revision of the terms, and that de Sandrouin had to be replaced.[19] Pergen was to obtain a modification of the 'onerous' obligation to purchase three per cent. bonds, without which, said Thugut, the cost of the loan would be only six per cent.[20] A further point for Pergen to investigate was how it came about that de Sandrouin negotiated the additional £3 millions without authority.[21]

Moreover, since the whole amount borrowed would now carry a British guarantee, the situation was quite different from that ruling in May 1794, when the first octroi was signed. The loan was now better than a mere obligation of the British government, since it was an obligation of Austria which was guaranteed by Britain. It was therefore quite inappropriate to compare it with the Irish loan, as Eden had done. Again, it was

15. Boyd to Pitt, 23 Feb., 1795, Chatham Papers, PRO, 30/8/115.
16. Boyd to Pitt, 25 March, 1795, Chatham Papers, PRO, 30/8/115.
17. *The Times*, 13 March, 1795. Supra. p. 74.
18. Starhemberg to Thugut, 24 Feb., 1795, Vivenot, *Quellen* op. cit., vol. V, p. 109.
19. Thugut to the Emperor, 27 March, 1795, Vivenot, op. cit., . . . pp. 145–150.
20. Thugut to Colloredo, 14 March, 1795, Vivenot, *Vertrauliche Briefe,* vol. I, p. 195.
21. Thugut to Colloredo, 29 April, 1795, Vivenot, op.cit., vol. I, p. 206.

clear that some of the interest paid by Austria went towards meeting the service of the British portion of £18 millions, which, Thugut said, whether regarded as a subsidy to Britain or as remuneration to Britain for the guarantee she had given, was equally repugnant to her generosity towards a faithful ally.[22]

Early in April, Pergen arrived in London, and de Sandrouin was withdrawn,[23] much to the disgust of Starhemberg.[24] Pergen lost not time in getting down to business, and only a few days after his arrival, he was in conference with Pitt and Boyd.[25] From the outset, he seems to have adopted a somewhat high-handed attitude. On April 14, Starhemberg was reporting to Thugut 'The language which Count Pergen used in speaking, in my presence, to the banker Boyd, who will probably give an account of it to Mr. Pitt, could be interpreted as a desire on our part to give up the idea of a loan.' With this attitude, no progress could be expected, and within a month he had been told by Grenville that the Cabinet had decided to transfer negotiations to Vienna.[26]

Officials in London assumed that Austria would accept the terms offered,[27] and on April 8 Eden was advised that arrangements were being made to have money available at various places on the Continent, so that immediately the convention with Austria was signed, the money could be remitted.[28] Boyd encountered some difficulties in making these arrangements. He started by offering each of three Hamburg houses, Schubach, Parish and Dorner, a one-third share in the remittance of £300,000, to be reimbursed by drafts on the Treasury. Schubach declined and Parish would have preferred to do the same, for he, like Schubach, had doubts about Boyd's position. However, Dorner accepted, and Parish, not wishing to break with Boyd, took up his own share of £100,000 and Schubach's as well. A further £100,000 was taken by houses in Vienna, Frankfurt, Genoa, Leipzig, Leghorn and Augsburg, who were given the option of drawing on Hamburg instead of on London. The whole operation, totalling £400,000, centred on Hamburg, and it was there that Boyd, Junior, was sent with letters of authority to the firms concerned, and with instructions to keep Eden informed of progress.[29]

Boyd was confident that there would be no difficulty in making the remittances in this way. 'I flatter myself', he wrote to Grenville, 'all will be accomplished in that respect before the operation can have been even suspected this side of the water'.[30] His confidence was justified, for a few

22. Thugut to Starhemberg, [?] April, 1795. Vivenot, *Quellen* . . . vol. V, p. 194.
23. Starhemberg to Thugut, 7 April, 1795, Vivenot, op.cit., vol. V, pp. 155–6.
24. Starhemberg to Grenville, 4 April, 1795, PRO, F.O. 7/40.
25. *The Times*, 13 and 14 April, 1795.
26. Starhemberg's dispatches to Thugut, 14 April and 24 April, 1795, quoted by Helleiner, op.cit., pp. 43 and 45–6.
27. *The Times*, 30 March 1795.
28. Grenville to Eden, 8 April 1795, PRO, F.O. 7/40; Thugut to Colloredo, 29 April 1795, Vivenot, *Vertrauliche Briefe* . . . vol. I, p. 209.
29. Memorandum by Boyd, Benfield & Co., 10 April 1795, PRO, F.O. 7/40; Boyd to Pitt, 10 April 1795, Chatham Papers, PRO, 30/8/115; Parish, op.cit., pp. 75–7. For the names of the firms involved see Helleiner, op.cit., pp. 47–8.
30. Boyd to Grenville, 17 April, 1795, PRO, F.O. 7/41.

days after the signature of the convention on 4 May 1795, Eden was able to hand over £400,000 to representatives of the Imperial Treasury.[31] For carrying out this operation, the Treasury offered Boyd, Benfield & Co. a commission. Boyd, seldom averse to accepting remuneration from the Government, felt that on this occasion it would be wise to refuse, as the advance made by the Treasury undoubtedly facilitated the loan for which his firm were agents.[32]

Although Vienna professed great dissatisfaction with the loan as negotiated by de Sandrouin, the pressure of events afforded them little room for bargaining. Pergen, in London, had hardly had time to familiarise himself with the problem before Thugut decided reluctantly that better terms could not be obtained, and that Austria had to choose between accepting what was offered, or getting nothing. Thugut accordingly advised the Emperor to agree.[33] In a note to Eden, Thugut entered a protest against what he described as exorbitant terms, and reserved the right to raise later the question of the interpretation of clause 8 of the octroi, which dealt with the sinking fund.[34]

The convention, signed in Vienna on 4 May 1795, provided that in consideration of Austria's raising a force of 200,000 men, Great Britain would guarantee the payment of dividends on a loan of £4,600,000, of which £550,000 was to be used to repay temporary advances.[35] With the object of strengthening the lenders' position, the convention provided that the loan was to be secured on all the hereditary dominions of the Emperor, and holders of the bonds were granted the right to sue the receivers or treasurers of the various dominions in the event of default, a clause not in the octroi. Debentures of the Bank of Vienna were also to be deposited as security. An octroi for £3,000,000 had already been signed in May 1794, and another in similar terms was signed for the balance of £1,600,000.[36]

A bill providing for the guarantee of the loan was introduced by Pitt at the end of May. It met with considerable opposition, for many people doubted Austria's ability and willingness to meet her financial and military obligations. Doubts were increased by the news that on the same day as the Emperor accepted the second portion of the loan, he announced his readiness to make peace with France.[37] Fox invited the House of Commons to reflect that if peace should be concluded between France and Austria, 'we shall have given the whole of our four millions six hundred thousand pounds absolutely for nothing'. William Smith criticised the terms of the loan, saying that 'if the money was lent to the Emperor to enable him to make the greatest possible exertion in the common cause,

31.   Eden to Grenville, 20 May, 1795, PRO, F.O. 7/41.
32.   Boyd to Pitt, 16 May, 1795, Chatham Papers, PRO, 30/8/115., Pitt Correspondence, CUL., Add 6958/10.
33.   Thugut to the Emperor, 2 May, 1795, Vivenot, *Quellen*, op. cit., vol. V, pp. 195–6.
34.   Thugut to Eden, 4 May, 1795, Vivenot, op.cit., vol. V, p. 196.
35.   Lords Committee of Secrecy, 1797, Appendix 19.
36.   A translation of the Convention and the two octrois is in *Commons Journals*, vol. 51, pp. 554; Accounts and Papers, 1821, vol. 23: *Parliamentary History*, vol. 31, cols. 1558–64; *The Times*, 28 May 1795.
37.   *Morning Chronicle*, 30 May 1795.

we ought certainly to have procured it for him on the easiest terms without making any advantage of it for ourselves . . . We ought not to have suffered him to pay £250,000 commission on it, when we might have procured it for him without that expense.[38]

Boyd, led, as he said, by 'curiosity' to listen to the debate from the gallery of the House was greatly upset at this reference to commission. To doubt the good faith of the Emperor was one thing: to question the propriety of his firm's remuneration was entirely different. On reflection, he decided to raise the matter with Pitt. In a letter dated 31 May 1795 he said that he was 'much surprised and hurt' at this reference to commission. He pointed out that no objection had been made to the commission when the first part of the loan was negotiated in March 1794, or even when the second part was arranged in the following December. 'But for the certainty of the commission being allowed us', he continued, 'I could never have made the numerous sacrifices that I found it necessary to make in the progress of the negotiation, when so many prejudices were to be overcome and so much opposition to be encountered.' In reply to criticism of the payment of dividends out of capital, he claimed that this should be considered as a merit, not as a subject for reproach.[39] The bill passed the Commons without delay, but with time short, Boyd wrote urging Grenville to get quick action in the Lords. Fortunately, there was little opposition, and three days later the bill became law.

For each £100 advanced, the lenders received three per cent. annuities and twenty-five year annuities worth £121, at the market prices of sixty-five and thirteen-and-three-eighths respectively, representing a profit of twenty-one per cent. on the Austrian loan by itself, or four-and-a-half per cent. on the total of £22,600,000 for both loans. The Act provided for the guarantee of the half-yearly interest and annuities, but not the sinking fund, and introduced some modification in the payment arrangements. Boyd, Benfield & Co. instead of acting as the paying agents, could under the Act, pay to the Bank of England the sum required on or before May 1 and November 1 of each year. Any deficiency was to be issued out of the Consolidated Fund, and paid to the holders of the loan by the Bank on the following July 5 and January 5. Provision was also made for depositing the bonds issued by Boyd, Benfield & Co. with the Bank, so that both the three per cent. annuities and the twenty-five year annuities would be registered in the Bank's books, and be transferable in the usual way. They had become, for all practical purposes, British government stocks.

Once the guarantee had been approved by Parliament, the loan could be issued, and the proceeds remitted abroad as instalments were paid. The £550,000 advanced to General Clerfayt for use of the Imperial forces,[42]

38. *Morning Chronicle*, 29 May 1795. William Smith (1756–1835) was member for Camelford, Cornwall, and a close associate of Henry Thornton. He was a partner in the Lombard Street house of Samuel Smith Sons & Co., merchants and bankers.
39. Boyd to Pitt, 31 May 1795, Pitt Correspondence, CUL, Add 6958/10.
40. Boyd to Grenville, 16 June 1795, PRO, F.O. 7/41.
41. 35 Geo. III, c. 93.
42. F.S.C.J. de Croix de Drumez, Comte de Clerfayt (1735–1798) became commander-in-chief of the imperial forces in 1795.

was to be repaid out of the instalments on the loan falling due in November and December, but was in fact repaid in October.[43] Furthermore, the advance of £400,000, which has already been described, had to be deducted. Just over £295,000 had been paid out for loan service up to May, and Boyd retained a further year's loan service, requiring £345,000. Finally, Boyd, Benfield & Co's commission of £250,000 and expenses had to be deducted. The amount still to be remitted was thus about £2,750,000, 'a Matter of infinite Difficulty and Delicacy', said Boyd, particularly as he had to find the best means of remittance within the limits laid down by Vienna.[44]

Nearly £1,200,000 was sent in silver dollars, louis d'ors and foreign bullion, most of which was silver. All the purchases were made through the Bank of England's brokers, Mocatta and Goldsmid, and the 'greatest part' came from the Bank itself.[45] A shipment of silver dollars had been made in the autumn of 1794, but for some months thereafter the exchanges favoured sterling, so that it paid better to remit in bills. By the middle of the year, however, the Hamburg exchange had fallen. With shipments in metal thus becoming cheaper than sending bills, Boyd bought 1,910,000 silver dollars and 20,000 louis d'ors at a cost of £508,000. Purchases on this scale could hardly have been made in the market: all or most of this amount must have come from the Bank.

With French privateers in the Channel, it was not safe to ship large amounts unprotected. The Admiralty accordingly arranged for the frigates Ambuscade and Circe to take the metal to Hamburg, sailing in convoy, £250,000 on each being as much as could be insured.[46] Nothing was shipped in August, and in September, Thugut, complaining about Boyd, Benfield & Co's inaction, instructed Pergen to ask for permission to purchase gold and silver from the Bank.[47] This approach evidently proved effective, for in October Boyd was able to purchase a further amount of about £500,000. The metal, packed in barrels, was sent to Portsmouth,[48] and about £258,000 of it was shipped on the frigate Venus, the rest remaining to await transport. It was only after Starhemberg had made representations to Grenville[49] that the Admiralty provided the frigate Vestal, which sailed to Cuxhaven in December with £244,000. The Bank of England, concerned about the 'very large and continued drain of bullion and specie', was now reluctant to provide further amounts.[50] It is therefore possible that the remaining shipments of £22,000 by the packet in December and £109,000 by the frigate Doris in February had been bought in the market.[51]

Large as these shipments of coin and bullion were, the greater part of

43. Grenville to Eden, 25 Aug. 1795, PRO, F.O. 7/42; Helleiner, op.cit., pp. 54–5.
44. Lords Committee of Secrecy, 1797, Evidence of Boyd.
45. Commons Committee of Secrecy, 1797, Evidence of Boyd.
46. Pergen to Starhemberg, 18 Nov. 1795, PRO, F.O. 7/42.
47. Eden to Grenville, 17 Sept. 1795, PRO, F.O. 7/42.
48. Long to Customs, 19 Oct. 1795, PRO, T 11/38, p. 173.
49. Pergen to Starhemberg, 19 Nov. 1795, PRO, F.O. 7/42.
50. Helleiner, op.cit., pp. 53–4.
51. For a list of shipments, see Commons Committee of Secrecy, 1797, Evidence, Appendix 3.

the loan (£1,600,000) was sent in bills. These remittances no doubt involved several European places, with Hamburg as the central point, as in the earlier remittance of £400,000, but details have not been found. Boyd said that he never sent bills if it paid better to send coin or bullion, a normal banking approach. On the whole, he said, remitting in bills was not quite as favourable, not a surprising conclusion, since it was sometimes impossible to obtain coin and bullion in the amounts required.[52] Even Boyd's skill could not prevent some bills being negotiated at unfavourable rates.[53] In the first quarter of 1795 the exchange was well above the theoretical par of 34/3½d: by August it was 32, a fall of seven per cent., recovering only slightly by the end of the year. In fact, the nature and size of the whole operation made it inevitable that it would cause pressure on sterling, which would be reflected in a falling exchange.

This was something that Boyd was reluctant to admit, and in a long memorandum to Sir William Pulteney, written in the early hours of 9 March 1797, he tried to defend his remittances to the Emperor. He argued that by sending foreign coin and bullion, 'no effect was, or ever could be produced on the Exchange'; and that if remittances in bills caused the exchange to depreciate, 'this very circumstance becomes the source of a new and more extended exertion of national industry', by which he presumably meant that exports would be encouraged. He then abandoned economic argument, saying that if the same amount as was remitted to the Emperor had been used to support British armies on the Continent', no one would have complained. His final point was that the disappearance of guineas was due to hoarding at home, not to export abroad. Boyd, obviously on the defensive, was doing his best to support a rather weak case and it is unnecessary to examine his arguments in detail. When the Commons debate on the loans to the Emperor eventually took place in April, Pulteney made a short speech supporting further lending to Austria (without using Boyd's brief), and the debate ended as usual with a substantial majority for the Government.[54]

52. Lords Committee of Secrecy, 1797, Evidence of Boyd.
53. *Morning Post*, 11 Feb. 1796.
54. Boyd to Pulteney, 9 Mar. 1797, and enclosure, Henry Dundas Papers, Kress Library, Harvard University; *Parliamentary History* vol. 33, 1797–8, col. 251.

CHAPTER VI

The Hamburg Bill Transaction

'This was a transaction exceedingly disgraceful to the Government of this country; it was so in the opinion of every man in the Kingdom possessed of the least commercial experience. No house of character would be seen in such a transaction. . .'

Charles James Fox in the House of
Commons, 26 February 1796.

The war inevitably brought problems as well as opportunities. In the spring of 1794, the rapid advance of the French alarmed wealthy merchants in the United Provinces. London firms involved in Dutch trade also became anxious and diverted cargoes from Dutch ports to Hamburg, Bremen and elsewhere. The question received a good deal of attention in the City, and Boyd, as partner in a mercantile house with many links with the Continent, felt that this was a matter which he was entitled to raise with the Government. He did so, submitting certain suggestions for preventing Dutch cargoes from falling into enemy hands. Lord Grenville, to whom the matter was referred, consulted the British Ambassador at the Hague, Lord St. Helens, who, in due course reported that the cargoes concerned consisted chiefly of tobacco and sugar which were originally intended for the northern markets.[1] No action was therefore taken.

Three months later, nervousness in the United Provinces was increasing owing to the growing threat of invasion, and merchants were seeking a place of safety for their property. Merchandise was being shipped to Hamburg and Bremen, but it was obviously undesirable for Dutch merchants to have to rely entirely on these ports. Not only might the political independence of these places be threatened by the progress of the French, but the credit status of the individual merchants there might not warrant their being entrusted with large quantities of valuable merchandise.

In these circumstances Henry Hope, of Hope & Co., Amsterdam, wrote to Boyd urging immediate action. Boyd decided to raise the matter again, and at the end of July, after consulting Benfield,[2] he asked to see Pitt. The request was granted readily, but owing to pressure of public business Pitt had to cancel the interview, and Boyd had to submit his case in writing. He said that Hope had suggested to him that it would be 'highly politic' if

1. St. Helens to Grenville, 9 April 1794, *Dropmore Papers*, vol. II, p. 540.
2. Boyd to Benfield. 30 July 1794, Paul Benfield Papers, IO, Eur. c 307/5

England were to open her ports for the free admission of any goods or property which the inhabitants of Holland wished to send here. Goods so imported, Boyd explained, should not be chargeable to customs duties, but should be placed in bonded warehouses pending export to other countries. Any goods eventually admitted to the home market would pay the normal customs duties. The measure should be adopted, said Boyd, 'with great liberality', contraband goods should be admitted, and the scheme should apply whether the goods were imported in British ships or not. There was a very good precedent for action of this sort, as Hope had pointed out, for just before the occupation of Ostend by the French, Holland had opened her ports to receive goods of all kinds, and had thus prevented much valuable property from falling into enemy hands. Boyd admitted that the measure proposed might have a bad effect upon morale, but thought that this disadvantage was not to be compared with 'the irreparable certain consequences of such an access to their wealth as the French would receive' if Amsterdam fell into their hands with its warehouses full.

That, in substance, was Hope's plan. Boyd then went a step further. If such a measure could be applied to merchandise, should it not also extend to the specie and other valuables in the Bank of Amsterdam? 'So strongly am I impressed', he wrote, 'with the importance of this subject that by the last mail for Holland I suggested to my friend Mr. Hope in addition to his idea for securing *Goods*, that it would be of the highest importance that the Treasure in the Bank of Amsterdam, which is represented by Accounts in the Books of the Bank, but cannot be realised by the Proprietors as being contrary to the Constitution of the Bank, should be removed from the vaults of the Bank of Amsterdam to the Shipping in the harbour to be ready to be removed at first appearance of immediate danger, or rather that this Treasure should immediately be shipped off for this Country and lodged in the Bank of England. Such a measure, said Boyd, would maintain the value of Bank money as long as Amsterdam was not occupied by the French, and if the city did fall, the treasure would be saved.[3] Hope's reply, received a few days later, was that the idea was very much to the point, but he thought that it would 'meet with many local or constitutional objections which only extreme danger can surmount.' However, he said that he would discuss the plan with leading men in the regency and let Boyd know the result.[4]

Meantime, Pitt had communicated to Grenville the plan for opening British ports. Grenville doubted the wisdom of introducing it, as he considered that it would indicate a lack of confidence in the ability of the Allies to defend the Netherlands successfully, but he instructed St. Helens to discuss it confidentially with the Grand Pensionary of the United Provinces, Lorenz Pieter van de Spiegel. The latter turned out to be stongly opposed to any such measure. St. Helens reported: 'The Pensionary reprobates *in toto* Mr. Boyd's plan for opening the ports of

---

3. Boyd to Pitt, 31 July 1794, Chatham Papers, PRO, 30/8/115. In fact, when the French occupied Amsterdam, they found very little in the Bank: *Annual Register*, 1795, p. 52.
4. Hope to Boyd, 5 Aug., 1794, Chatham Papers, PRO, 30/8/115.

Great Britain for the reception of *flight goods* from this country . . . a contrary regulation would, if it were feasible, be far more expedient, in order to leave to the Hopes and other over-grown capitalists of this country no other chance for saving their property than the giving or at least the lending a part of it to supply the wants of the Government.[5]

Months passed without anything being done, and Boyd, despairing of a general solution, decided in October to put his own case to the Treasury. In so doing, he revealed that Boyd, Benfield & Co. had a direct interest in the matter, in that they held 800,000 pounds of tea in Amsterdam, which they were anxious to ship to England. The Treasury were not sympathetic and gave a brusque refusal.[6] This was not the answer he expected, for in anticipation of something more accommodating, he had already arranged with one of his Amsterdam correspondents, Wilkiesons, to have the tea shipped to England. He accordingly made a further appeal to the Treasury on the following day (for time was short), pointing out that it was too late to let Wilkiesons know of the decision, as the ships bringing the tea would already be at sea, and were expected to arrive hourly. He therefore asked that the Customs be directed not to seize the tea, when it was landed. He recognised that such a procedure might create an awkward precedent, and proposed that the Treasury should authorise the East India Company to purchase the tea. Boyd, Benfield & Co. already had an important contract with the East India Company, under which they had purchased on the Continent and shipped to England for account of the Company several million pounds of tea. Since ships carrying this tea were arriving in London almost daily, no comment would be caused if the tea from Wilkiesons were treated similarly. The tea, it was true, was not of the grade usually taken by the East India Company, but he was prepared to offer the Company a thirty per cent. profit on whatever price they were able to obtain.[7] But the Treasury were adamant and refused.[8] As to what happened to Boyd's tea, the official records are silent.

There were many other cases not greatly different from Boyd's, and pressure on the government to permit some relaxation continued. At the end of November, Lord Auckland wrote to Pitt expressing his regret that British ports were still closed. 'The panic of the Dutch', he wrote, 'cannot be materially increased by such permission, and I understand that much property has already been sent to Hamburg, Bremen &c.[9] Eventually Boyd's plan was adopted, and Orders in Council issued early in 1795 allowed the import into Great Britain of goods from the United Provinces or from ships bound for the United Provinces.[10]

5. Grenville to St. Helens, 5 Aug. 1794; St. Helens to Grenville, 19 Aug. 1794, *Dropmore Papers*, vol. II, pp. 610 and 622.
6. Rose to Boyd, Benfield & Co, 15 Oct. 1794, PRO, T. 27/44. Treasury Board Minutes, PRO, T. 29/67, p. 195.
7. Boyd, Benfield & Co. to Rose, 17 Oct. 1794, Treasury In-Letters, PRO, T. 1/735/2649.
8. Rose to Boyd, Benfield & Co., 18 Oct. 1794, PRO. T. 27/45; Treasury Board, Minutes, PRO, T. 29/67, p. 254.
9. *Journal and Correspondence of William, Lord Auckland*, London, Richard Bentley, 1862, p. 273.
10. Orders in Council 16 Jan. and 21 Jan. 1795. These were later superseded by 35 Geo. III, c. 15 and c. 80.

As mentioned already, Boyd made a new departure in bidding for the Irish loan and lottery issued in March 1795.[11] The loan was for only £1,500,000, of which the greater part, £1,100,000, was transferable at the Bank of England, the balance of £400,000 being on the books of the Bank of Ireland. Bids had to be submitted to the Irish Chancellor of the Exchequer, Lord Milton, and could be for one or more parts of the loan. Boyd decided not to bid in person – it was obviously inconvenient to have to travel to Dublin – but to employ for the purpose J.C. Beresford & Co., one of the four banking firms in Dublin. A Dublin agent would eventually have been necessary, and there was therefore a good case for bringing in a local banking house at the outset. For each £100 advanced, subscribers were to receive £100 five per cent. Irish annuities, together with an amount of fifteen-year terminable annuities in which the bidding was to be made. For the English portion of the loan, Beresford & Co, on behalf of Boyd, Benfield & Co., bid £1.1.11. of fifteen-year annuities, and for the 40,000 lottery tickets £6.12.6. a ticket. They made no bid for the Irish portion.

Boyd, Benfield & Co., were successful, but when the results were announced, it was seen that they had bid much higher than anyone else. Their nearest competitors were Nesbitt & Stewart, merchants of Aldermanbury, London, who offered £1.9.0. annuities for the loan and £6.1.6. in cash for lottery tickets.[12] The Irish portion of the loan went to Robert Shaw & Co. of Fleet Street, Dublin, whose bid of £1.5.0. annuities reflected their preference for the local stock over the English portion, for which they wanted £1.12.6. annuities.[13] Whether Boyd's unnecessarily high bids were the result of faulty advice from Beresford & Co. or of his own insistance on getting the loan and lottery at all costs, is not apparent, but it was said in Dublin that those concerned were 'considerable gainers' by the purchase, in spite of the fact that the lottery tickets were £1.10.0 higher than those of the previous year.[14]

It is questionable whether Boyd found the lottery as profitable as this comment indicates. He could not sell tickets direct to the public, for only persons holding a licence were allowed to do this. Tickets were accordingly sold to the public through licensed dealers, including the well-known Nicholson's State Lottery Office in Bank Street, Cornhill. Dealings started at around £6.4.0., compared with the price of £6.12.6. paid by Boyd, but the price rose steadily, although it was only a few days before November 16, when drawings commenced, that it rose above Boyd's figure. On November 13 the price touched £7.0.0., and before drawings were completed it reached £8.1.0.[15] These prices give no clear indication of the results as far as Boyd, Benfield & Co. were concerned: if allowance is made for the dealers' profit there could have been little left for Boyd.

In spite of the large amounts raised by means of the loan for 1795, and subsequent borrowing from the Bank of England, the summer of 1795

11. Authorised by 35 Geo. III, c. 6. (Ireland).
12. According to Boyd, James Morgan was associated with Nesbitt & Stewart in this bid, *Commons Journals*, vol. 51, p. 387.
13. *The Times*, 13 March 1795.
14. *Saunders News-Letter*(Dublin), 11 March 1795.
15. *The Times*, 23 Oct. 14 Nov. and 21 Nov. 1795.

found Pitt in need of more money. In July he applied to the Bank. The Bank directors regarded these requests with considerable misgivings, and passed on 6 August 1795 a dignified but firmly-worded resolution to the effect that 'this Court cannot take his Letter [requesting further accommodation] into consideration until it has received Satisfaction respecting the Re-payment of the Monies already advanced for Payment of Treasury Bills of Exchange, to reduce that Account under the stipulated Sum of £5,000,000 . . . and until it has had sufficient Security held out that it shall not be called upon to make further Advances on this Account in future. . . .'[16] A similar answer was given to a request for a loan of £2,500,000 on Exchequer Bills. Clearly, there was no prospect of getting anything out of the Bank.

Early in August, Pitt sent for Boyd. His firm had already been able to render valuable service to the Government. Through their agency a remittance of £400,000 on account of the Austrian loan had been made with speed and secrecy in the previous May. They had made substantial purchases of silver for shipment abroad, for which, incidentally, they had not yet been paid.[17] Now, however, something even bigger was in prospect.

Pitt opened the interview by asking whether it would be 'quite convenient' for Boyd to anticipate instalments of the £18,000,000 loan and lottery falling due in November, December and January. The sum involved was large, for three instalments, each of fifteen per cent., fell due within this period, amounting together to £8,200,000, though part of these instalments would have been paid up in advance under discount, leaving perhaps one-half of the total outstanding. Boyd replied that in view of the prevailing abundance of money he had not doubt whatsoever of being able to do it. Asked what he would charge, he explained that he could not do it at less than the usual rate of five per cent., for although money was abundant — bills were being dealt in at four-and-a-half and four per cent. – it would be dangerous to reckon on that state of affairs continuing in view of the large amount of borrowing contemplated. In addition, he pointed out, he might have to raise the sum required by negotiating bills through brokers, to whom a commission would be payable, and less than five per cent. would therefore involve him in loss. The rate was accordingly fixed at five per cent.

Pitt then suggested reimbursement by Treasury warrant. This did not suit Boyd. He replied that he could not sell Treasury warrants in the market, 'nor would it be consistent with the respectability of my house to endeavour to raise money on these warrants in case the advances became inconvenient.' He promised to think the matter over, but impressed upon Pitt the necessity of secrecy, as knowledge of the operation 'would produce a very great scarcity of money, thus rendering the operation extremely difficult.' Reflection only strengthened Boyd's view that Treasury warrants would not be suitable. At a further interview he pointed out that however 'full of money' his firm might be occasionally, he had to have negotiable securities, which he could realise in case of need. It was

16.   Commons Committee of Secrecy, 1797, Appendix 9.
17.   Boyd to Pitt, 14 Aug. 1795, Chatham Papers, PRO, 30/8/115.

accordingly agreed that he should receive bills of exchange drawn on the Treasury, which suited him admirably, for he had 'much Experience in the discounting of Bills between Merchants and also with the Bank of England;[18] and a transaction in this form would attract the minimum amount of attention.

Meanwhile, Pitt was trying other measures to raise money. The £550,000 advanced to Austria was repayable at the end of the year. Could not Austria repay earlier? Grenville accordingly instructed Eden to endeavour to arrange for repayment in October, instead of in November and December, as originally agreed. He said that the British Government could easily arrange with the subscribers to the loan to pay in October, thus making it unnecessary to vary the dates on which remittances were made. All that was needed was for the Austrian Government to instruct Boyd, Benfield & Co. to make the payment in October.[19] The Austrians raised no objections, and Pergen was instructed to make appropriate arrangements. Their ready compliance with the proposal was no doubt due to the fact that they had substantial balances with Boyd, Benfield & Co., although Vienna had apparently only the most general idea of their amount.[20]

Boyd realised that this manoeuvre could give the Treasury only limited assistance, and he therefore wrote on August 20, repeating that he was ready to grant a credit on the basis of acceptances of the Treasury, and hinting that he would like an early decision. He took the opportunity of suggesting, in view of possible military operations to deal with the slave insurrection in the West Indies, 'that Government may have occasion for extraordinary supplies in that quarter and perhaps on a larger Scale than the general run of Houses chuse to do Business.' He continued: 'If this should be the case, I beg to inform you that we have very intimate Connections in every place in Europe and also in America & the West Indies and that all our exertions and Credit can do for the Service of Government shall, on the slightest hint, be employed for furnishing the Supplies'.[21]

Nothing came of this last proposal, but a few days later, Boyd had yet another interview with Pitt, at which he again pressed for a definite decision. Pitt told him that the amount would be substantially less than the £2,000,000 to £2,500,000 originally mentioned, but was vague as to the exact amount and period of the loan. Boyd seems to have been anxious to make a deal, although he deemed it wise to profess indifference. 'My only Object in the Business', he wrote on August 26, 'is to accomplish in a satisfactory Manner the Wish of Government, and taking beforehand the necessary Steps for insuring Success; if upon Examination you find you can dispense with the Whole . . . I shall be extremely happy at it, because the Business is by no Means so much an Object of Desire as of Care and Anxiety; 'tis not an Advantage that I long to reap, but a Service of some Difficulty and Delicacy which I am solicitous to perform with Success'.[22]

18. Lords' Committee of Secrecy, 1797, Evidence of Boyd, 7 April 1797.
19. Grenville to Eden 25 Aug. 1795, PRO, F.O. 7/42.
20. Eden to Grenville, 17 Sept. 1795. PRO, F.O. 7/42. The Ministry of Finance thought that the amount should be £2,000,000, but it might, they said, be only £1,500,000.
21. Boyd to Pitt 20 Aug. 1795, Chatham Papers, PRO, 30/8/115.
22. Boyd to Pitt 26 Aug. 1795, *Commons Journals*, vol. 51, p. 355.

Agreement was not made easier by a slight misunderstanding which had arisen. Boyd, Benfield & Co. had purchased silver for government account a month or so previously, and George Rose, (Parliamentary) Secretary to the Treasury, had mentioned to Pitt that Boyd, Benfield & Co. had charged commission as well as brokerage on the transaction, which the Treasury considered unusual, if not improper. Boyd took strong exception to this attitude, and wrote a very forthright letter to Pitt. 'Every man acquainted as Mr. Rose is with the details of business must know that *Brokerage* is no part of a Merchant's Commission, but on the contrary a Commission which he pays out of his pocket to the intermediate Agent between the Buyer and Seller, and that if the Merchant is not reimbursed for what he pays to the Broker, he does not receive his own commission in full: if Mr. Rose had attended to the *Rate* of the Commission charged, he would have found that it is fully 1/6 p.ct. below the general rate of charging over all Europe even by Merchant to Merchant, the regular commission for buying and forwarding silver being ½ p.ct. beside Brokerage, while the Commission I charged is only 1/3 p.ct.' Then Boyd added a masterly touch. 'I should have been very happy to have done the business for nothing, and certainly would have done so, had it not occurred to me that Government might have been slow in applying to me in future while we declined any remuneration for our Services'. Finally he drew attention to the favourable terms on which he had made the purchase, which, he said, had been made two per cent. better than the market price at the time, and now the market price was more than four per cent. above the price he paid. 'Commission earned under such circumstances no man need blush to accept of', he concluded with better logic than grammar.[23]

Boyd was correct: the normal commission was a half per cent., excluding brokerage, which was extra, although merchants undertaking a large bullion business would frequently reduce their commission, as Boyd did, to one-third per cent. He was right, too, in saying that the purchase would have cost more at the end of August, for bar silver was then quoted in London at 5s. 5d. per fine ounce, compared with 5s. 2d. in June and 5s. 1d. in May. Whether the rise was foreseen by Boyd is less certain: he may to some extent have been responsible for it by his purchases in July of foreign coin and bullion worth over £500,000, for remittance to the Austrian Government.[24] In any case his having these remittances to make, placed him in a strong position, and he suggested to Pitt that if the silver were not required after all for the public service, he would be very glad to keep it.[25] The result of this discussion is not known, but it can safely be assumed that Pitt kept his silver, and Boyd his commission.[26]

These differences were not serious enough to prevent an agreement being made for advances to the Treasury. Early in September Pitt told Boyd that the amount required would not exceed £1,000,000, payable one-half on September 20, and one-half a month later. These terms were

23. Boyd to Pitt, 26 Aug. 1795, Pitt Correspondence, CUL, Add. 6958/9.
24. Commons Committee of Secrecy, 1797, Minutes of Evidence, Appendix 3.
25. Boyd to Pitt 26 Aug. 1795. Pitt Correspondence, CUL, Add. 6958/9.
26. The commission on a shipment of £50,000 in guineas or gold bullion from Hamburg to London made by Goldsmid & Eliason for government account in February 1797 was also a third per cent., Lords Committee of Secrecy, Appendix 9.

embodied in a letter from the Treasury to Boyd, instructing him to arrange for bills to be drawn on the Treasury amounting in total to £1,000,000, together with interest at five per cent., one half payable on 7 December 1795 and the other half on 31 January 1796.[27]

Boyd, of course, had no intention of advancing this money himself. At the same time the greatest care had to be taken to keep the transaction secret. He hit on the idea of making the bills appear similar to those ordinarily drawn on the Treasury to meet war expenditure abroad. It would not have been difficult to have arranged for one of his Hamburg correspondents to draw the bills, but Boyd thought he had a better plan. He explained later: 'My cousin, Mr. Boyd Junior, having been at Hamburg the 30th August, I though it proper (sic) to get him to draw the Bills, in order to keep the Operation as much as possible within the Knowledge of my own House and to save the Expence of a Commission, which we must have paid had we employed any House to draw on their Lordships'. Boyd, Junior, drew bills on the Treasury payable to Boyd, Benfield & Co., using unstamped paper,[28] and dating them 'Hamburg, 31st August', as though they had actually been drawn there. Of the total of £1,000,000 agreed upon, only £700,000 was advanced, bills totalling this amount and maturing at various dates between 10 December 1795 and 3 February 1796[29] being negotiated by Boyd, Benfield & Co. in the market. To conceal the transaction from the Bank, the proceeds were paid into the account of the Paymaster-General, instead of to the Bank of England as provided by law.[30]

This was not the only credit arranged by Boyd, Benfield & Co. for Government account. Since May, 1795, Benfield & Co. had been making remittances to the Continent for Lieutenant–Colonel Craufurd.[31] In the following September Lord Grenville wrote to the Treasury, saying that it was necessary that Colonel Craufurd, — who had been sent on a special mission to the headquarters of the Austrian army, — should have an additional credit of £100,000 and asking that Boyd, Benfield & Co., 'or such other person your Lordships shall judge proper', should be authorised to accept Colonel Craufurd's bills on them to that amount.[32] This was business that suited Boyd admirably, and within a week he had discussed the matter with Pitt and confirmed to the Foreign Office and the Treasury his willingness to open the credit.[33] From 25 May 1795 to the end of 1796 the total amount provided in this way was £140,000.[34]

Although Boyd took such care to keep the Hamburg bill transaction secret, he was successful only for a while. Officially, the Bank of England knew nothing of the business, but Daniel Giles, the Governor, had a fairly accurate idea of what was going on, and even discounted two or three of

27. Long to Boyd, 17 Sept. 1795, *Commons Journals*, vol 51, p. 356, Appendix 10.
28. Bills drawn abroad and negotiated in the United Kingdom bear an adhesive stamp: bills drawn in the United Kingdom are on paper bearing an impressed stamp.
29. *Morning Chronicle*, 1 March 1796.
30. Repayment was made by the Treasury: £505,548 at the end of 1795, £200,000 on 1 February 1796. Paymaster-General Ledger, PRO, PMG 2/50.
31. later Lieutenant-General Sir Charles Gregan-Craufurd.
32. Grenville to the Treasury 9 Sept. 1795, PRO, F.O. 366/427.
33. Boyd to Aust, 15 Sept.[1795], PRO, F.O. 7/42.
34. Controller's Office to the Treasury, 18 July 1797, PRO, F.O. 83/6.

the bills in a private capacity.[35] But the Bank remained aloof, and refused some of the bills which were tendered for discount. Gradually the story leaked out, and when at the end of October the matter was raised in Parliament, further attempts at concealment became useless.

On October 30, Joseph Jekyll, lawyer and member for Calne, Wiltshire, asked in the House of Commons whether Pitt 'had not been drawing fresh loans upon bills, without the concurrence and indemnity of Parliament, thereby . . . aggravating the National Debt by an exorbitant discount'. He understood, he said, 'that it had lately been the practice to negotiate bills dated Hamburgh, and drawn upon a banker in London of the name of Boyd, which were made payable in four months and in consequence discounted at the Bank'.[36] This last statement was wide of the mark. There is no evidence that the Bank discounted any of the bills, and in any case the Bank did not discount bills which had four months to run. Pitt replied to the effect that the borrowing was not in excess of amounts authorised by Parliament, but he was clearly somewhat disturbed by the possibility of criticism of the rate of interest paid for the accommodation.

He accordingly summoned Boyd to Downing Street, where, on November 3, the situation caused by Jekyll's disclosure was fully discussed. The rate charged by Boyd, Benfield & Co. was five per cent., and Boyd was pressed to reduce it to four per cent., which was the market rate for first class bills. Boyd resisted this suggestion strongly, setting out his case in writing on the following day in a forceful and closely-reasoned letter. 'The rate of 5 per cent.', he wrote, 'is so much a matter of course of even the smallest sums that it appears to me there might be just ground of objection to the stipulating of a *lower* rate for sums of such a magnitude as are not usually within the reach of a private House. – five per cent. is the rate at which the Bank of England discounts Bills. – It is the rate at which Bankers discount for their Customers, and it is the rate at which all advances by Merchants to each other are calculated, over and above the commission which is charged upon all mercantile Transactions, it being a principle universally acknowledged that when a Merchant draws only the natural and legal interest of his money he only *does not lose* by the Trans-action . . . I leave it to you to judge whether it would not be apt to strike Mercantile people as unnatural that a House of Business should receive orders from and enter into correspondence with the Treasury, get large sums of Bills drawn, go thro' the forms of office in paying money for account of Government, wait the gradual negotiation of these Bills for the reimbursement of these advances, pay Brokers for negotiating the Bills, and after all receive only 4 per cent. interest for the Money so advanced . . . No man of Business would believe that there was not some secret under-standing beyond the bare 4 per cent., and such a suspicion would certainly do infinitely more harm than the open and fair avowal of the real state of the transaction. . .'

He went on to point out that he negotiated a large proportion of the bills at four and a half per cent., in addition to which he had to pay brokerage, making the total cost fully equal to, if not more than, five per

35. Giles was a partner in the merchant firm of Giles & Bottelin.
36. Morning Chronicle, 31 Oct. 1795.

cent. He concluded by expressing his regret that the secrecy, which he had been so anxious to see preserved, had not been maintained. 'If the operation had been kept quite secret, in all probability none, or at least very few of the Bills would ever have seen the light, because many other resources would then have remained untouched, whereas the publicity unfortunately given to the Transaction produced that scarcity of money which a certain wealthy Corporation can create at pleasure'.[37]

Further reflection brought Boyd to the view that he had perhaps not stressed sufficiently the undesirability of a public investigation. He accordingly wrote a letter on the following day suggesting that 'however honourable it may be found', the transaction would 'prove to all Europe that the public Treasury of this Country had felt the pressure of a temporary distress, and (what is worse) that the Bank of England had refused or had been unable to relieve it . . . If I had a wish upon the subject which had only for object the extinction of the reputation of my House, I certainly ought to desire that the Investigation may go on, but if there is a Chance of giving any comfort or hope to our Enemies, it is my duty to wish it had not taken place'.[38] Boyd's arguments apparently won the day: interest was paid at five per cent. and Pitt gave no further opportunity for talk of an investigation.

Successful as the operation was, Boyd later regarded it as marking the beginning of the Bank's hostility to him. Four years later he wrote to Pitt: 'The hostility of the Bank to all my views . . . began with the liberality in the pecuniary negotiations to which you had been but little accustomed before your first public transaction with the party to which I belonged . . . Its highest point was the advance made in the autumn of 1795'. Furthermore the transaction involved the discount of bills in the market, and made him vulnerable to the contraction of discounts by the Bank of England at the close of the year.[39] There were signs, even earlier, that Boyd, Benfield & Co.'s position was becoming strained. Sir John Call, holding a maturing note of Benfield's for £1,900, wrote to him asking for payment, adding, 'I cannot by any means think of applying to Mr Boyd's knowing how many other calls he must have for money'.[40] From this time on, calls for money would increase.

37. Boyd to Pitt, 4 Nov. 1795 Pitt Correspondence, CUL, Add. 6958/9. The 'wealthy Corporation' was the Bank of England.
38. Boyd to Pitt, 5 Nov. 1795, Chatham Papers, PRO, 30/8/115.
39. Boyd to Pitt, 7 Oct. 1799, Chatham Papers, PRO, 30/8/115. Pitt Correspondence, CUL Add. 6958/13.
40. Call to Benfield, 1 Sept. 1795, Paul Benfield Papers, IO, Eur, c., 307/1.

CHAPTER VII

A Question of Competition

'As to the claim of Mr. Boyd . . . I at first testified strong prejudices and great reluctance, which were not overcome till it was brought forward in a shape in which it was no longer controvertible.'

William Pitt in the House of Commons,
26 February 1796.

In the autumn of 1795 it was apparent that Pitt would have to borrow considerable sums in the following year. Boyd, who had headed the group which contracted for the loan for 1795, and who had also bid successfully for the Irish loan and lottery in March 1795, had no intention of relinquishing the dominant position he had gained in the money market. He could hardly afford to do so, for at the end of November his group still held £1,500,000 of the previous loan, of which his firm's share was between £400,000 and £500,000, and if another group contracted for the loan for 1796 he would no longer be able to control the market. Scrip of the 1795 loan which he was holding was 'heavy', for only three instalments remained to be paid. The new loan, on the other hand, would at first be only ten per cent. paid, and the amount of cash required to hold a given nominal amount of scrip would obviously be far less. Thus a newcomer, with the same resources as Boyd, could hold a nominal amount several times as large, and would be able to exercise a disproportionate affect on prices.

Boyd therefore approached Pitt in October, and put forward the view that since three instalments of the loan for 1795 were still to be paid, his group, as contractors, were entitled to the new loan without competition. He undertook that if his right were admitted, it would be exercised 'with great liberality'.[1] Pitt was in a difficulty. He had received considerable assistance from Boyd, Benfield & Co. in the matter of the Hamburg bills only a month or so previously, yet he realised that the oppositon were always ready to seize on any suggestion of favouritism. He therefore temporized by refusing to admit Boyd's claim, promising, however, to hear what he had to say before putting the loan to competition.

The Chancellor of the Exchequer relied very much on the Governor of the Bank of England for advice on loan contracts. It was therefore clearly to Boyd's advantage that such an influential person should have a direct

---

1. The minutes of evidence of the Select Committee appointed to enquire into . . . the Late Loan form the main source of material for this chapter. *Commons Journals,* vol. 51, pp. 309–60.

interest in seeing that Boyd's group received the contract. Meeting the Governor, Daniel Giles, accidentally in the street, Boyd mentioned that he was forming a list for the loan, and said that it would 'give him great pleasure' to accommodate him. Giles did not refuse and was put down for £165,000, which was additional to the allocation he would receive as Governor. Boyd's next step was to eliminate possible competitors. One experienced group which might compete consisted of Godschall Johnson, J.J. Angerstein, and James Morgan. Boyd therefore offered them a share in his list, but all three declined.

There were others, however, who did not intend to let Boyd have the loan without a fight. James and William Mellish, partners in an old-established mercantile firm, formed a list with the object of bidding. Morgan, hearing of this, was somewhat impressed, and called on Giles, who said that although Pitt had told him that he would offer the loan to competition, he (Giles) was sceptical, since Boyd and his friends seemed so confident. Two days later, Morgan told Giles that he would form a list. Giles reiterated his doubts about competition, saying that the loan would go to Boyd, as 'something would be done' to prevent competition. Morgan, undeterred, went on with his list, which he opened to the public on October 29. He thought that if competition were not allowed, it would be because provision had to be made for a loan to the Emperor of Austria. He therefore wrote to Pitt to say that he was forming a list, and would be prepared to bid for an Austrian loan, if it were guaranteed by Parliament.[2]

Meantime, Boyd's confident attitude became the talk of the City. 'Odds were repeatedly offered that there would be no competition, and even on the supposition of a competition, that Boyd & Co. would get it'.[3] These views were reflected in the anxiety shown to get on Boyd's list. One investor offered to exchange £5,000 on Morgan's list for £3,000 on Boyd's. Another offered three for one.[4] Boyd said afterwards that he was 'overwhelmed with demands for shares in his list'. Even a well-known banking house like Newnham, Everett & Co., who had applied for 'a very large sum', were glad to accept £30,000. One reason why Boyd's chances were favoured was no doubt the knowledge that he was in touch with Pitt. There was correspondence between the two at least as early as mid-November, when Pitt mentioned the possibility that the initial deposit might be twenty per cent. instead of the usual ten per cent. Giles heard of this, and a day or so later, in conversation with Boyd, mentioned that he had been informed 'from the most respectable authority', that Pitt had settled that the initial deposit should be twenty per cent., and asked whether this was true. Boyd was not to be caught in a trap of this sort. He replied immediately, not wholly truthfully, that he had had no conversation with Pitt on the subject, and that he never had been and probably never would be consulted on it. Giles, perhaps only half convinced, endeavoured to impress upon Boyd the harm which such an unusually large deposit would cause, to which Boyd replied cautiously that no doubt

2. Morgan to Pitt, 16 Nov. 1795, *Commons Journals, vol. 51, p. 350.*
3. *William Smith, 7 Dec. 1795, Parliamentary History*, vol. 32, p. 568.
4. *Morning Chronicle*, 23 Feb. 1796.

the Governor's opinion was entitled to considerable weight.[5]

A few days later, when Boyd, accompanied by Robarts, called at the Bank to see Giles, he stated that he had the right to object to the loan until the last payment on the preceding loan had been completed, although whatever right he had, he would not exercise in an illiberal or unfair way. Giles said that he had always considered that Boyd's group had the right to object, but thought, nevertheless, that the loan would be offered to competition.

On November 24 Boyd and Robarts saw Pitt. Boyd argued that he contracted for the loan for 1795 on condition that no other public loan would be issued until the last payment on the earlier loan had been made. Pitt said that he did not recollect any positive engagement to this effect, to which Boyd replied that the right, positive or implied, existed 'from the nature of things'. Pitt admitted, somewhat incautiously, that if the loan had been put forward in June, he would have considered an objection well founded, a remark which gave Boyd the opportunity of saying that if the right existed in June, it also existed in November, and could terminate only when the loan became fully paid. Pitt replied that as the sum to be paid was so small it could not seriously be urged as a reason for not making the loan. Small as it was, retorted Boyd, it was fifteen per cent. on £5,000,000.[6] Boyd, realising that Pitt was determined to present at least a façade of open competition, offered to waive his right to prevent the negotiation, if the injury which he and the other contractors would thereby suffer were offset by an advantage to be gained from the new loan. He was willing, he said, to allow the loan to be offered for competition, if the option were reserved to his group to take the loan at one-half per cent. above the highest offer. Pitt asked Boyd to submit these points in writing, which he did.[7]

At noon on the following day, November 25, James Morgan, James and William Mellish,[8] and Boyd and his associates — Abraham Goldsmid, Abraham Robarts, E.P. Salomons and Rawson Aislabie, met in the Chancellor's house in Downing Street. However outwardly friendly, they must all have been conscious of a certain tension in the atmosphere, for in the preceding few days there had been much talk in the City regarding Boyd's position. Thus they waited for an hour. Meantime, the Chancellor, apparently still undecided, was in conference behind closed doors with the Governor and Deputy Governor of the Bank. There, Pitt read out Boyd's letter claiming preference, and asked Giles whether he recollected making any promise of the kind claimed by Boyd. Giles replied that he considered that Pitt had to some extent committed himself, for when one of the contractors had asked for the last instalment of the previous loan to be payable in February 1796, instead of a month earlier, Pitt had refused on the

5. Boyd to Pitt, 17 Nov. 1795, Chatham Papers, PRO, 30/8/115. The initial deposit was eventually fixed at ten per cent.
6. This estimate was too high: the amount was less than £3.500,000. *Commons Journals*, vol. 51, p. 341.
7. Boyd and Robarts to Pitt, 24 Nov. 1795, *Commons Journals*, vol. 51, pp. 353–4.
8. William Mellish (1764–1838) was member for Grimsby and a director of the Bank of England.

grounds that he might want to raise a loan in the January. This, indefinite as it was, seems to have tilted the scales in favour of Boyd.

Pitt then called in Boyd and Robarts. The matter, he explained, was not free from difficulty, but he thought that a 'considerable degree of attention' was due to Boyd's claim. If, he asked, the other parties would not agree to the qualified bidding, would he (Boyd) agree to take the loan on whatever terms Pitt fixed. To this Boyd and Robarts readily assented. Victory was in sight. Boyd and Robarts then rejoined the other competitors, and Pitt, the two Secretaries to the Treasury and the Governor and Deputy Governor of the Bank came in soon afterwards. Pitt opened the proceedings by saying that the contractors for the previous loan considered that they had a right to prevent the negotiation of another loan until the last payment on the previous loan had been made, but that they were prepared to give up that right if they were allowed to contract at one-half per cent. better than the highest offer.

Morgan and the Mellish brothers immediately objected. Morgan pointed out with sound logic that 'if there was any Agreement not to bring forward a Loan it must concern the Public, the then Holders of the former Loan, who were the Persons that would be injured by bringing forward another Loan, and did not justify any Claim of Preference of Behalf of the Contractors.' Furthermore, the contractors appeared to him to be 'highly blameable' rather than deserving a preference, for taking part in a loan before the expiry of the period fixed in the agreement, if such an agreement had in fact been made. Abraham Goldsmid then spoke in support of Boyd, and recalled that when, at the previous bidding, Salomons had proposed postponing the last payment to February 1796, this had been refused, as it might interfere with the loan for 1796. William Mellish interposed that he thought this was a point which should be settled by the Chancellor and Boyd, for not being present at the meeting, he could not say what took place.

There followed a sharp exchange between Boyd and Morgan, in which Morgan maintained that if there were any preference it should be given to the present stockholders. To this Boyd retorted that he himself was a substantial stockholder. The proceedings threatened to become acrimonious, so Pitt intervened to say that he thought there was no obligation, although there might be some consideration due to the contractors. He then asked the Mellishes whether they would like to consider the matter, to which William Mellish replied that he was astonished to hear such proposals from one set of mercantile men to another, but would consult his friends. Morgan said emphatically that he could not entertain the proposition for a moment, and at this the Mellishes came into line and refused as well. All three thereupon left the meeting.

The Chancellor then gave the usual preliminary details; the amount of borrowing over the ensuing year, and the technical details of the loan to be bid for. He then retired with the Governor and Deputy Governor. The Governor gave Pitt the current prices for stocks, and Pitt, after being assured that sixty-five was a 'fair price' for five per cent. Consols – the market quotation that morning was sixty-seven and one half – decided upon the amount of Long Annuity to be given. Pitt then returned and announced to Boyd and his party the terms he had fixed. For every £100 advanced, they were to receive £120 three per cent. Consols, £25 Reduced

Consols and 6s. 6d. Long Annuity.[9] Boyd was delighted, and said afterwards that he and his friends were struck by the 'wonderful coincidence' between the terms fixed by the Chancellor and those he had worked on.

The news caused a sensation in the City, and Pitt was openly accused of partiality. The *Morning Post* spoke bluntly. 'The manner in which this loan has been made and the beneficial terms granted to the contractors are such as must ruin Mr. Pitt's character for fair dealing, and must show at once his compleat disregard of the Public interest.'[10] That there was at least a prima facie case for the allegation that public interests had been disregarded was shown by the first day's dealings, which started at seven premium. The episode continued to attract attention, and it was said freely that Boyd had been favoured because of the Hamburg bill transaction of the previous September. On the Monday following, Morgan met with his subscribers at Garraway's Coffee House, when it was agreed to petition Parliament not to confirm the bargain.[11] Pitt, somewhat concerned, postponed the budget, and sent a soothing message to Morgan, asking him not to take any action until he (Pitt) had had an opportunity of making an explanation which he hoped would be satisfactory.[12]

Morgan had an interview with Pitt a few days later. Pitt explained the reasons which led him to think that 'some consideration' was due to Boyd, and said that it was impossible to make any alteration in the loan. He hinted, however, that compensation might be given on some other occasion, and hoped that Morgan 'would not do anything to agitate the Public mind in these dangerous times.'[13] This vague promise failed to tempt Morgan, and on December 4 his petition, bearing between 150 and 200 names, was presented by William Smith and referred to the Ways and Means Committee of the House of Commons.[14] Three days later, Morgan wrote to Pitt offering to take the loan at 2s. 0d. less of Long Annuity than was to be given to Boyd, and asked that his letter be read in the Commons.[15] This was a shrewd move, for it put the contract given to Boyd in an unfavourable light, although since the funds had risen over the period, Morgan's offer, in relation to actual market conditions, was not better than Boyd's.

In this budget speech Pitt explained that he was faced with the choice between deferring the loan until February (by which time the 1795 loan would have become fully paid), or issuing it against the wishes of the subscribers to that loan. As neither course appealed to him, he made the arrangement under discussion. The debate which followed threw little fresh light on the transaction, and after what a somewhat bored reporter described as 'a long and desultory conversation', Pitt's resolutions were passed.[16]

9.   The full terms are in *Commons Journals*, vol. 51, p. 588.
10. *Morning Post*, 25 Nov. 1795.
11. *Morning Post*, 1 Dec. 1795.
12. *Morning Post*, 2 Dec. 1795.
13. *Morning Post*, 5 Dec. 1795. The account given in *Commons Journals*, vol. 51, p. 349, is slightly different and suggests that Morgan was not present at this interview.
14. *Commons Journal*, vol. 51, p. 189; *Morning Post*, 5 Dec. 1795.
15. Morgan to Pitt, 7 Dec. 1795, *Commons Journals*, vol. 51, p. 354.
16. *The Times*, 8 Dec. 1795.

There the matter might have rested, had it not been for Pitt's announcement on December 8 of a message from the King, indicating the Government's willingness to negotiate a peace with France.[17] Prices on the Stock Exchange responded immediately, and the new loan rose from seven to thirteen premium. This greatly strengthened the hands of Morgan and his supporters. It was pointed out that 'A profit of no less than six per cent. (on eighteen millions, £1,080,000) was, in addition to the high profit which the contractors had by their own dexterity secured, actually given in one day, by a Message delivered by Mr. Pitt from the King, announcing his disposition to treat with the Republic of France . . . Had Mr. Pitt any idea of such a Message when he negotiated the Loan?'[18] This was the sort of question which many people beside the *Morning Post's* contributor were asking.

A premium of thirteen per cent. was too much, even in an age accustomed to high profits on government contracts. When, therefore, on 15 December 1795, William Smith moved in the House of Commons that a Committee of Inquiry be appointed, Pitt agreed, taking care, that its membership included a generous proportion of his own supporters.[19] At the end of the year, the premium on omnium was ten per cent . . . and a statistically-minded writer calculated that 'the annual subsistence of one hundred and fifty thousand inhabitants of Great Britain has been at one blow, given by Mr. Pitt to gorge the voracious maw of a gang of Loan Contractors.'[20]

Before the Committee could report, fresh fuel had been added to the controversy. On 22 December 1795 the *Morning Post* published an open letter to Daniel Giles, signed under the pseudonym of 'Gideon', drawing attention to the way in which the five Commissioners for the Reduction of the National Debt (of whom Giles was one) had applied the money lying in their hands.[21] It appeared that on November 3, some three weeks before the loan agreement was made with Boyd, the Commissioners, who usually purchased three per cent. Consols, began to purchase four per cent. Consols, with the result that the price rose two-and-three-quarter points between October 31 and November 6, while three per cent. Consols rose only three-quarters. The loan agreement having been signed, the Commissioners, it was said, reverted to the purchase of three per cent. Consols.[22]

'Gideon' made no specific allegations, but his meaning was plain. At the end of October it was known that the loan would be mainly in three per cent. stock. Contractors based their bids on market prices, and were accordingly anxious that the price of the stock they were to bid for should not be raised in any way. This feeling would be even stronger if competitive bidding were absent. It would therefore suit the contractors far better if the Commissioners bought four per cent. stock, instead of the three per

17. *Commons Journals*, vol. 51, p. 198.
18. *Morning Post*, 14 Dec. 1795.
19. The names of members of the Committee are in *Commons Journals*, vol. 51, pp. 235 and 241.
20. *Morning Post*, 26 Dec. 1795.
21. *Morning Post*, 22 and 29 Dec. 1795.
22. John J. Grellier, *Terms of all the Loans* . . . John Richardson and J.M. Richardson, London, 1812, p. 60.

cent. stock to be contracted for. In short, it was suggested that the Commissioners had deliberately favoured the contractors by a judicious manipulation of the funds under their control, 'making the loan', wrote William Morgan, 'one of the most distinguished for its extravagance of all the loans made in this country.'[23] This was not all. Some £649,000 of four per cent. Consols created in 1795 were pledged at the Bank of England as security for advances, and an additional or alternative motive for the action of the Commissioners might have been a desire to assist the owners of these stocks. This was the sort of criticism which came from several directions, in spite of the fact that the whole matter was under investigation by a Commons Committee, and might therefore be regarded as sub judice. Criticism reached such a pitch that Boyd approached Smith, the Committee's Chairman, and asked him to stop irresponsible newspaper comment which he (Boyd) was precluded from answering. But veiled innuendo could not be stopped, and when the *Morning Chronicle* defined competition as 'a predetermination to give a certain thing to a certain person', all the world knew that the certain person referred to was Walter Boyd.[24]

It was against this background that the Committee began its work. Numerous witnesses were examined, of whom Boyd and Morgan were the chief. The examination brought to light a great deal of information on the events already described, much of which those concerned were most reluctant to disclose. The Committee did not record any general conclusions and reported only the evidence. On February 9, William Smith, as Chairman, laid the report before the House, and shortly afterwards moved no less than forty resolutions, each setting out one or other of the criticisms which had been levelled against the procedure adopted. The last resolution ran: 'That in every part of the Transaction of the late Loan, the Public Interest has been sacrificed by the Chancellor of the Exchequer; and that the Profit to the Contributors, at the Expense of the Nation, has been so exorbitantly swelled, as to have risen . . . to the enormous and incredible Sum of Two Millions One hundred and Sixty thousand Pounds Sterling.'

The debate covered the same ground as those of previous occasions, and all the familiar arguments were made from both sides of the House. In the end, Smith's resolutions were heavily defeated, and a Government resolution was passed stating 'That the Terms of the Loan were fixed with a due Regard to the Magnitude of the Sums borrowed, and provided for, as well as to the Market Price of the Funds, and the Situation of Public Affairs, at the Time the Bargain was concluded', and 'That, in every part of the Transaction of the late Loan, the Conduct of the Chancellor of the Exchequer was actuated by a View to the Public Interest; and that there is no Ground to suppose that any Interference took place on the Part of any Persons connected with Government, in the Distribution of any Part of the said Loan'.

A few days later Joseph Jekyll moved three resolutions condemning the Hamburg bill transaction. Their general tenor can be gauged from the

---

23. William Morgan, *Facts addressed to the Serious Attention of the People of Great Britain* . . . J. Debrett and T. Cadell jun., and W. Davies. London. 1796, pp. 17–18.
24. *Morning Chronicle*, 6 and 14 Jan. 1795.

third, which ran: 'That the Practice of drawing such Bills of Exchange, not duly stamped, with fictitious Dates of Time and Place, accepted by the Lords Commissioners of the Treasury . . . is illegal, unconstitutional and highly injurious to the public Credit, and that the Chancellor of the Exchequer, by the Introduction of such Practice, has brought into Disrepute and Suspicion the Acceptance of His Majesty's Treasury, and sanctioned a System of Fraud and Collusion unprecedented in the Administration of the Finance of this Country.'[25] The chief government spokesman to defend the transaction was Charles Long, the Junior (Financial) Secretary to the Treasury who had been concerned in the negotiations, which drew the comment that 'Had Mr. Long's father (a West India merchant) fabricated Bills in the same way, he would not have obtained so much credit *in the City,* as his son has done *in the House of Commons.*'[26] Like those of Smith, Jekyll's resolutions were decisively defeated.

Boyd had won. His contract had been upheld. Moreover, the principle had been accepted that no loan could be made until the previous one was fully paid, unless the contractors for that loan gave their consent. Since the last instalment on the loan was not due until 15 December 1796, Boyd must have felt sure of his grip on the market, for it was all but certain that Pitt would have to borrow before that date. An historian, viewing the inconclusive and often conflicting evidence, may feel less sure of the merits of Boyd's case.

Much remains obscure in spite of the Committee's labours. The reason for the Commissioners' action in buying four per cent. Consols was never investigated. The facts are that from 31 January to 30 October 1795 the sinking fund moneys went entirely into three per cent. stocks. At the beginning of November, the Commissioners changed over suddenly to four per cent. Consols, some £507,000 being purchased in November and December 1795, while purchases of three per cent. stocks were negligible. At the end of December the former practice of buying three per cent. stocks was resumed.[27] The Commissioners could hardly have adopted a policy more calculated to suit the interests of the contractors and prejudice those of the Treasury, and it was no doubt mainly due to their action that the 'spread' between the price of three per cent. and four per cent. Consols increased just when every effort should have been made to narrow it. The Commissioners were apparently not asked for an explanation, nor did they offer one. Nor did Pitt ever explain the curious circumstance that the terms of the loan were fixed just before the Government's intention to negotiate with France was announced. It might have been just a coincidence.

Apart from side issues, such as these, there were two main questions. First, was there justification for Boyd's claim to be allotted the loan without competition? There was nothing in writing to support it, nor was there an explicit oral agreement. The point seems to have been one on which there was no settled practice. Abraham Newland had not been able to find an instance of a new loan being issued before the old one was fully

25. *Commons Journals*, vol. 51, p. 451.
26. *Morning Post*, 10 March 1796.
27. *Commons Journals, vol. 51, pp. 394–7. An Account . . . by the Commissioners . . . for the Reduction of the National Debt.*

paid, but this did not show how, if the case had arisen, it would have been decided. Pitt, throughout, appeared indecisive, torn between an interest in giving Boyd the loan and a reluctance to pay the political price of going against the principle of competition. In the end, escape from the dilemma having been blocked, he did what all along he had wanted to do, which was to give the contract to Boyd. One result of the case was that it established a rule that a contractor whose loan was not fully paid could object to a new loan being given to someone else, a rule which was invoked subsequently on several occasions.

The second main question concerns the terms on which the loan was allotted. Whatever doubt may remain on the first question, there is none on the second. On the basis of prevailing market prices, the terms were unduly favourable to the contractors. Onmium opened at seven premium, it rose later to thirteen premium, and although contractors did not by a long way benefit to this extent, there is little doubt that Pitt could have done better by insisting on open competition.

Boyd's victory was not without cost. Details of the Hamburg bill transaction, which he had been at such pains to keep secret, were laid open to the whole world, Publicity in another direction, too, was most unwelcome. The Committee had directed the Bank to produce lists of the names in which the scrip was to be issued, and these were made public. Boyd, Benfield & Co's list accounted for £5,704,000, out of a loan of £18,000,000: in addition to their own list they had £285,000 in E.P. Salomon's list making £5,989,000. Of this, £1,878,000 was taken in the firm's name, the rest being in the names of customers. About a third of the £1,878,000 – £694,000 – was for customers who found it convenient to have scrip issued in the name of Boyd, Benfield & Co. as their nominees; thus the firm's own holding amounted to £1,184,000. This was a very large commitment, and it explains Boyd's anxiety to get the loan on his own terms. He was playing for big stakes. Even assuming that his average selling price was only five premium, he would have secured a profit of nearly £60,000.[28]

Boyd, Benfield & Co's customers were allotted £4,111,000. This was divided among 135 names, the amounts allotted to each ranging between £350,000 and £3,000. Banking houses took £1,168,000 – just over a quarter – but of this, £650,000 went to various nominees of Smith, Payne & Smiths. Presumably, they received such a large share because they were Boyd, Benfield & Co's bankers. Perhaps this was one of 'the immense advantages' which Boyd claimed they had derived from their connection with him.[29] Other bankers took amounts which varied from £100,000 taken by Walwyn, Petrie & Co.[30] to a mere £5,000 by Lockharts, Maxtone, Wallis & Clarke for one of their customers. The other names on the list were mainly those of London merchants and brokers, who took, in all, nearly £300,000. The individual amounts varied as widely as did those of the bankers, although the average was much lower. The two largest

28. *Five per cent on the firm's holding of £1,184,000.*
29. *Boyd to Pitt, 7 Oct. 1799, Chatham Papers, PRO, 30/8/115; CUL, Pitt Correspondence, Add. 6958†13.*
30. Partners in this firm were James Walwyn, John Ward, William McGeorge and the brothers John and William Petrie: the Petrie brothers were also partners in J. Petrie, Campbell & Co.

participations were those of J.J. Angerstein and Godschall Johnson & Co., each of whom took £350,000, the size of their allocations reflecting Boyd's anxiety to eliminate them as competitors. Both were known to be dealers in the funds in a large way and had contracted for previous loans. Charles Herries & Co., who were close to Boyd, Benfield & Co., had £250,000, a large sum for a firm of their size, and Walter Boyd, Junior, and John William Ker £150,000 each. Directors and officials of the Bank of England received special consideration. Giles received £90,000 (in addition to larger amounts in other lists), and his son £20,000. Samuel Beachcroft, Samuel Bosanquet and Godfrey Thornton, all directors, received in all £50,000. Abraham Newland, Chief Cashier, had £20,000 and other officials smaller sums.[31] Boyd was doing his best to keep in with those who might be useful to him.

For Boyd, the episode carried an important lesson. It showed the importance of having political allies, for when it came to loan contracting, Whitehall was as least as important as Threadneedle Street. Boyd was not slow to learn. In February 1796 he announced his intention of entering Parliament.[32] The seat he selected was Taunton in Somerset, one of whose representatives, Alexander Popham, was about to retire. At first, Boyd was confident of success, but the other candidates, Sir Benjamin Hammet and William Morland, had the advantage of being well known in the constituency, and after three months of much effort and lavish expenditure he found he could make little progress. Like a good speculator, he decided to cut his losses – which amounted to some £3300 — and find another constituency where prospects were better.[33] The prospects of nearly Minehead were canvassed, but there the candidate had been received so favourably that Boyd quickly abandoned all thought of contesting the seat.[34]

This was in early May, and time was running short. Arrangements were therefore quickly made for Boyd to stand for the pocket borough of Shaftesbury, Dorset, one of whose two members was Benfield, who had been elected in 1793. Since the voting was largely in Benfield's hands, the result was a foregone conclusion; Benfield and Boyd were duly returned with 224 and 190 votes respectively, their two opponents, James Milnes and William Dawson, polling 143 and 105 votes respectively.[35]

Boyd seems to have been reluctant to sit for Shaftesbury, possibly because he did not want to feel dependent on Benfield. Almost as soon as he had been returned, he was considering contesting Yarmouth. One of Yarmouth's two members, Lord Charles Patrick Townshend, had been found shot two days after his election,[36] and Boyd thought that he might be able to gain sufficient support to get the seat. He soon found that he was on dangerous ground. The Townshend family, wealthy and influential

31. The contractors' lists were published in *Commons Journals,* vol. 51, pp. 350–353; they are not complete, as some subscribers objected to their names being revealed.
32. *The Times,* 11 Feb. 1796.
33. Joshus Toulain, *History of Taunton,* new edition by James Savage, John Poole, Taunton, 1822, p. 340; *Morning Chronicle,* 2 May 1796; Boyd to Benfield, 4 Oct. 1796, Forbes of Fettercairn Papers, NLS.
34. *The Times,* 11 May 1796.
35. *The Times,* 31 May 1796.
36. *Morning Chronicle,* 28 May 1796.

in Norfolk, regarded the seat as theirs. This view was made known to Boyd in unmistakeable terms, and he had to assure Pitt, through Fordyce, that he had no intention of opposing the Townshend family at Yarmouth, and would stand only if the family were not interested.[37] Unfortunately for Boyd, the family were interested, and were supporting the candidature of the son-in-law of the Marquis of Townshend, Major-General William Loftus, who a few months later was elected.

Boyd's political activities gave rise to some sly comments in the press. The *Morning Chronicle* – bitterly opposed to Pitt and his supporters – related the story of a contractor for a foreign loan (obviously Boyd, although no name was mentioned) who held himself out to be one who had a great stake in the commerce of the country. A voter asked one of his friends 'Pray in what particular branch is M. —— chiefly engaged?' 'Why', said the other, 'I believe that he is largely concerned in the Export Trade.'[38]

The 1796 loan affair showed Boyd's skill as a negotiator, manipulating a pliant Chancellor, who was none too sure of himself, and eliminating powerful competitors. Much, however, remains obscure. There was the unexplained action of the Commissioners for the National Debt in switching their purchases to four and five per cent. stocks. Daniel Giles was one of the Commissioners; he was also Governor of the Bank, and as such would receive the customary loan allocation. Inevitably, he was an interested party, the more so since Boyd gave him an additional allocation, and he would be tempted to use his position as Commissioner, to his own advantage. Had Boyd himself any inkling of how the sinking fund was being applied? He was never asked – publicly.

Finally, there was the announcement of intention to negotiate with France. It is unlikely that the diplomats, immersed in the intricacies of their own negotiations, gave much thought to the market implications of their actions. Pitt and the Cabinet should have done so, but apparently did not. While it might have been impossible to advance the date of the announcement about negotiations with France, it should have been possible to postpone the loan, at least for a few days. None of those responsible for these decisions seems to have benefitted personally from them. The timing, as it turned out, was unfortunate, perhaps maladroit, but not corrupt.

37. Fordyce to Pitt, 31 May 1796, Chatham Papers, PRO, 30/8/136. John Fordyce, c. 1738–1809, was an old friend of Boyd's. He was member for New Romney, 1796–1802, and Surveyor-General of the Land Revenue Office.
38. *Morning Chronicle*, 9 June, 1796.

CHAPTER VIII

Boyd and the Bank of England

'The Bank Directors seem to forget that the Institution was formed for a National Benefit, not a National Misfortune.'

True Briton, 5 April 1796.

'To the Bank of England, to its energy and wisdom — to its disregard of clamour and misrepresentation, to its intrepidity and steadiness in pursuing the good old and wholesome system of English caution Great Britain is indebted perhaps for her salvation.'

Morning Chronicle, 7 April 1796.

During the whole of 1795, the economy had been subjected to strain, which, as the year drew to a close, increased rather than diminished. The exchanges moved adversely, partly because of heavy remittances abroad for loans and subsidies to allies and for the support of British armies overseas. The export of guineas was prohibited, but there was a considerable clandestine trade between England and the Continent, as the export of melted-down guineas showed a profit of some seven and a half per cent.[1] The resumption of dealings in gold in France increased the flow of gold across the Channel, despite the fact that France and Britain were at war.[2]

Internally, too, there were difficulties. Most of the additional government expenditure caused by the war had been met, not out of taxes, but by the issue of loans which stretched to the limit the market's capacity to take them up. Even with the inducement of an extra discount of a quarter per cent. on payments made before December 31, only one-tenth of the £18,000,000 loan had been paid up in full by the end of the year. There was a great deal of government short-term paper in the market, such as Navy and Victualling Bills and Exchequer Bills. Despite the Bank's protests, short-term borrowing from the Bank of England had risen from £9,000,000 to nearly £13,000,000 by the end of 1795. The credit position was further weakened by the existence of a large amount of accommodation bills.[3]

In these circumstances, the Bank directors, precluded by the usury laws from raising their rate of discount above five per cent. opted for a quantitative limitation of discounts. According, on 31 December 1795, they resolved that the sum to be employed in discounts was to be fixed for each day in advance, and that any excess was to be dealt with by returning 'a pro rata proportion of such bills in each parcel as are not otherwise objec-

---

1. *Morning Chronicle*, 6 Jan. 1796.
2. Hawtrey, op.cit., pp. 326–9.
3. *Morning Chronicle*, 2 and 6 Jan. 1796.

tionable . . . without regard to the respectability of the party sending in the bills or solidarity of the bills themselves.'[4]

The decision caused great concern in the City. Bills became increasingly difficult to discount, and the funds fell as much as one point in a single day. The difficulties in the stock market were increased by the incidence of four payments in January; the last payment on the loan of December 1794, an instalment on the Imperial loan, a payment on the lottery, and ten per cent. on the latest £18,000,000 loan. The Bank of England relented to the extent of advancing the fifteen per cent. due on the loan of December 1794, but it was clear that the assistance which the Bank was willing to give holders of partly-paid loans was to be very limited. The end of January saw continuation for the last settling day in February at a quarter per cent.,[5] and the price of omnium at 9 premium, compared with 12½ premium in December.

Boyd, Benfield & Co. were still holding substantial amounts of stock, which they were reluctant to sell for fear of causing a further fall, and although they had reduced their holding in the £18,000,000 loan to £125,000,[6] they lacked the resources to hold indefinitely even the reduced amount. Early in February, the Bank announced that they would advance the third payment on the loan, which was 'a great accommodation to the holders,'[7] but when Boyd, Benfield & Co. applied for advances to pay the fourth instalment due in March, the Bank refused. The extent of their involvement can only be conjectured; many of their operations were in the newly-issued scrip, which passed from hand to hand in bearer form, and there is no record of their 'jobbing' transactions, which were settled by payment of 'differences' at the settlement dates, without actual delivery of stock. Boyd, Benfield & Co's holdings which were in the names of Boyd and Drummond therefore show only part of the picture. In three per cent. Consols, the Bank of England stock ledgers show them, with few exceptions, as having few transactions, with small amounts held for only short periods.

Only in the Imperial loans were large balances held for any length of time. In Imperial three per cent. annuities, Boyd's and Drummond's accounts taken together show holdings around £150,000 in the late summer and autumn of 1795. From November, their holdings remained above £50,000 until April, when they dropped to £1,000. Thereafter, the amounts were insignificant. In the Imperial twenty-five-year annuities, their holdings remained above £28,000 from July to October 1795, falling to £18,000 in November and to £6,000 in March, virtually nothing being held thereafter.[8] At their peak in the autumn of 1795, the holdings of the two Imperial loans in the Bank's books were worth £475,000, and were possible only because the firm held large balances for the Austrian government. As these balances were remitted, the Imperial stocks had to be sold.

4. Wilfrid Marston Acres, *The Bank of England from Within, 1694–1900*, London, Oxford University Press, 1931, vol. I. p. 270.
5. *Morning Chronicle*, 16 and 22 Jan. 1796.
6. They paid £12,560 on 22 Jan. 1796, as the second instalment, Select Committee on the Tenth Naval Report, Evidence of Drummond, p. 75.
7. *Morning Chronicle*, 5 Feb. 1796.
8. Bank of England, Stock Ledgers.

For the reasons given above, the story of Boyd, Benfield & Co's dealings in the funds can be told only in very general terms. There was undoubtedly much bull speculation in the funds from the end of 1795, based on the expectation of an early peace with France, which had been aroused by the King's message of 8 December 1795. On February 5, William Wickham, British Minister in Switzerland, was instructed to approach François Barthélémy, the French minister, with a view to opening peace negotiations.[9] Although no public statement was made for a month, the news soon leaked out, for speculation flared up on the very day that the despatch was sent to Wickham.[10]

The movement in prices was noticeable, although not spectacular. Three per cent. Consols, which were around sixty-eight at the beginning of March, touched seventy before the month was out. The *Morning Chronicle* expressed the view that more was involved than a simple bull speculation on hopes of an early peace, and that 'a foreign click, who have introduced into this country all the science of the French agiotage', was responsible. It was alleged that this group had bought at least £3,000,000 in the funds, for which they were paying twenty-five per cent. per annum for continuation to April 12. Hope of peace would not by itself justify paying such a price: therefore there must be other reasons. 'It is more probable', the *Morning Chronicle* continued, 'that the proprietors of the speculation, being men of great funded opulence, but distressed for the present by the Bank having refused to take in the scrip, have artificially raised the price to sell real stock for ready money to a large amount, trusting to their own powers to regulate the market in future.'[11] Two days later there were further reports in the same strain, the reason put forward this time being that 'a body of eminent Scrip-holders have entered into an engagement to accommodate Government with a large sum of money: to do which they were desirous to force the Stock up by bargains for time, that they might sell their stock for ready money at a higher price.'[12]

Although possibly exaggerated in the press, it was clear there was a big speculative position in the market, and that Boyd, Benfield & Co, and others of their group, were involved. The most plausible explanation is that the group held large amounts of the £18,000,000 loan issued in 1795. If these were suddenly thrown on the market, the premium would disappear. The longer the scrip was held, however, the more was the cash required, as instalments were falling due nearly every month, and the Bank had refused to advance money for their payment. The group were apparently selling stock for ready money and buying it back for time in order to provide the funds to enable them to meet instalments. This was expensive, and Boyd's active mind canvassed various alternatives. Aid from the Bank, even if obtainable, was limited, and might be withdrawn at short notice. What he needed was an entirely fresh source on which to draw.

There were many who shared Boyd's views on this subject. Merchants

---

9.   Grenville to Wickham, 5 Feb. 1796, General Correspondence-Switzerland, PRO, F.O. 74/15.
10. *Morning Chronicle*, 12 April 1796.
11. *Morning Chronicle*, 24 March 1796.
12. *Morning Chronicle*, 26 March 1796.

depended very much on being able to discount at the Bank of England, and quickly experienced difficulties when discounts were restricted. On 23 February 1796 a 'very respectable Meeting of Bank Proprietors' at the London Tavern agreed to send a deputation to the Bank to protest against the restriction, and to ask for the reason, but when they did so, no explanation was forthcoming,[13] In March stories appeared that an important mercantile house had sent in for discount bills amounting to £36,000, and had had all but £1,400 returned. For another firm the Bank discounted £150 out of a parcel of bills totalling £8,000.[14] This naturally gave rise to much criticism, all the more because the Bank did not publish any statement of its position which might have justified its action.

Foremost among the critics was Boyd. At a time when the Bank would not advance a penny more to the Government, Boyd had provided Pitt with funds. He had made remittances abroad for government account when the Bank was trying to prevent a drain of gold. He had protested against the Bank's credit policy. He now proposed a more radical step in the formation of a credit institution which could only be regarded as a rival to the Bank of England.

To carry out this plan, Boyd and a number of his friends constituted themselves a committee. That something was afoot became known at the end of March, and it aroused suspecion immediately. 'It is not impossible', wrote the *Morning Chronicle*, 'that the Minister's own friends are to be the Members of this Committee, and that however they may bear the title of Merchants, their commerce is in the article of money only and that they are none other than the body of Capitalists who are the authors of the difficulty they affect to deplore.'[15] This was a direct thrust, but Boyd, undeterred, went ahead with his scheme. A few days later, he invited twenty leading bankers and merchants to a meeting at the London Tavern on 2 April 1796. None of the West End bankers was included, as Boyd felt that they would be against any scheme, just because it was new, and because they were not sympathetic to the needs of the trading community.[16] In the City, Boyd wisely confined his invitations to those he knew and who were unconnected with the Bank of England. Even so, several declined, possibly agreeing with *The Times* that 'the difficulties in the money market were due as much to the immense speculations which have been carried on in the funds,'[17] as to any restrictive credit policy on the part of the Bank of England, and that the remedy lay, in part a least, in the hands of contractors such as Boyd, whose anxiety to contract for loans was not equalled by the willingness of the investing public to subscribe.

13.   Bank of England, Committee of Treasury, 23 Feb. 1796.
14.   *Morning Chronicle*, 28 March 1796.
15.   *Morning Chronicle*, 29 March 1796.
16.   'They have no interest whatsoever in, nor acquaintance with Trade — Their occupation is to keep the Cash of people out of Business, and to employ in Stocks and Mortgages such part of it as they may venture to employ; but whether Discount is easy in the City, whether merchants are able to execute the Commissions they receive, whether they are able to encourage Consignments to this Country by the necessary Advances, are all objects in which they feel little immediate concern.' Boyd to Pitt, 14 April, 1796, Chatham Papers, PRO, 30/8/115.
17.   *The Times* 5 April 1796.

Some fifteen merchants, however, duly met, with Sir Stephen Lushington in the chair. The meeting passed a number of resolutions to the effect that the alarming scarcity of money was due chiefly to an increase in commerce and a great diminution in the discounts made by the Bank of England, that the trade of the country was sound, but that the lack of discount facilities threatened 'the most serious calamities', as no merchant could count on getting bills discounted, and that since appeals to the Bank were useless, it was necessary that means of augmenting the circulating medium of the country should be devised. The meeting accordingly appointed a committee of seven to study the matter. A copy of these resolutions was sent to the Chancellor of the Exchequer, and a conference requested.

The Committee, not unnaturally, contained no representatives of the merchant houses from which the Bank directors were drawn. Nevertheless, it was not without influence. Four of its members were in the House of Commons. William Lushington and John William Anderson represented London, and both were also aldermen of the City. Lushington was a Grenada merchant, and had been a customer of Boyd, Ker et Cie. Anderson, soon to become Lord Mayor, was agent and commissary of the City of Danzig. He had been on the Select Committee which considered the plan for issuing Exchequer bills to merchants in need, and he was one of the Commissioners for making advances to Grenada merchants. Sir James Sanderson had taken Benfield's seat as a member for Malmesbury in 1792. He had been Lord Mayor in 1792/3, and it was his banking house in Southwark which had been saved by the Bank of England during the 1793 crisis. The fourth member of Parliament was Sir Stephen Lushington, member for Helston in Cornwall, and a prominent East India Company director, three times Chairman. The other three members were John Julius Angerstein, a loan contractor and a leading figure at Lloyds; John Inglis, a merchant and later an East India Company director; and, of course, Boyd. Under Sir Stephen Lushington's chairmanship, this was a distinguished group.

The Committee met on April 2, and three days later, approved a report, drawn up by Boyd, which, if not actually written beforehand, must have been thought out in advance. The report described the system of issuing Bank of England and country bank notes, and concluded that without infringing the Bank's monopoly, a new note-issuing authority could be formed to supplement existing currency, and alleviate the shortage of funds in the market.[18] The Committee proposed that a board of twenty-five members, acting without remuneration, should be created by Act of Parliament. The board would issue promissory notes payable at six months' date against gold or silver, Bank notes, or bills of exchange having not more than three months to run. The notes would carry interest at the rate of a penny farthing per £100, equivalent to 1.9 per cent. per annum. To provide for their redemption a 'ready-money-fund will easily be provided by the voluntary deposits of the Bankers, Merchants, and others

18.   The text of the report is in Walter Boyd, *A Letter to the Right Honourable William Pitt, on the . . . Stoppage of Issues in Specie at the Bank of England . . .* Second edition, With additional Notes; and a Preface, London, J. Wright, 1801, Appendix, pp. 7–18.

who will be happy, in order to promote the general good . . . to carry a part of their ready money to the Board, and receive a return in the new notes at six months' date which . . . will, to all intents and purposes, perform the functions of money.' The Committee insisted that this ready money fund must consist of Bank of England notes and not specie, 'the grand object of the establishment of this Board being merely to supply the deficiency of the circulation . . . and not, by any means, to diminish that circulation.'[19] There was a revealing postscript to the letter Boyd sent to Pitt enclosing a copy of the plan and resolutions: 'the idea generally entertained at the close of the discussions', he wrote, 'was that it would infallibly bring the Bank-Directors to their senses and thus may never be carried into execution. The true way to do so (if that is desirable) is to appear to consider the present or some other new plan as indispensably necessary.'[20]

Pitt duly received Boyd's Committee on April 5, and, according to the *True Briton*, gave them a most cordial reception, discussing the subject with them for nearly an hour and a half. The Committee was told that the Bank felt that a restrictive policy was made necessary by the large advances, amounting to some £14,000,000, made by the Bank to government; by the drain of gold abroad, estimated at £16,000,000; by monopolies, especially of grain; and by speculation in the funds. Already, these evils had been checked. The exchange on Hamburg had risen from thirty-one to thirty-five, wheat was 80s. a quarter, instead of 120s., and the funds had fallen. The need now, said the Bank, was to fund the floating debt. Boyd admitted all this, but insisted that the problem was to devise some means of giving temporary assistance to the Government and to trade, which was suffering from the Bank's stringent credit policy.

In the course of these discussions, Boyd's plan was examined in some detail. Pitt suggested that the notes of the proposed note-issuing institution should be backed by Exchequer Bills and bear a name which made this clear. Boyd differed. He pointed out that the term 'Exchequer Bill' had long denoted a security subject to sharp fluctuations in value: the proposed paper, on the other hand 'ought to be assimilated as much as possible to Bank notes'. If, however, the connection had to be emphasised, he thought they could be called 'Exchequer notes'. The discussion, which seems to have centred on Boyd's plan, was exploratory only, and no definite decisions were reached. According to the *Morning Chronicle*, 'various new and ingenious schemes' were considered, a report which the *True Briton* hotly denied, describing such schemes as 'mere creatures of the writer's imagination.'[21]

The scheme had a mixed reception. Opposition papers such as the *Oracle* and the *Morning Chronicle* attacked it vehemently. The *Oracle* drew a parallel between French assignats and the notes of the proposed board, and called the scheme 'a design pregnant with the greatest danger', continuing, 'If any paper is created that will supply the place of Bank Notes it will certainly try the strength of the Company. If on the contrary it

19.   Boyd, op.cit., Appendix, p. 15.
20.   Boyd to Pitt, 4 April 1796, Chatham Papers, PRO, 30/8/115.
21.   *Morning Chronicle*, 7 April 1796, *True Briton*, 9 April 1796.

does not answer the purpose of a circulating medium for payments from hand to hand, then the intended purpose will be frustrated — it will pass at a discount and discredit both the government and commerce of this country.'[22] The *Morning Chronicle* could hardly find words strong enough to express its dislike of the scheme. 'It is too delicate a topic for newspaper discussion. We shudder at the precipice to which we are brought. We feelingly lament the distress, which we hear is universal; but we know of no calamity equal to that into which we may be plunged by a departure from the established safe and prudent practice which has governed our forefathers. For Godsake let us have no new schemes of finance.'[23]

In newspapers supporting the Government the scheme was warmly defended. The *True Briton* assured its readers 'that neither the Government of this Country not the Committee of Gentlemen who proposed it, have reason to blush for the invention when the nature of it comes to be fairly explained . . . the miserable false insinuation of its being in any degree similar to the Bankrupt Paper of a neighbouring Country will be exposed to the contempt and indignation it deserves. It will then be demonstrated, that the honest endeavours of the Committee, formed for the express purpose of warding off a great general calamity, deserve the thanks of their Countrymen and even of the Bank of England itself.'[24]

One influential voice in the city was openly hostile. 'The paper of Mr. Boyd', wrote Sir Francis Baring, 'cannot answer the purpose of those who wish to make a daily interest, because the Exchequer Bills afford an interest so very much superior . . . although Exchequer Bills carry an interest of three-and-a-half pence per day, they never did serve the purpose of foundation upon which Mr. Boyd's plan rests. The paper proposed by him not only bears a less rate of interest, but the holder must wait six months for the payment, and at last receive Bank Notes, which the Public may have every day at the Bank of England without the least delay. But if Mr. Boyd finds fault with the conduct of the Bank, are the Public inclined to repose more confidence in the twenty-four Directors of the new Bank, chosen, or perhaps guided by himself? . . . I cannot discover what description of persons would be disposed to receive and to circulate paper under the circumstances I have described . . . it will neither suit the convenience, nor prove for the interest of Bankers or Merchants nor advantageous for any commercial purpose whatever.'[25]

These were practical objections, and, as far as they went, they were valid. There were, however, more fundamental objections of a theoretical character. Boyd's plan was based on an incorrect diagnosis. It implied that the causes underlying the crisis of 1793 and the conditions existing in 1796 were similar. In 1793, the Bank's losses of gold were internal, and were caused by a loss of confidence within the country. Confidence was immediately restored by the knowledge that Exchequer Bills could be obtained by merchants in need, and that they would be accepted by the mercantile community. The drain of gold which started in September 1795, however,

22. *Oracle*, 9 April 1796.
23. *Morning Chronicle*, 7 April 1796.
24. *True Briton* 11th April 1796.
25. Sir Francis Baring. *Observations on the Publication of Walter Boyd, Esq., M.P.*, J. Sewell and J. Debrett, London, 1801, pp. 27–29.

was external, and was caused by an adverse balance of payments, which was reflected in a depreciation of sterling on the exchanges. Such a state of affairs could only be made worse, not cured, by a plan such as Boyd's.

In a letter to Pitt written on the day after the interview, Boyd developed the idea that the scarcity of money was engineered as part of a plot to eliminate his influence in the money market and to undermine Pitt's administration. 'Great pains have been taken by the authors of the present scarcity of Money to circulate Stories of Speculation (in which they give me a principal share) to an immense amount, and to insinuate with no small share of plausibility but without any foundation in truth that the Scarcity of Money proceeds from what they well know to be only a consequence and not a cause . . . The authors . . . have the same object in view, viz. to prevent the possibility of carrying on the war and to throw difficulties in the way of your Administration. . . .'[26]

Certainly the attitude of the opposition papers lent colour to this view. The *Morning Chronicle* came out with an attack on the 'greatest speculators ever known.' 'By their immense bargains they have caused all the floating specie to be absorbed in the vortex of continuation, and as the stock thus held must necessarily be the more valuable in proportion to the abundance of money, they are now goading the Ministers to measures which may be thought to tend to such effect.'[27] This was a direct attack on Boyd, to which the *True Briton* replied vigorously the next day. 'A certain Morning paper has lately dwelt much upon the evils arising from a certain great speculation in the Funds to which it attributes the present scarcity of money . . . the immense purchases so frequently alluded to and so roundly asserted to have been made by a certain great House have never existed but in the minds of a set of Stock jobbers, who to favour their own schemes, attribute to that House the operations they themselves set on foot . . . It was certainly well imagined . . . to attribute them to a house of eminence, possessing the most extensive connections abroad, and the fairest character at home.'[28]

The Bank of England continued to follow what the *Morning Chronicle* called 'the good, old and wholesome system of English caution.'[29] When, a few days later, the Governor had an interview with Pitt, he made it clear that the Bank directors would have none of these new-fangled schemes. Their solution was strictly orthodox – a funding of the floating debt, which for long had been causing them concern. They had felt compelled to take up Treasury bills, when they would have preferred not to do so, and the amount of Treasury bills and Exchequer Bills they held was always greatly in excess in their commercial discounts. In the market, the availability of short-term government paper, which yielded more than five per cent., attracted from individuals as well as from banks, funds which would otherwise be employed, directly or indirectly, in discounting commercial bills. The point was made by the *Oracle* of April 23, and it was soundly based.

Boyd was not alone in thinking that there was a scarcity of means of payment. Sir John Sinclair, that indefatigable writer on agriculture and

---

26. Boyd to Pitt, 6 April 1796, Pitt Correspondence, CUL, Add. 6958/10.
27. *Morning Chronicle*, 6 April 1796.
28. *True Briton*, 7 April 1796.
29. *Morning Chronicle*, 7 April 1796.

finance, had the same approach as Boyd. His view was that 'a greater quantity of representative signs or circulating medium' was required. In April he put to Pitt, in their barest outline, three schemes based on this idea. The first was that £3,000,000 of three per cent. stock should be issued, and that £1,000,000 or £2,000,000 of it should be converted into £20 bills, bearing three per cent. interest. The second, a variant on the first, was that £5,000,000 of three per cent. stock should be issued, and that holders would have the option of converting into three per cent. 'share notes', according to the price of the day, and could reconvert back into stock. Said Sir John: 'no man would keep in his coffer £10 in money when he could make an interest of it.' Thirdly, in a memorandum to Pitt of 29th April, he made the simple proposal that the Bank should issue £1 and £2 notes, not redeemable in specie, which he thought could be done safely up to £500,000.[30] This last plan was in effect adopted after the suspension of cash payments in 1797. The time for this experiment, however, was not ripe. In face of the indifference, or even hostility, of the leading houses in the City, the opposition of the Bank, and the reluctance of the Government to take a decisive lead, these schemes could make little progress, and Boyd's Committee of Merchants adjourned sine die.[31]

Boyd, however, was not one to give up the struggle as long as there was the remotest chance of success. Within a few days of the adjournment of his Committee he was writing to Pitt on the same theme. His letter contained a closely reasoned argument in favour of a 'board of credit'. he claimed that there was 'nothing new in principle or practice in the measure recommended', and that 'the issuing of Government-paper to the extent of four of five millions and providing a fund for exchanging for Bank-Notes such of that paper as should occasionally be presented for that purpose would not . . . produce the slightest effect to the prejudice of public Credit. On the contrary, . . . not only would it form a Barrier against the oppression of the Bank of England, but it would infallibly in time, prove the most fertile of all the sources of Revenue'. He suggested that the Chancellor should obtain authority from Parliament to fund the floating debt, and also to create the board, but that he should proceed with the second step only if the first did not produce the results desired. 'The knowledge of the existence of such a Board, even if they should never act at all, would operate as a powerful stimulus to the Bank to do their Duty, and prevent the possibility of the necessities of Government and of Trade becoming (as they have lately been) the sport of certain disaffected Men whose influence in the Bank unfortunately predominates too much.'

As evidence of this 'disaffection', Boyd repeated a story he had heard from a member of his Committee. At the end of 1795, some days before the resolution of the Bank directors to contract their discounts (so the story ran), a letter was addressed to the directors taxing them with having been too liberal in their support of the government, and insisting on a change of policy, and threatening that unless a change were made, nine proprietors of Bank stock would call a general meeting and charge the

30. Sir John Sinclair, Memorandum to Pitt, April, 1796, Letter to Pitt, April, 1796, and Memorandum for Mr. Pitt, 29 April 1796, Chatham Papers, PRO, 30/8/178.
31. *Morning Chronicle*, 11 April 1796.

directors with abusing their powers. As a consequence of this demarche, the Bank directors passed the resoution. What truth, if any, there was in this story it is impossible to say: to Boyd, at any rate, it was useful as propaganda.[32]

Pitt was not inclined to embark on any new schemes, however plausibly presented, and proceeded to implement the Bank's proposal, which was to fund Exchequer and Navy Bills. Here difficulties presented themselves immediately. When the £18,000,000 loan was being negotiated with Boyd in the previous November, Pitt had fixed the amount of Navy bills to be funded in 1796, and Boyd would certainly be entitled to object if any attempt were made to increase this amount without his concurrence. Furthermore, the £18,000,000 loan was far from being fully paid, and the contractors would no doubt object if a loan were offered to competition. The *Morning Chronicle* thought that the solution was simple. 'Here then is an opportunity for Mr. Boyd as Contractor for the Loan, to do a most essential service to his Country, and a most splendid thing for himself. Let him relieve Mr. Pitt from his engagement, and permit him to fund the oustanding navy up to the end of 1795. The market will thus be cleared of an enormous mass of paper, the hands of the Bank will be eased, public credit will be reassured, and all the tribe of speculators will be left to their fate.'[33]

Newspaper comment of this sort, accompanied by talk in the City of the possibility of competition, was little to the liking of Boyd's group, who, fearing that perhaps Boyd might agree to waive his (and their) rights, made their views known to Drummond in unmistakable terms. As soon as Boyd heard of the trouble, he immediately made it clear to his colleagues that he had said or done nothing which could in any way bind them, and that he had merely indicated in official quarters a desire to meet the Government's wishes. Their firm attitude suited Boyd, for he could now negotiate with Pitt in the knowledge that his colleagues supported him. He accordingly wrote to Pitt on April 12, setting out the arguments against competition. 'In the present scarcity of money', he wrote, 'the idea of Competition will undoubtedly render any Bargain worse for the Country than it would otherwise be, as many Lists will be forming and of course several preparations be making for the same object. This I only mention as the natural Consequence of all times of Competition, which, in the present state of Money-Matters, must operate with double force.'[34]

On the following day, April 13, Boyd, Robarts, Salomons and Abraham Goldsmid attended at Downing Street for the preliminary negotiations. At the meeting Pitt announced his intention of offering the loan to competition. Possibly, he really thought that Boyd and his group did not want to take the loan themselves, in view of their already heavy commitments, and that notwithstanding Boyd's letter, they would not object to competition. If so, he was badly advised, for Boyd immediately protested that the

32. Boyd to Pitt, 14 April 1796, Chatham Papers, PRO, 30/8/115. The Bank of England has no record of this incident.
33. *Morning Chronicle*, 7 April 1796.
34. Boyd to Pitt, 12 April 1796, Chatham Papers, PRO, 30/8/115. The term 'preparations' means selling existing stocks in order to have money available for a new issue, which, incidentally, depresses their price.

agreement made in the previous December provided that no further sums were to be raised during 1796. Pitt, however, insisted that a loan had to be raised. Anxious as they were to prevent a loan being offered to competition, Boyd and his group had no particular desire to take it themselves, especially as Pitt wanted forty per cent. paid within a month, thus putting the new loan on the same basis as the old. They had enough on their hands. After a two-hour discussion, there was still no agreement, and the meeting was adjourned.[35] At a further meeting on the following day Pitt accepted Boyd's point to the extent that he agreed not to offer the loan to competition,[36] and reduced the early instalments, so that the loan did not become forty per cent. paid until the latter part of June. Pitt and the Governor of the Bank also gave Boyd an assurance that there would be 'a total change of system on the part of the Bank.' On the strength of this assurance Boyd took the loan on what he described later as 'very liberal terms.'[37]

That, at least, was the published account of what happened. It is possible that Pitt announced his intention to allow competition merely to forestall criticism in Parliament, and that Boyd's protest and the subsequent negotiations were merely moves in a game, settled beforehand by the contending parties. On the other hand, there is some evidence of hard bargaining. The adjourned meeting, the change in instalments dates, and the relatively unfavourable terms on which the loan was taken, all indicate that Boyd was able to retain control of the market only by sacrificing the profit normally obtainable from a loan contract. For each £100 advanced, subscribers received £120 three per cent. Consols, £25 three per cent. Reduced Consols and 5s 6d. in Long Annuity, worth in the aggregate £101.19.9. at current market prices.[38] Of the total of £7,500,000, Boyd, Benfield & Co. took £2,389,000 for themselves and their customers,[39] roughly the same proportion as they had in the previous loan.

Pitt's action in giving the loan to Boyd's group raised a storm of criticism. In the House of Commons there was some very plain speaking. Alderman Newnham said that 'it was, to all intents and purposes, and contrary to the approved system, a shut up Loan, and competition, to his knowledge, had been offered by fifteen or sixteen respectable Houses in the City, but they had received no answer nor any reason why. . . . He wished to know . . . why this exclusive right to all Government Loans was invested in the present Contractors'. Newnham, admittedly, was not disinterested. He was a partner in the banking house of Newnham, Everett & Co., and it is probable that some of the 'fifteen or sixteen respectable Houses' were members of a group formed by his firm. He no doubt considered, too, that Boyd had treated him badly in giving his firm only a small share in the loan of 1796. But there were other critics who had no axes to grind. Grey was very outspoken, and wanted to know 'when this Loan Leviathan was to be satisfied, or how long he was to have Loans on

---

35. *London Chronicle*, 14 April 1796.
36. *The Times*, 16 April 1796.
37. Boyd, *Letter to Pitt*, op.cit., Appendix, p. 18.
38. 36 Geo. III, c. 74.
39. Select Committee on the Tenth Naval Report, Evidence of Drummond.

his own terms.'[40] To all this Pitt replied by explaining that the terms of the agreement he had made prevented him from offering the loan to competition. He hoped that 'the monied men in the City would become indirectly sharers in it', and added meaningly that 'there was no other set of men who had less inducement from the Scrip which they held, to raise the terms of this Loan than the present Contractors.'[41]

In the City, Pitt's idea of being 'indirect sharers' had little attraction for the houses who were not on the list of one or other of the contractors. Indignation was increased by reports of the arbitrary manner in which the contractors allotted the loan to their customers. Boyd, in particular, made no attempt to divide his share among those who had participated in the previous loan: several houses were told that their shares were already allocated, while those who received a small amount were expected to consider that they had received a favour, and were told that Boyd had included them 'from personal regard.'[42] Even insurance companies and public bodies who normally received shares were excluded: only the Bank of England and the East India Company received the normal amounts.[43]

There was much comment in the press. The *Morning Chronicle*, for example, pointed out that the loan agreement provided that Exchequer Bills to the amount of £2,000,000 were to be accepted at par, in satisfaction of loan payments. To those who were. in the know, and who acted accordingly, this provided a considerable profit, for only a fortnight before, Exchequer Bills could be bought at £1.3.0. per cent. discount.[44] But most criticism was directed to the absence of competition '. . . the sagacity of Mr. Boyd approaches to the second sight, for he foresaw another loan, he knew his Minister, and not content with trusting this year as he did the last to the spirit of his contract, he would not trust Mr. Pitt without a positive written letter, . . . To talk of competition is ridiculous. There is but one booth in the fair.'[45] The *Oracle* remarked on April 15: 'Messrs. B. & B. are to have the new Loan – because they had the last; and . . . they had the last because they had the former. This is a chain and let no man say it is a counterfeit – it is pure sterling gold.'

In fact, the chain was not quite as golden as the *Oracle* suggested. Unofficial dealings started at three and a half premium,[46] it is true, but the market generally was vulnerable owing to the existence of a large speculative position. So far, the price of the funds had been well maintained. Just before April 12, the settling day, there had been a considerable amount of selling, causing a drop of two points in three per cent. Consols, and about £1,500,000 of stock had been dealt in for the May account, but, in spite of this, Consols were higher than they were in March and February. Fortunately, the settlement was carried out without much difficulty, although the existence of a bull position was revealed in the wide

40. *Morning Chronicle*, 19 April 1796. Charles Grey (1764–1845) was member for Northumberland, and supported Fox.
41. *The Times*, 19 April 1796.
42. *Morning Chronicle*, 18 April 1796.
43. *Morning Chronicle*, 16 April 1796.
44. *Morning Chronicle*, 18 April 1796.
45. *Morning Chronicle*, 14 April 1796.
46. *Evening Mail*, 18 April 1796.

spread between the price of Consols for cash and the price for the May account.[47] By early May, omnium had fallen to two-and-three-quarters premium, and Boyd and certain other members of his group sent a petition to the Bank, asking for advances to enable them to pay the ten per cent. instalment due on May 20 on the loan of £18,000,000. The Bank refused. A few days later, the Bank also refused to advance the second instalment of the £7,500,000 loan, adding bleakly that they would 'decline to take into consideration the possibility of making advances on the future payments'.[48] The second answer was understandable, for the loan was only ten per cent. paid.[49]

For Boyd, the next few weeks were disastrous. 'All at once', he wrote to Benfield later, 'there burst upon me such a Variety of Disasters that I was not equal to the Shock'.[50] At the end of April, Walckiers, who for two years had been carrying on a mercantile business in Hamburg, failed, owing considerable sums to Boyd, Benfield & Co. Of more immediate significance was the steady fall in the funds. Consols, standing at sixty-seven at the beginning of May, had fallen to sixty-four by May 25, while omnium, over the same period, had fallen from three-and-a-half premium to one-and-a-half discount. When the settling day, May 26 arrived, Boyd, with a heavy bull position, found himself at the mercy of the jobbers. To one of them, Mark Sprott, he had to pay two points for continuation, equivalent to forty per cent. per annum. Consols were dealt in at one time at sixty, although they recovered towards the close of business to sixty-three-and-a-half.[51] Boyd, writing later of the events of this period, blamed the 'existence of so unexampled a scarcity of money' and complained that the Bank directors had gone back on their promise of a liberal credit policy. 'How this prospect was realised', he wrote to Pitt, 'the distresses of the City at the end of May 1796 can testify . . . when I represented to you and others the tendency of the wretched system they were pursuing, it was answered that I was mistaken, and that the Bank had never been more liberal. . . .'[52]

Liberal was hardly the word to apply to the Bank's policy at this time. Samuel Thornton, soon to be Deputy Governor, admitted later that 'the directors thought it prudent to restrain their engagements';[53] their refusal to advance the instalments on the loan was the principal way of putting this policy into effect, and one which was calculated to cause the minimum amount of dislocation to trade and to curb speculation in the funds most effectively. A restrictive policy seems to have been carried out with moderation, for the Bank agreed to advance the instalment due in June, in order to ease the situation, and there is no evidence that when it came to discounting commercial bills, the Bank directors were unreasonably strict. During 1794, some £124,000 of bills had been discounted for Boyd, Benfield & Co., the average amount outstanding being £14,360. In the first

47. The spread was one-and-a-half points, equivalent to nineteen per cent. per annum.
48. *London Chronicle*, 8 May 1796.
49. Bank of England, Court Minutes, 12 May 1796.
50. Boyd, *Letter to the Creditors*, op.cit., p. 21.
51. *St. James' Chronicle*, 25 and 27 May 1796.
52. Boyd, Letter to Pitt, op.cit., p. 5, Appendix, pp. 4, 18.
53. Select Committee on the Tenth Naval Report, Evidence of Samuel Thornton.

four months of 1795, the Bank had discounted £95,402 of bills for them, roughly £24,000 a month. Then for a year there was a gap, the reason being that Boyd, Benfield & Co. had had such substantial amounts in their hands from the proceeds of the Imperial Loan that they did not need to discount. May 1796 saw the resumption of regular discounts, which were to continue at roughly £15,000 a month until the middle of 1798.[54] Thomas Raikes, the Deputy Governor, told Boyd that they would discount for him in exactly the same way as they would for any other house of the most respectable situation, but Boyd wanted six times as much.[55]

It was probably about this time (May 1796) that Boyd made a final attempt to persuade Pitt to set up a parliamentary 'board of credit'. He realised that his tactics would have to be more subtle than they had been before, and the plan he drew up for submission to the Chancellor commenced with the orthodox suggestion of an issue of £1,500,000 or £2,000,000 of Commercial Exchequer Bills to Commissioners appointed for the purpose. Similar plans had been adopted successfully to meet the crisis of March 1793, and to assist the St. Vincent and Grenada merchants in 1795. Here, at least, was no frightening innovation. A measure on these lines, said Boyd, would meet with little opposition in Parliament, and it would only be at one of the stages of the bill that clauses would be introduced giving the Commissioners powers for the superintendence and support of credit and authorising them to issue Exchequer-Notes, carrying interest at a penny farthing per day for every £100 and exchangeable on demand for Bank of England notes. 'Thus the measure of establishing this paper-Circulation would gradually be brought forward and in a great measure be established almost before any opposition could be formed against it.'[56] But these tactics met with no more success than did the earlier ones, and Boyd was forced to realise that he would have to struggle on without any adventitious aid.

54. Bank of England Drawing Account.
55. Select Committee on the Tenth Naval Report, Evidence of Thomas Raikes, p. 52.
56. Idea of the mode of carrying into Execution the Scheme of circulating Exchequer-Notes. Undated memorandum by Boyd [May 1796?], Chatham Papers, PRO, 30/8/115.

CHAPTER IX

Further Lending to Austria

'We never acquiesced in any point with an idea of an imperial loan taking place, but always deprecated an imperial loan as dangerous.'
Thomas Raikes, Deputy Governor of the Bank,
giving evidence before the Lords Committee of Secrecy
relating to the Bank, 1797.

In the autumn of 1795 reports were current that Pitt intended to grant further aid to Austria of £1,400,000[1] and Giles, Governor of the Bank, alarmed at the prospect of a further drain of gold, sought an interview. At a meeting on October 23, Pitt, asked whether he proposed to make further advances to Austria, protested that 'he had not at present the most distant Idea of it',[2] although he was cautious enough to add that 'he did not pledge himself that on no occasion such a Thing might happen.' In spite of this denial, rumours of a loan persisted. These rumours were, in fact, not without foundation, for over a month earlier, Grenville had sounded Starhemberg in confidence about Austria's requirements, indicating that a request for a subsidy would be a waste of time, and that Austria could only hope for a loan on the basis of the previous one of £4,600,000.[3] Conversations with Austria continued, and in November Pitt admitted to Giles that 'Ministry now had it in Contemplation to let the Emperor have another Loan, not exceeding Two Millions.'[4]

The prospect of a further drain on their reserves was most unwelcome to the Bank directors, and they soon made their views known to the Government. '. . . the Court of Directors,' ran a resolution passed on 3 December 1795, '. . . are unanimously of Opinion that should such a Loan take place, they are but too well grounded in declaring (from the actual Effects of the Emperor's last Loan, and the continued Drains of Specie and Bullion they still experience) that they have the most cogent Reasons to apprehend very momentous and alarming Consequences.' The Chancellor replied that he should not think at present of bringing forward such a Measure, adding that 'though he should, in opening the Budget, make it known that he had made Reserve with the present Contractors for the Loan to permit the Emperor's raising Three Millions, should circumstances require it, he

1 Précis of correspondence to and from Berlin, *Dropmore Papers*, vol. III, p. 148.
2 Lords Committee of Secrecy, 1797, Papers and Accounts, 1796–7.
3 Starhemberg to Thugut, 14 Sept. 1795, Vivenot, op. cit., vol. V, pp. 373–4.
4 Copies of all Communications between the Directors of the Bank and the Chancellor, Accounts and Papers, 1796–7.

should lay aside all Thoughts of it, unless the Situation of Things relative to the Bank should so alter as to render such a Loan of no Importance or Inconvenience to them.'[5]

The Bank directors were not alone in seeing a connection between the Austrian Loan and the drain of gold overseas, and the *Morning Post* of December 23 was expressing a view widely held in the City when it wrote: 'The loads of Gold exported to pay for the last Austrian loan have been very injurious to the Circulation of Specie in this Country. . . .' Boyd, undeterred by the general feeling against foreign lending, not only persisted in his efforts to obtain sanction for the Imperial loan, but even put forward, early in January 1796, tentative proposals for a loan to Portugal. It appears that the Portuguese Minister in London had been trying for some time to persuade Boyd to issue a loan for Portugal of £400,000, secured by diamonds to be deposited with the Bank of England. The amount was relatively small, but Boyd, realising that Austria's needs were as much as he could handle, did not appear anxious to undertake the transaction. The Minister, however, pressed for a final answer, and Boyd decided to submit the proposition to Pitt, although he did so in a somewhat half-hearted fashion. 'From the first mention of the Business', he wrote, 'I had resolved, within myself, to have nothing to do with it, in case the Measure happens in any respect to thwart any views of yours, and if this should be the case, you have only to give me a hint of it and I shall decline the Business without assigning this as the reason.'[6] Pitt was obviously averse to another foreign loan. 'There are circumstances', he wrote to Boyd, 'which make me think that just at present it would be desirable to discourage the Loan to the Court of Portugal and . . . I shall be glad if you can with Propriety decline the Transaction.'[7] Pitt did not give any reasons for this attitude, but he presumably had in mind the adverse exchange, which, since September 1795, had been below the export point. In any event Boyd deemed it wise to drop the matter.

Pitt, possibly prompted by Boyd, then considered the possibility of raising at Frankfurt, at Hamburg, or in Italy, an Imperial loan guaranteed by Great Britain, an idea which had been discussed tentatively in 1794, and Eden was told that he might mention the point to Thugut, without committing himself in any way.[8] The Bank directors liked this scheme no better than the earlier one. The Committee of Treasury gave their opinion on 14 January 1796 'that they cannot look upon the Scheme of assisting the Emperor to raise a loan in Germany by the Guarantee of the Parliament of Great Britain, in any Light which will not, one way or other be detrimental to this Country, even if a Law were passed by Parliament to prevent British subjects from taking any share therein.'

The reasons given for this opinion throw some light on the mobility of capital at the end of the eighteenth century. They continued: '. . . such a call for money in Germany will occasion demands of it from hence: Germans, Italians, and other foreign capitalists, who have property here, will be induced to draw it away. People in Holland, who by the late Acts,

5   Lords Committee of Secrecy, 1797, Papers and Accounts, No. 4.
6   Boyd to Pitt, 2 Jan. 1796, Chatham Papers, PRO., 30/8/115.
7   Pitt to Boyd, 4 Jan. 1796, Chatham Papers, PRO, 30/8/102.
8   Grenville to Eden, 22 Dec. 1795, PRO, F.O. 7/42.

have money locked up here, may go to Germany and draw for it from thence . . . funds which would otherwise be employed in speculations of trade with England, may, by such an opportunity of investment at home, be diverted. . . '.[9] It is unnecessary to consider in detail the merits of these arguments. They indicate the Bank's determination to prevent the issue of an Imperial loan, whatever its guise, and wherever it was issued. Thugut also considered the idea impracticable, although for different reasons. Eden reported that although Thugut 'thought that there was much Specie, particularly at Hamburg, yet he was persuaded that no considerable Sum could be procured, the Merchants being able to employ their Money to much greater advantage in Commercial Speculations and in Stock-jobbing.'[10] Pitt therefore abandoned the idea.

If the difficulties involved in floating a loan in London were great, the needs of the Austrian treasury were pressing. In November 1795, Thugut had been urging the need for a £3,000,000 loan, but without much success. The British view was that 'the drain of specie from this Country in consequence of the numerous and extensive remittances of Money to the Continent . . . preclude the possibility . . . to comply with this request. It must depend on the state of exchange and the situation of the Country with respect to its circulating specie.'[11] By early 1796, however, Grenville seems to have accepted the idea of a loan of £3,000,000 spread over a six-months period from June or July.[12] Thugut soon made it clear that although payment could be deferred for three months, he wanted the guarantee to be arranged immediately.[13] This did not help, for the British Government considered that it was impossible to bring forward a loan until it was clear that the shortage of specie was only temporary. Grenville told Eden, however, that consideration was to be given to a plan whereby a loan might be raised and guaranteed, the Government being given authority to suspend remittances if necessary, in which eventuality money could be raised on the Continent.[14]

Early in February it was rumoured in the City that the terms for a new loan of £3,000,000 had been agreed, and that Boyd, Benfield & Co. as agents for the Imperial Government would be the contractors.[15] *The Times* promptly denied that a contract had been made, admitting, however, that the Cabinet might have approved a loan, to be raised if the war continued.[16] In fact what had happened was that Pitt had promised a deputation from the Bank which waited on him on 5 February 1796 'that he would not commit himself to any Engagement for a further Loan to the Emperor, without a previous Communication on the Subject with the Gentlemen of the Bank.'[17] This did not satisfy the directors, who passed

9   Lords Committee of Secrecy, 1797; *Parliamentary History, vol. 33, cols. 322–3.*
10 Eden to Grenville, 19 Feb. 1796, PRO, F.O. 7/44.
11 Grenville to Eden, 22 Dec. 1795, PRO, F.O. 7/43.
12 Grenville to Eden, 22 Jan. and 9 Feb. 1796, PRO, F.O. 7/44.
13 Eden to Grenville, 19 Feb. 1796, PRO, F.O. 7/44.
14 Grenville to Eden, 8 March 1796, PRO, F.O. 7/44.
15 *Morning Chronicle*, 9 Feb. 1796.
16 *The Times* 11 Feb. 1796.
17 Lords Committee of Secrecy, 1797, Papers and Accounts, No 5 (15).

an emphatic resolution on February 11 that '. . . any further loan or advance of money to the Emperor or to any other Foreign State . . . will, in all probability, prove fatal to the Bank of England'. Pitt replied somewhat petulantly that 'after the repeated Intimations he had given to the Governor and Deputy Governor . . . he did not see any Reason for these Resolutions; that he did suppose they were adopted in a Moment of Alarm and that he would consider them in that Light.'[18]

Public opinion supported the Bank. According to the *Morning Chronicle*, it had been stated 'upon high authority' that £16,000,000 of bullion had left the country since the beginning of the war.[19] 'Every million in bullion or specie sent to a foreign land is a greater injury to the nation than five millions squandered at home.'[20] In deference to such views, Pitt considered making a loan partly in goods, with the object of minimising the adverse effect on the exchanges. Both Giles, the Governor, and Bosanquet, a director, considered that ultimately the drain on the exchanges was the same, whether specie or goods were sent, and the idea was not taken up.[21] The strength of the opposition to foreign lending, whatever its form, was shown by a motion in the House of Commons by Maurice Robinson, member for Boroughbridge, for leave to introduce a bill to prevent any member from having any share in a contract, commission or agreement for a foreign loan. This might conceivably have been effective, for many, if not most, of the leading mercantile houses who contracted for loans, including Boyd, Benfield & Co., had one of their partners in the Commons. Members, however, showed little enthusiasm for a self-denying ordinance of this sort, and the motion was lost.[22]

Throughout the first half of 1796, Boyd was busy in negotiations with Pitt and Starhemberg, but progress was slow. On March 13, he submitted to Pitt a plan, which, he said, would solve all difficulties. According to Starhemberg, who was privy to it, the plan provided for payments to the Emperor to be made by Boyd, Benfield & Co's correspondents in Europe, who would re-imburse themselves by drawing on London. Boyd made it clear that the firm had no funds of their own on the Continent, and that the operation would be based solely on credit.[23]

Pitt had no intention of acting hastily, and when he met with Boyd early in April, he told him that the Government felt unable to promise a guarantee, but thought that a decision might perhaps be possible in a few weeks' time. Starhemberg, anxious for news, called on Boyd shortly afterwards to learn the result of the interview with Pitt. Boyd explained the Government's attitude to a guarantee, and said that Starhemberg should be empowered by his court to conclude an arrangement as soon as the decision was taken in London. Starhemberg thought that it was unlikely that Thugut would commit himself to this extent, as he was very much afraid of being sold 'a pig in a poke'. He therefore suggested that Boyd

18 Lord Committee of Secrecy, 1797, Papers and Accounts, No 4.
19 *Morning Chronicle*, 5 Feb. 1796.
20 *Morning Chronicle*, 28 Jan. 1796.
21 Lords Committee of Secrecy, 1797, Evidence of Giles and Bosanquet.
22 *Morning Chronicle*, 12 Feb. 1796; *Commons Journals*, vol. 51, p. 382.
23 Starhemberg to Thugut, 19 Feb, 8 and 15 March 1796, cited by Helleiner, op.cit., pp. 66–7.

should give him a plan in outline, setting out the range within which the price would ultimately be fixed, according to when the loan was issued. If Vienna approved the terms. Starhemberg would be authorised to sign when the political conditions were fulfilled. If the terms were rejected, the idea of a loan would have to be given up.[24]

Much discussion was taking place in Government circles about the practicability of a loan. Early in April, Lord Auckland consulted one of the Hopes, then in London, on the various plans which had been put forward. Hope felt that only small sums could be raised on the Continent, and that the mere fact of having to borrow there would damage British credit. He thought that it was hardly practicable to remit by purchasing bills, as although at the moment the exchange was favourable, owing to recent exports of bullion to Hamburg, the large sums which would shortly be drawn to pay for the import of corn and naval stores were likely to turn the exchanges against London. His general opinion was that if the Austrian loan were not more than £2,500,000, it could best be arranged by placing specie in the hands of Boyd, Benfield & Co., as the Emperor's London Agents, leaving to them the transmission of the money as they thought best. Some advantage might be derived from making part of the loan in manufactured goods, and from buying bills in London and drawing from the Continent while the exchange was favourable, but he considered that, on the whole, manoeuvres such as these would only disturb the course of the exchange.[25]

In spite of all this advice, much of which was sound, Pitt still hesitated, and attempts to make him say whether or not he would advance money to the Emperor met with evasive replies. Challenged in the Commons on the subject early in May 1796, he replied that it was not his intention in the current session to make any proposals for a loan, although when pressed, he admitted that he had not given up the idea of making an Austrian loan later in 1796.[26]

A week later Boyd tried to clinch matters by making definite proposals. He suggested to Pitt that the best way of giving the Austrians the help they needed, before the meeting of the new Parliament in September, was to adopt the method used in 1795, when £400,000 was remitted to the Emperor. This had been done by arranging for Boyd, Benfield & Co's correspondents at Frankfurt, Augsburg, Leghorn and Genoa to hold the money at the disposal of Vienna on instructions from Eden, which were to be given only when the treaty regarding the loan was signed. Boyd continued: 'It appears highly probable that they are in want of money, and that they must soon be so, very seriously, seeing they never reckoned on being able to go on further than the month of June, and they have already drawn upon us 50,000 1. more than they had in our hands. Perhaps they had not reckoned upon 172,500 1. for half a year's dividend due the 1st May, which I paid in to the Bank the 30th April.'

24 Starhemberg to Grenville, 12 April 1796, *Dropmore Papers*, vol. III. p. 192.
25 Auckland to Pitt, 10 April 1796, Pitt Correspondence, CUL, Add. 6958/10.
26 Debrett's *Parliamentary Register*, vol. XLIV, p. 651. He later admitted that he became convinced of the necessity for advances shortly before the end of the session, 19 May 1796; *Parliamentary History*, vol. 32, col. 1320.

As to the method of remitting, Boyd said that for some time past the Austrians had preferred drawing on Boyd, Benfield & Co., and that this was likely to be 'the most easy and agreeable mode of furnishing the supplies.' Boyd clearly attached great importance to keeping remittances secret and in his own hands. He continued, 'To prevent remarks by the Public, we cd order all the Drafts to be negotiated upon our House and the Drafts in reimbursement upon the Treasury to be sent to us.' As with the previous remittances in anticipation of a loan, no commission would be payable, as, said Boyd, the remittances tended to facilitate the Austrian loan for which Boyd, Benfield & Co. were agents. Boyd concluded by urging immediate action. The exchange was favourable, and if a public loan were subsequently arranged, the private remittances now would turn out to have been done on terms more favourable than for those made later.

On the assumption that a loan would be made, there was every justification for Boyd's policy : This, however, was not certain, and in trying to show that remittances would be an advantage, even if no loan were made, Boyd produced arguments which were ingenious rather than sound. He continued: 'It would be still advantageous in another imporant point of view, as the re-drawing of the 3 or 400,000 l. would furnish the opportunity of improving the Exchange very considerably and thus rendering Money abundant'. It must have been obvious that to remit money abroad would tend to turn the exchanges against this country, and that to bring it back would tend to improve the exchanges, leaving rates hardly changed on balance. Characteristically, Boyd drew attention only to the favourable aspects of the operation. The cost of the remittance, Boyd thought, could not exceed four or five per cent. 'which is certainly small compared with the importance of saving a faithful ally'.[27]

Meantime the 'faithful ally' was becoming increasingly impatient, and in May, Baron von Müller, formerly the Emperor's Secretary of State at Brussels, was sent to London to negotiate a new loan.[28] As a prelude to these negotiations, there were discussions regarding the sinking fund for the £4,600,000 loan, which had never been implemented. Progress was slow, and it was only after several months that it was agreed, subject to the consent of the Imperial Court, to set up a board which would be responsible for making monthly purchases of three per cent. annuities.[29] The Austrians accepted this arrangement only as a result of pressure from London – although a similar provision had been made in the original agreement – and it is doubtful whether they ever intended to carry it out. Boyd had anticipated a greater willingness on their part, and had provided in February the first monthly instalment, which had been applied in the purchase of £11,790.12.6. of Imperial three per cent. annuities.[30]

The second, and far more important matter, was to raise fresh funds for

27 Boyd to Pitt, 16 May 1796, Pitt Correspondence, CUL, Add. 6958/10.
28 Morton Eden to Auckland, 15 May 1796, *Journal and Correspondence of Lord Auckland*, op.cit., vol. III., p. 332.
29 Boyd to Long, 14 Dec. 1796. Account of what Sums have been remitted . . . for . . . the loan of 1795, Accounts and Papers 1796–7, vol. 44.
30 *Morning Post*, 24 Feb. 1796; Bank of England Stock Ledgers; Account . . . relative to Imperial three per cent. Annuities, Accounts and Papers 1796–7.

Austria. The exchanges had improved; the Hamburg exchange was now at 34.0, compared with 33.0 in January, and Grenville was confident that if the exchanges continued to be favourable, and if the other points in connection with the loan were settled, there would be no difficulty in proposing the guarantee. Meantime, Colonel Craufurd was authorised to increase the £100,000 he had been authorised to advance in April, to £150,000,[31] and Starhemberg was given to understand that further monthly advances would follow. Pitt was still uncertain whether Austria would continue to fight, for in June there were vague but disturbing reports that the Emperor was endeavouring to make a separate peace. Pitt considered, however, that even if these reports were false, only the first £300,000 should be advanced, pending clarification of Austrian intentions.[32]

In these circumstances a public loan was out of the question. Boyd himself was strongly of this view, and repeated the advice he had given to Pitt in May, that any proposition to guarantee a fresh loan to Austria would seriously affect the money market and depreciate the funds.[33] Boyd, Benfield & Co. and the other members of their group had good reason for not wanting a public loan. They still held large amounts of the loans of 1795 and 1796, and from May onwards had become increasingly embarrassed by the weakness of the funds. Three per cent. Consols, which touched sixty-seven in May, were fifty-four in September. In fact, Boyd's sense of the 'growing embarrassment' of the money market was very much a reflection of the increasing difficulties of his own position. A private loan, however, was quite another matter. Boyd, Benfield & Co. would not be required to provide any money; on the contrary, substantial sums would probably be placed in their hands for remittance broad.

The Government's view of their relationship to Boyd, Benfield & Co. in the loan negotiations was set out at some length for Eden's benefit. '. . . this Government', wrote Grenville, 'has no other interest than that which the Court of Vienna must have in obtaining the sum required at the lowest possible rate . . . the persons employed by His Imperial Majesty will be left at full liberty to make their bargain with whom and in whatever manner they shall think best: provided only that in the arrangement of the business provision is made for a sinking fund as part thereof as large as least . . . as that which included in the Austrian loan of last year. Whatever assistance His Majesty's Ministers can afford by their advice or otherwise in negotiating the loan will be readily given, but the final arrangement of the terms will be left to the Austrian Agents themselves.'[34]

This official aloofness was somewhat unrealistic. Boyd, Benfield & Co. were theoretically free to make what terms they could, yet in fact they could not hope to float a loan without a British guarantee. The temporary advances to Austria, moreover, were made by the Treasury and not by Boyd, Benfield & Co., which gave the Government an interest they could not well avoid. In addition, there were the military and diplomatic implications of a loan which might materially affect the course of the war. Lastly, there was the effect of foreign remittances on the exchanges, and the

31 Grenville to Eden, 29 April and 20 May 1796, PRO, F.O. 7/45.
32 Pitt to Grenville, 23 June 1796, *Dropmore Papers*, vol. III, p. 214.
33 *Parliamentary History*, vol. 32, col. 1320.
34 Grenville to Eden, 24 May 1796. PRO, F.O. 7/45.

possibility of a loss of gold, which neither the Government nor the Bank of England could regard with equanimity.

For the moment, it was the exchanges which were of overriding importance. Renewed weakness of the exchanges in May and June made a public issue impossible,[35] and Pitt had to resort again to temporary advances. In June, he agreed to advance £300,000 to the military chest of the Imperial Army, further advances of £150,000 a month from the end of August onwards being promised.[36] Early in July, an agreement having been signed with the Imperial representatives, the Treasury instructed Boyd, Benfield & Co. to 'take the speediest and most effectual means' for remitting to the Emperor's agents on the Continent £900,000, which the British Government had agreed to advance 'until by a favourable Change of Circumstances, the Loan which was in Contemplation may be carried into effect.' Of the £900,000, one-third was to be remitted as soon as possible, and the remaining two-thirds in four monthly instalments of £150,000, commencing in September. Remittances had to be so arranged that they could be stopped on a month's notice.

If Boyd had hoped that the transaction would put large sums into his hands, he was to be disappointed, for the Treasury went on to point out that the same considerations which prevented the issue of a loan to the Emperor, also prevented payments being made in advance in respect of the instalments on the loan of 1796, as would be expected were conditions in the money market more normal. There were therefore no funds in the Treasury out of which advances would be made immediately. They therefore proposed that, instead of receiving cash, Boyd, Benfield & Co. should draw on the Treasury £900,000 of bills, maturing at the rate of £150,000 a month, commencing in October 1796, and finishing in March 1797. As before, secrecy was to be maintained. 'If the money can be raised upon the Continent without circulating the Bills of Exchange to be drawn upon their Lordships, it would be very desirable that they should not be negotiated, because their appearance in circulation would have a manifest tendency to lower the Course of Exchange.' As remuneration, Boyd, Benfield & Co. were to receive interest at five per cent. on all sums advanced by them 'besides all the necessary Charges which may be incurred.'[37] To arrange the remittance of these advances, Boyd sent his cousin to Hamburg in June or July, empowered to draw on the firm without limit.[38]

All this was carried out without the Bank of England being consulted, or even told what was going on. Giles, Governor of the Bank, suspected that remittances were being made, and told Pitt so, but Pitt, whatever he said to Giles privately, never informed the Bank officially of his plan. 'Had the Bank been informed', said Giles later, 'a protest would undoubtedly have been made'. Boyd claimed that 'the Influence of Foreign Loans [on the exchanges] was very small indeed, when considered as forming Part of the

35 Grenville to Eden, 10 June 1796, PRO, F.O. 7/45.
36 Grenville to Eden, 17 June 1796, PRO, F.O. 7/45.
37 Treasury to Boyd, July 1796; (draft in Boyd's handwriting), Chatham Papers, PRO., 30/8/339.
38 Benfield, op.cit., p.2; Select Committee on the Tenth Naval Report, Evidence of Drummond. p. 75.

whole Foreign Expenditure which this War . . . has occasioned'.[39] This claim can hardly be substantiated: contemporary opinion was quite the other way, and such statistical evidence as is available shows that loans and subsidies formed a substantial proportion of total foreign payments for military purposes.[40] However, much as the Bank directors disapproved of foreign loans, they were generous enough to pay tribute to the way Boyd had made the remittances. Asked whether 'the manner in which a Supply was remitted to the Emperor last year, tended in any Degree, to palliate the evil Consequences which . . . might result from an open Loan of the same Amount. . . .', they replied 'that an open loan to the Emperor would have given occasion for a good deal of Operation on the Course of Exchange, which would have produced much worse effects for this Country than the remitting of the Money, in the silent and gradual way in which it was done, did cause'.[41]

Although in May Boyd had urged that the transaction should be kept secret, he must have realised that sooner or later it would become known. The market soon discovered that something was going on, for in June there were press reports (which proved incorrect) of an Imperial loan being issued in July.[42] For nearly six months the news was kept from the public, but early in December the Army extraordinaries for 1796 revealed that £1,200,000 had been provided for the Emperor.[43] A few days later, Pitt presented to the Commons a message from the King stating that discussions with the Allies were in progress on concerted measures for the prosecution of the war, and that in the meantime such temporary advances to the Emperor as might be 'indispensably necessary' should be continued. In the course of the debate which followed, Fox delivered a bitter attack on the Government for advancing £1,200,000 without parliamentary authority. In defence, Pitt claimed that the Crown had the right to draw on money voted for extraordinaries, and that earlier disclosure would not have been in the national interest.

Even while these remittances were being made, the Austrians were pressing for further advances. During September and October Baron von Müller repeatedly expressed to Boyd his great anxiety about the payment of the interest due on 1st November, as it was impossible for Austria to make the necessary remittances, or even to earmark for this purpose the monthly advances which were being made under the May agreement. He urged that Boyd should recommend to Pitt that the British Government should advance £172,500 to enable the interest to be paid on its due date, instead of allowing Austria to default and having to meet the interest under the guarantee.

Boyd put the proposal to Pitt. In its support he put forward a typically specious argument '. . . it appears to me peculiarly useful', he wrote, 'to

39   Commons Committee of Secrecy, 1797, Evidence of Boyd.
40   Norman John Silberling, *Financial and monetary policy of Great Britain during the Napoleonic wars,* Quarterly Journal of Econonomics, Cambridge, Mass., vol. 38, 1924, p. 227.
41   Commons Committee of Secrecy, 1797, Evidence of Raikes, Giles and Bosanquet.
42   *Morning Chronicle,* 3 June 1796.
43   *The Times,* 8 Dec. 1796; Account . . . of the Sum of £2,500,000 . . . to defray any Extraordinary Expenses . . . for the Service of the Year 1796, 7 Dec. 1796.

swell the advance to the Emperor because there will be less objection to the Loan, if a large portion of it shall have been remitted or in train of being remitted than if it were all to appear as a Sum to be sent out of the Country.' He added (and this was perhaps a sound argument) 'The difference between the *advance* of the Interest and the *payment* of it in January is infinite in point of respectability and comfort for both Governments, and I shall therefore hope you would agree to furnish the necessary funds the end of October for making good the Interest in such a manner as that it may appear that they come from the Imperial Treasury'.[44] At the same time Starhemberg was making similar representations through Grenville, pointing out that it was important for the sake of British credit, as well as for Austrian, that the interest should be paid when it was due.[45] In the end, the interest was paid by Boyd, Benfield & Co., out of funds which were awaiting remittance.

In November, Starhemberg was urging the conclusion of a new convention, to provide for instalments of £200,000 a month,[46] instead of £150,000, from December 1796, with an additional amount of £400,000 for January. Pitt, although willing to grant some assistance, was not prepared to go to this length. The advance he proposed was limited to £500,000, but even this met with great opposition in the House of Commons, and was sanctioned on 19th December only after prolonged debate.[47] Of this amount, £300,000 was to be made available in January.

The remittance of these amounts did not run smoothly. Frankfurt was threatened by the French, and some of the leading houses had moved to Leipzig. The real trouble, however, lay nearer home. Boyd, Benfield & Co., as Starhemberg recognised, were pressed for funds, and did not always have the means to make remittances promptly. In a draft convention which he had drawn up in November, he had felt it advisable to provide for the payment of instalments to Boyd, Benfield & Co. on the first day of each month, and for any delay to be notified forthwith to him.[48] That the fault did not lie with the British Government is suggested by the equal insistence shown by Grenville that responsibility for remittances should be clearly defined. He wrote to Eden: '. . . to avoid great difficulties and inconveniences which have arisen here on the subject of remittance . . . fixed day or days in each Month shall be assigned for the Payment by His Imperial Majesty's Minister, after which the remittance shall be made by His Imperial Majesty's Agent alone.'[49]

Although responsibility for remittance was thus squarely placed on Boyd, Benfield & Co., there were still considerable delays. During January and February the Treasury issued £280,000, yet by the end of February, no part of this sum had been received in Vienna, for Starhemberg wrote to Boyd saying that the Austrian treasury wished to

44   Boyd to Pitt, 6 Oct. 1796, Chatham Papers, PRO, 30/8/115.
45   Starhemberg to Grenville, 13 Nov. 1796, *Dropmore Papers*, vol. III, p. 268. This letter appears to be incorrectly dated and was probably written around the middle of October.
46   Starhemberg to Grenville, 16 Nov. 1796, *Dropmore Papers*, vol. III, pp. 270–2.
47   *Parliamentary History*, vol. 32, col. 1389.
48   Project, (17 Nov. 1796) *Dropmore Papers*, vol. III, pp. 273–4.
49   Grenville to Eden, 3 Jan. 1797, PRO, F.O. 7/48.

draw on Boyd, Benfield & Co. immediately the £500,000 placed at Austria's disposal by the British Government. It was also urgent, he said, that Boyd should in turn draw on the Treasury for the amounts in question.[50] For some reason or other, the procedure laid down by Grenville does not seem to have been followed, and it is possible that funds awaiting remittance were lying in the hands of Boyd, Benfield & Co.

Some of the rather complicated remittance arrangements can be traced from an account Boyd, Benfield & Co. sent to the Emperor much later. The operation centred on Hamburg, and it was there, as already mentioned, that Boyd, Junior, was sent in the summer of 1796. The account opens, without giving details, with an amount of £66,800 remitted before he arrived. It then shows that from August to the end of the year £488,600 was sent, and in the following five months, January to May, £546,900, making a total of £1,102,300. Two different methods were employed. Some £212,900 was sent by Boyd, Benfield & Co. to two leading merchant benking houses, Johan Schubach and Martin Dorner, partly in sterling and partly in marcs banco, and these amounts were paid directly to an Austrian body in Hamburg referred to as the 'Direction of the Mines'.[51] The rest, £790,700, was drawn by the Direction on merchant banking firms in Hamburg, Rotterdam, Augsburg, Venice and Vienna, partly in marcs banco, but mainly in sterling, they in turn, drawing on Boyd, Benfield & Co. Altogether seventeen firms were involved, and at least 176 bills were drawn, most of them in broken amounts, to make them look like commercial bills, and ranging in amount from £25,000 to £30. When eventually the bills drawn by these firms reached London, prhaps even before, Boyd, Benfield & Co. drew bills on the Treasury, which they discounted, thus putting themselves in funds.

In addition to making these remittances, Boyd, Benfield & Co. withheld £349,300 required for the service payments on the loan of 1795, which the Austrian government had not furnished; £100,000 advanced to Col. Craufurd, which had to be repaid to the Treasury; £3,100 advanced to various Austrian officials (including a mysterious £100 paid to Mr. Scholl, the Emperor's gardener, at the Cape of Good Hope); £81,000 for Boyd, Benfield & Co's five per cent. commission, and £200 for brokerage on their remittances to Hamburg. The total came to £1,635,900,[52] £15,900 more than the amount of the loan, which was £1,620,000.

50 Account of the . . . Sums . . . drawn for . . . His Imperial Majesty, Accounts and Papers, 1796–7; Starhemberg to Boyd, 28 Feb. 1797, Pitt Correspondence, CUL., Add. 6958/11.
51 This was the Kaiserliche-Königliche-Bergwerks-Producten-Verschleiss-Direction, an agency of the Austrian government, set up in 1759, for selling copper, quicksilver and other minerals.
52 Copy of Account of 2nd Imperial Loan (undated, probably late 1798), Baring Archives. It has not been possible to reconcile this account with 'An Account of the Dates of the several Bills drawn from the Use of his Imperial Majesty' (Accounts and Papers, 1796–7 (44)), which covers the period June to September 1796, and which may relate to a different phase of what was probably a circuitous remittance process. The account was apparently Boyd's response to a claim made by the Austrians that the firm owed them £150,000. One item they objected to was the £81,000 for the firm's commission. The Account bears the notation 'Case prepared by Mr Romilly', no doubt Samuel Romilly, who became Solicitor-General in 1806.

Boyd's ability to arrange these remittances was partly due to his close connection with mercantile houses in Hamburg. Among these was John Parish & Co. The connection between Boyd and Parish was of long standing, and, as described earlier, Boyd, Ker et Cie, and Parish & Co. had joined together in exchange operations. As was customary, it was a two-way relationship; Parish & Co. acted as Boyd, Benfield & Co's Hamburg agents and correspondents, Boyd in London performing a similar service for Parish. It was in this capacity that Boyd, Benfield & Co. became involved in the provision of transports from the Elbe for the Commissioners for conducting His Majesty's Transport Service.

The Commissioners, who constituted the Transport Board, had appointed a naval officer, Captain Home Popham, to be their representative in Hamburg. In July 1795 Popham was instructed by Henry Dundas, Treasurer of the Navy, to charter ships to transport from North Germany the remnants of the Duke of York's ill-fated expedition to the Netherlands, which had retreated to Osnabrück. Popham approached Parish & Co., who had earlier handled the remittance of the British subsidy to Prussia, and found them confident of being able to obtain up to 30,000 tons of shipping.[53]

A few weeks later, Popham instructed Parish to charter the tonnage required. By various charter parties between August and October 1795, Parish obtained ninety-six ships, having a total tonnage of some 40,000 tons, at a cost for freight and primage, demurrage and other charges equivalent to £195,287. Payment was to be made by bills of exchange at thirty days' sight drawn by Popham on the Transport Board, and made payable to Parish & Co. These bills were then endorsed over to Boyd, Benfield & Co., as Parish's London correspondents, for presentation to the Transport Board for acceptance, together with Parish's statements of account and vouchers. By the end of November, the Transport Board had accepted bills totalling £97,000. When, however, Boyd, Benfield & Co. presented bills for a further £60,000, the Board refused 'for the present' to accept them[54] The reason was that serious divergences of view had developed over the measurement of the tonnage, the exchange rates used, and charges for demurrage and brokerage.[55] In September, Popham proposed to the Board that the differences should be submitted to arbitration, and, early in 1796, sailed to England to make a full statement to a somewhat critical Board.

As Parish's agent, Boyd was anxious to get the £60,000 bills accepted as soon as possible, and on February 9 he proposed to the Board that the bills should be accepted under his firm's guarantee.[56] To this the Treasury gave a somewhat reluctant consent, conditional on Boyd, Benfield & Co. giving 'sufficient legal Security to indemnify the Public'.[57] Accordingly, Boyd, Benfield & Co. signed a guarantee for £60,000, and entered into a

---

53 Popham to Transport Board, 26 July 1995, Report of Transport Office to George Rose, 8 Aug. 1796, PRO, Adm. 108/172, p. 5. Tonnages were expressed in lasts, roughly equivalent to two tons.
54 Parish & Co. to Popham, 19 Jan. 1796, PRO, Adm. 108/169.
55 Statement of Charges, PRO, Adm. 108/170.
56 Boyd, Benfield & Co. to Transport Board, 9 Feb. 1796, PRO, Adm. 108/5.
57 Rose to Transport Board, 9 Feb. 1796, PRO, Adm. 108/5.

bond in the penalty of £120,000, expiring on 24th August 1796.[58] The Board then accepted the bills, which made it possible for Boyd, Benfield & Co. to negotiate them in the market. According to Parish, Boyd had no authority to give a guarantee, and did not advise Parish until later of what he had done. The most likely explanation is that Boyd, pressed for funds, wanted the bills accepted to gain the temporary use of the money due to Parish by discounting them.

The Commissioners of the Transport Board examined the accounts and vouchers submitted on behalf of Parish, found sums aggregating over £60,000 disallowable or improper, and gave notice to Boyd, Benfield & Co., and to John Parish, junior, then in London, who managed the ship-chartering side of his father's business. This they followed by a formal request to Boyd, Benfield & Co. to pay £66,000 and interest to the Treasurer of the Navy, in the terms of their bond. Parish & Co., however, convinced of the merits of their case, refused to agree to payment being made, on the grounds that the Transport Board had not given proof of their contentions, and asked for further time.

John Parish was sixty-three years of age, and wanted to retire and hand over his business to his sons, John and Richard. He had accordingly given notice to his correspondents that the unsecured credits he had granted them should be repaid by 1 January 1796. For Boyd, however, he made an exception, for he considered it unlikely that Boyd, Benfield & Co. would be able to repay what they owed him by that date. Parish therefore gave Boyd an extra six months, hoping that this would give him sufficient time to repay. In May 1796, Boyd received a reminder that he could no longer draw on Parish & Co., and realised that this was final. The personal messages which Boyd was accustomed to add to his business letters to Parish no longer appeared, and the correspondence between the two houses became more and more formal. That summer, Boyd, Junior, was in Hamburg to arrange the remittances for Austria, and he took the opportunity of seeing Parish to persuade him to give further time. The attempt failed, and Boyd, senior, decided to break.

His first step was to demand of Parish either that he should pay the £60,000, which Boyd had guaranteed to the Transport Board, or approve his having given the guarantee. Parish considered that Boyd should not have given the guarantee, but in view of his close relations with Boyd, and the extent to which he was already committed, he decided, after consulting his son-in-law, Hercules Ross, who was then in Hamburg, to give it retrospective approval.[59] In the summer of 1796, Parish tried to induce Boyd to extend his guarantee, but Boyd, knowing only too well his own financial difficulties, and thinking, perhaps, that his guarantee and bond might no longer be acceptable to the Treasury, refused to extend it beyond 24 November 1796.[60] The break between the two houses was now almost complete. Parish proposed to the Transport Board that Ross should replace Boyd, Benfield & Co. as guarantor. This the Treasury would not accept, on the grounds that Ross was resident in Hamburg, but they

58 PRO, Adm. 108/170.
59 This account of the dispute over the guarantee is based on Ehrenberg, op.cit., pp. 71, 76–9, using Parish's memoirs. Boyd's version might have been different.
60 Parish, Junior, to Boyd, (Nov., 1796) PRO, Adm. 108/170.

agreed to have him as joint guarantor with David Scott,[61] founder of the agency house of David Scott & Co., for a period of six months to 28 May 1797, Boyd, Benfield & Co's guarantee being cancelled. At the end of 1796, after much correspondence, the Treasury agreed to arbitration, and in July 1797 Parish & Co. were awarded £29,536[62] – a good deal less than they had asked for.

The events described in this chapter showed Boyd from two aspects. From the one side, the arrangements for the remittance abroad of large sums for Austria showed him as a skilled technician ably serving his clients. From the other side, his unauthorised guarantee of Parish's bills saw him disregarding accepted business procedures in order to gain the temporary use, for his own purposes, of funds belonging to someone else.

61 David Scott (c1746–1805) member for Forfarshire and, later, Perth Burghs, and chairman, East India Company.
62 Award of Arbitration, 25 July 1795, PRO, Adm, 108/170.

CHAPTER X

Boyd, Benfield & Co. in Difficulties

'. . . the Expedients resorted to by the House, for preventing its Fall, were various. Every one of them, while it put off the evil Day, only tended to insure the ultimate Arrival of that Day . . .'

Walter Boyd, 5 May 1800.

The position of Boyd, Benfield & Co. deteriorated during the summer of 1796. In mercantile transactions, as well as on their extensive holdings in the funds, the firm had sustained considerable losses. By August, the position had become serious, and Boyd, on the advice of Benfield, applied for assistance to certain of the partners of Hope & Co, who were then living in London. From them Boyd obtained £55,000 by way of discount.[1] This, however, proved to be insufficient, for conditions in the money market made it impossible for the firm to strengthen their cash position by normal means.

Early in September, the Bank of England narrowed its discounts still further, and threw out bills of the most respectable houses. 'It is with difficulty', wrote the *Morning Chronicle* on 8 September, 'that cash is given for any bills whatever'. Even such an experienced dealer as Abraham Goldsmid found that not more than £1,000 or £2,000 of Navy bills or acceptances of the East India Company could be sold or used as collateral for loans.[2] The Bank was reluctant to make further advances on scrip of the loans for 1796. Boyd realised that an attempt to sell in the market sufficient of the £7,500,000 loan of May 1796, of which his firm were the principal holders, would force the price still lower (it was already at 13–15 discount), and would increase their losses. In addition, they held nearly £270,000 of the £18,000,000 loan, on which an instalment of fifteen per cent., requiring £40,000, was payable on September 9.

These circumstances forced Boyd to take the one step he had been trying to avoid. With the full knowledge and approval of Benfield, he revealed the firm's position to Pitt and Dundas, and asked for aid.[3] Two years earlier, Pitt had been the borrower and Boyd the lender: now the roles were reversed. Boyd had to explain the 'great pecuniary difficulty and embarrassment of his house', and said that the Bank of England had

---

1. Boyd, *Letter to the Creditors*, op.cit., p. 10.
2. Select Committee on the Tenth Naval Report, Evidence of Abraham Goldsmid, p. 62.
3. Boyd, op.cit., p. 10.

refused to discount the firm's bills,[4] and that although they had ample securities in their possession, they found themselves unable to pay the next instalment on the loan.

Quite apart from any personal regard he might have had for Boyd, Pitt, for his own sake, was anxious to prevent Boyd, Benfield & Co's failure, for it would inevitably cause a further fall in the funds, which might precipitate other failures. Moreover, there would be great difficulty in finding other contractors to take over their holdings. That, at any rate, was the opinion of Samuel Thornton, who was a director of the Bank at the time. He said later: '. . . there would have been great difficulty in negotiating a fresh Loan for the supplies of that year . . . cancelling a contract for a Loan at that period of the year would have been as calamitous as it would have been unprecedented . . . it would have shaken public credit, and have materially affected the money market'.[5] Moreover, as bankers for the Imperial Loan, Boyd, Benfield & Co. were due to pay to the Bank of England £186,000 for interest and charges due on November 1, and were still engaged in remitting abroad the balance of this loan. Their failure would have international, as well as domestic, repercussions.

Considerations such as these led Pitt to the conclusion that Boyd, Benfield & Co. should be assisted. He made no attempt to enquire into the firm's position, nor did he consult the Bank of England, who might be presumed to be in a position to advise him on such a matter '. . . I had a strong persuasion', he said later, 'of the solidarity of the house, and a belief that their difficulties were only occasioned by the temporary scarcity of money; and I did not hesitate to make the advance, because I conceived the security for its repayment to be unquestionable'.[6] The Bank directors had apparently no idea of the extent of the firm's difficulties. 'Except their engagements with the Public', said Samuel Thornton, 'Messrs. Boyd and Company had no engagements, that were known to the Bank, to be of a nature or extent that precluded them from receiving the same accommodation as other houses of the first credit . . . I had no apprehension of their insolvency in 1796'.[7]

Having decided that Boyd, Benfield & Co. ought to be assisted, Pitt's next problem was to obtain the necessary funds without going to Parliament or calling on the Bank of England. Dundas, whose handling of public money later led to a motion of impeachment,[8] suggested to Pitt that the £40,000 required by Boyd should be drawn from naval funds. Pitt, although he recognised the irregularity of such a step, was so impressed with the urgency of the need that he agreed to it in principle, leaving the details to be worked out by Dundas.

Accordingly, on 9 September 1796, Dundas summoned Charles Long, the junior Secretary to the Treasury, to his office in Parliament Street, and explained to him the reasons for supporting Boyd, Benfield & Co.

4. Samuel Thornton, Governor of the Bank of England, stated in evidence before the Select Committee on the Tenth Naval Report (p. 57) that 'except the advances on the Loan, they received all, or nearly all the accommodation they asked for. . . .'
5. Select Committee on the Tenth Naval Report, Evidence of Thornton, p. 58.
6. Select Committee on the Tenth Naval Report, Evidence of Pitt, p. 50.
7. Select Committee on the Tenth Naval Report, Evidence of Thornton, p. 57.
8. Henry Dundas was Treasurer of the Navy from 1784 to 1800.

He then handed Long £40,000 in Bank of England notes, saying that Boyd would call on him at the Treasury to receive them, against delivery of 'undoubted security'. Dundas impressed upon him the necessity of secrecy, as otherwise the credit of Boyd, Benfield & Co. would be irreparably injured. Dundas had already been in touch with Boyd, for by the time Long had returned to his office, Boyd was waiting there with a parcel of East India Company, Victualling Office and Treasury Bills totalling £40,704. Long took the securities and sent them under sealed cover to Dundas,[9] while Boyd returned to the City with the money. The £40,000 advanced had been drawn on Dundas' authority from the Bank of England; of this sum £29,000 was repaid before the end of November, and the balance between August 1797 and January 1798. All concerned seem to have been anxious to keep the transaction secret. No record was made in the books of the Navy Office, the advance apearing in the monthly accounts as part of the balance due to the public, and no interest on it was paid. In Boyd, Benfield & Co's books it was shown as a discount operation, and even Drummond was not told that the money had come from Government.[10]

Early in October, Boyd felt that he should place a full statement of the firm's position before his partner, Benfield.[11] That any such action was necessary at all shows how little Benfield participated in the conduct of the firm's affairs. The statement which Drummond drew up and sent to Benfield listed assets totalling £994,000 and liabilities of £730,000, the difference being made up of the capital of £85,000, and what Drummond described as 'balance' of £179,000. That at that stage in their affairs they really had a surplus as large as this, or indeed any surplus at all, seems most unlikely.

The statement has to be viewed with caution for other reasons as well. The firm's bookkeeping does not seem to have been of a very high standard. The assets side of the statement bears a note: 'There is an Error in the cast of £10,000', and a similar note on the liabilities side, of an error of £20,000. A number of important accounts show balances in round figures, which suggests that Drummond had been obliged to make estimates, for lack of actual figures. There are no accounts in the names of brokers, even though the firm were still operating in the funds, although several accounts in the names of individual partners might have represented the firm's Stock Exchange transactions. With all these reservations, the statement is useful in indicating some of the firm's problems.

It showed large amounts advanced to firms whose position had become precarious. Charles Herries & Co. was one such firm. They had been badly hit when the Compagnie des Indes took from them its valuable London business and gave it to Bourdieu, Chollet & Bourdieu and John Henry Cazenove & Co., and the dissolution of the company three years later must have created further problems. Boyd was always reluctant to turn down business with a fellow Scot, and although the situation of Herries & Co. was known in the market, he continued to work with them. As already

9.   Select Committee on the Tenth Naval Report, Evidence of Charles Long, pp. 39–43.
10. Ibid.
11. James Drummond, Account purporting to be a statement of the House, [October 1796], Forbes of Fettercairn Papers, NLS.

mentioned, he gave them a generous share in the loan for 1796, allotting them £250,000, of which £100,000 was for their customers.[12] He continued to provide them with advances. In the spring of 1793, they were in debt to Boyd, Benfield & Co. to the extent of at least £20,000. In October 1796 Drummond's statement showed their debt at a round and undoubtedly under-estimated figure of £60,000. By this time Charles Herries seems to have become more interested in the activities of the Light Horse Volunteers of London and Westminster, of which he was colonel, than in his mercantile business.[13] Whatever the precise cause, Herries & Co. failed in July 1798,[14] owing substantial sums to Boyd, Benfield & Co. An extent made two years later showed them as owing £107,000 on current account, £75,000 on 'security account' and £6,000 on an account cryptically marked 'TN', making in all £188,000.[15]

Édouard de Walckiers also owed large amounts. Boyd, although aware in 1793 of Walckiers' difficulties, believed that his debt would ultimately be paid.[16] As already noted, Walckiers left France in March 1794, and went to Hamburg, where, with characteristic enterprise, he set up a mercantile business almost at once, primarily to supply stores and provisions to the French. He arranged shipments of rice and wheat to French ports, and negotiated contracts for the supply of corn with agents of the republic sent to Hamburg for that purpose.[17] Unfortunately, Boyd's confidence proved to be ill-founded, for Walckiers failed in April 1796,[18] owing large amounts to Boyd, Benfield & Co. There was, for example, an amount of £9,070 for acceptances on a consignment of claret made in 1795.[19] In addition, there were the amounts which Boyd, Benfield & Co. had advanced to meet Walckiers' liabilities to Herries, and which were included in an amount of £65,340,[20] which was guaranteed by Boyd, Ker & Co. These figures do not represent the total liability of Walckiers to Boyd, Benfield & Co., whose books contained obscure accounts in the names of fictitious firms, such as that of Paul Stepper of Lausanne, which showed a debit balance of £12,061, and which, according to Benfield, really represented advances to Walckiers.[21]

Another advance, which, if not a loss, had at least become unrealisable, was one to the firm's Brussels correspondents, Veuve Nettine et Fils. Boyd, Benfield & Co. had allowed them to run up a debit balance of over £33,000 on the understanding that, if required, they would remit to cover it and then redraw. This was common mercantile practice, and the arrange-

12. *Commons Journals*, vol. 51, p. 350.
13. J.N. Collyer and J.H. Pocock, *Historical Record of the Light Horse Volunteers,* London, 1843, p. 10.
14. *London Gazette*, 21–24 July 1798. Several dividends in the liquidation were paid, but details are not known as the bankruptcy records have been destroyed.
15. Inquisition of 23 April 1800, Schedule B, PRO, E. 144/40.
16. Boyd, op.cit., p. 5.
17. Bouchary, op.cit., vol I, p. 207.
18. *Morning Chronicle*, 30 April 1796, *The Times*, 29 and 30 April and 2 May 1796.
19. Boyd, op.cit., p. 6.
20. The amounts due, according to Boyd, Benfield & Co's books were £40,705 on current account, £9,070 on account 'VB' and £16,057 on account 'P'. Inquisition of 23 April 1800, Schedule A, PRO, E. 144/40.
21. Benfield, op.cit., p. 3.

ment had been in force for some time without inconvenience to either party, until the war made it impossible for Nettine to cover. Criticised later for this policy, Boyd defended himself vigorously. 'If the House of Boyd, Benfield & Co.', he wrote, 'had refused to Nettine and Son, a Credit of £30,000, they would probably have been the only House in London, acquainted with the Fortune and Prudence of that antient Establishment, that would have given such a Refusal; and with what sort of Grace would it have come from Boyd, Benfield and Co. who owe to their Connection with them, through me, all the Advantages which have resulted from the Loans for the Emperor?'[22]

In a somewhat similar category were the advances made to Laborde's relations. Members of a wealthy, titled family, they had been compelled to leave France, and had come to England. Jean Joseph de Laborde had been able to send money out of France: at his death he had £9,000 with Harman, Hoare & Co., and Hope & Co. subsequently remitted £46,000. But so far the family had not benefited greatly, as the funds were held in Chancery, pending the grant of letters of administration.[23] Boyd, Benfield & Co. came to the assistance of François Laborde and others connected with the family, by lending £29,190, apparently without security. Boyd wrote afterwards, in an attempt to justify his action. 'I am confident, that if the House of Boyd, Benfield and Co. had refused these Advances, and thus tacitly waved their Title to the Correspondence and Friendship of so wealthy a Family, more than one House in London would gladly have made such Advances, not only from a Principle of Regard for that Family, but also from the Hopes of the Advantages, which on the return of Peace, a connection with such a Family would have held out.'[24] Boyd's optimism was not justified. François Laborde never recovered any of the family estates and other property in France, and he died in London in 1801.

Among Boyd's other troubles was the firm's financing of Alexander Houston & Co., into which, as already related, he had entered rather precipitately in 1793. Houston's debt to the firm at the end of that year was £138,000. Four months later, further advances of nearly £150,000 had been made, to enable Houston to repay the balance of the government aid received in Exchequer Bills, and to make further advances to their Grenada agents, and Houston's debt had become £284,000. During 1794 and 1795, Houston & Co. were very active, and the connection brought much profitable business. Boyd, Benfield & Co. handled consignments from Houston's West Indies agents of such products as sugar, coffee and cocoa, often in quite small lots. They also covered insurance on these and other commodity shipments to London, to Scottish ports and to Amsterdam and Hamburg. The Houston account gives some idea of the amount of business handled: in the year ending 30 April 1795, payments and receipts each totalled over £1,000,000, by which time Houston's indebtedness to Boyd, Benfield & Co. had risen to £378,000, nearly £100,000 higher than it had been a year earlier.

At this moment, the long-smouldering unrest among the slaves in the West Indies broke out, this time, in a slave revolt of great violence in

22. Boyd, op.cit., p. 7.
23. de Calonne v. Harman, PRO., Chancery Proceedings (Equity Side) C. 12/692/18.
24. Boyd, op.cit., p. 7.

Grenada and St Vincent. It caused much havoc, the crop was destroyed, buildings and installations were damaged, and the whole commercial life of the islands was disorganised. Alexander Houston & Co. and George Baillie & Co., who were the largest of the West India merchant houses, sought government aid.

Pitt hesitated, but eventually agreed to support a bill to authorise the issue of £1,500,000 of Exchequer Bills, repayable in January and October 1797 and July 1798. The Act was passed in June, 1795 (35 Geo. III, c. 127), but the security requirements were so stringent as to prevent the merchants receiving what they needed. Only £590,000 of bills could be issued, of which Houston received £170,000 in August and September 1795. McDowall, William Lushington and other Grenada merchants therefore pressed Pitt in July and August 1796[25] for some relaxation to enable the balance of £910,000 to be used. Pitt was sympathetic, and promised to bring in the bill which would be necessary.

Both Boyd and Benfield had kept in close touch with these discussions, for it was of great importance to them that Houston & Co. be provided with Exchequer Bills which could be sold to reduce Boyd, Benfield & Co's advances.[26] Pitt's statement, although not providing immediate relief, was reassuring, and Boyd, Benfield & Co. continued to support Houston & Co. It therefore came as a shock when, early in November 1796, Boyd learned that at a meeting between Pitt and Lushington, doubts had been expressed as to whether the whole of the £1,500,000 authorised would ever be issued.

Boyd, greatly alarmed, sent an urgent appeal to McDowall: 'I have been daily making advances during a period unexampled in the Annals of Trade for scarcity of money, and which many causes contributed to render still more severe upon *me* than any other Man. You *must*, my dear Sir, immediately take the most vigorous measures for getting the Bill brought in. You must not admit of any delay'.[27] McDowall was unable to get the Government to act quickly, and it was not until the end of December that an Act was passed which relaxed the security requirements and extended the repayment period by two years.[28] The Act made it possible for Houston to obtain a further £70,000 in Exchequer Bills in April, enabling them to reduce their debt to Boyd, Benfield & Co. to £209,000, and in the end the whole of it was repaid.[29] This, of course, Boyd could not have known in September 1796, but even if he had, the knowledge would have given him little help in his immediate difficulties.

Drummond's statement revealed that substantial amounts were owing by the firm's partners and associates, which Boyd had difficulty in justifying to Benfield. 'There is a large sum due by my Cousin;' he wrote, 'this is of a very recent contracting, and a great part of it is loss in the Funds, in which,

---

25. Lushington to Pitt, 21 July and 2 Aug. 1796, Chatham Papers, PRO, 30/8/153.
26. Benfield to Boyd, Aug. 1796, Boyd, op.cit., p. 10, and Appendix 5.
27. Boyd to McDowall, 9 Nov., 1796, Melville Papers, NLS, MS 1041.
28. 37 Geo. III, c. 27.
29. For a general account of Scottish West India merchants in this period see T.M. Devine, *An eighteenth century business élite: Glasgow West India merchants, c. 1750–1815*, Scottish Historical Review, April 1978; Sydney George Checkland, *Two Scottish West India liquidations after 1793*, Scottish Journal of Political Economy, June, 1957.

since his departure for Hamburgh, I find, by his own confession, that he had speculated in the month of April last. He used to operate for his own account in Exchanges, by which means he threw a good deal of money into our hands, and he had gained upwards of £17,000. I was thus without any suspicion of him; and it was not 'till I wrote to Hamburgh for an explanation why he appeared to owe so much, that I learned the fatal secret . . . I am persuaded that we shall recover it all; but I dont expect him to pay more than half of it for some time'.[30] James Drummond owed the firm nearly £17,000 as a result of similar speculations. Boyd, himself, owed £42,000, but refused to admit that this was unduly large. 'I leave it to the Feelings of every Gentleman', he wrote in 1800, 'whether the Partner who had brought £60,000 Capital into the House, and whose Name, Connections and Exertions, had carried it to the Pitch of Celebrity it had acquired, could possibly feel any Scruple in having, for the necessary Purposes of his Situation, taken up a Sum of £40,000 . . . in the space of Four Years, while he knew himself entitled to so large a Share of Profits'.[31] There were, however, other accounts in Boyd's name which showed large debit balances: on one of them, marked with the letter 'S', there was a debt balance of over £260,000. The precise nature of these accounts is not clear: it is possible that they related to Stock Exchange operations, either for Boyd himself, or for the firm. It is however, obvious that these amounts, which together totalled nearly £1,000,000 did not represent assets which could readily be realised, if at all.[32]

Drummond's statement throws little light on the firm's business in merchandise. It shows them holding coffee, rice, cotton and other goods in London to an amount of £5,000, and coffee in Hamburg amounting to £800. Hamburg was in fact one of the few important centres on the Continent which was open to British merchants, and a somewhat later document shows them as having consigned sugar and coffee to Martin Dorner of Hamburg to an amount of over £34,000. As already mentioned, they handled a considerable commodity business for Alexander Houston & Co., and it is probable that Edward MacCulloch & Co., and William Lushington – both West India merchants – also gave them commodity business on a smaller scale.[33] They were also in the West Indies trade with Edward Maxwell of Albemarle Street, exporting British manufacturers and importing sugar, cotton and coffee. Samuel Thornton summed up their merchandising activities by remarking '. . . the manufacturers of this Country, and the Importers of East and West India Produce had not any great Concerns with them'. At one stage they had a contract with the East India Company for tea, which they imported from the Continent. In the first year of the contract, 1794, they sold £400,000 of tea; in 1795 the amount was £25,000, and in 1796 a mere £10,000,[34] the decline no doubt reflecting the difficulty of trading with the Continent in time of war. As far

30. Benfield, op.cit., p. 2. Boyd, Junior, was in Hamburg to arrange remittances for Austria.
31. Boyd, op.cit., p. 8.
32. Benfield, op.cit., p. 4.
33. Inquisition of 23 April 1800, Schedule B, PRO., Exchequer, Extents and Inquisitions, E. 144/40.
34. East India Company, Court Minute Book.

as is known, their shipping interests were very small. They had a one-sixteenth share in a ship, the 'Walter Boyd', a vessel of 792 tons, built in Holland in 1794 and registered A1 at Lloyds. Carrying twenty-three nine-pound guns as a defence against privateers, she was used in the East Indies trade.[35]

One of the few investments held by the partners individually was in the British Cast Plate Glass Company, which was incorporated under an Act of 1773 (13 Geo. III, c. 38), for a term of twenty-one years. Its early history was disastrous, and it was only in 1792, with new management, that it turned the corner. When its charter expired in 1794, the shareholders, unable to get a new Act, decided to continue unincorporated, but by that time the company was heavily in debt. To avoid bankruptcy, an arrangement was worked out with the creditors; and the company was recapitalised. In the process several new shareholders came in, and some of the old ones went out. Three of the partners of Pybus, Call, Grant and Hale, who were bankers to the company, as well as being one of Boyd, Benfield & Co's bankers, became shareholders, and possibly played a part in the reorganisation. Benfield and Boyd became shareholders during this period, Benfield apparently with £18,000 of shares and Boyd with £12,000. While this reorganisation put the company on a sound basis, it was still far from being able to pay dividends, and Benfield and Boyd found themselves unable to sell their holdings at a time when they badly needed funds. Ultimately their faith in the company was vindicated, for the shareholders were able to obtain incorporation in 1798 (38 Geo. III, c. 17), and by 1804 they were receiving dividends. Boyd sold his shares in 1799 for £12,000, but Benfield still held his shares when he died in 1810.[36]

The only other investments held by the partners individually, apart from what Benfield might have held in India, were the holdings of Boyd and Drummond in East India Company stock. Each bought £10,000 of stock in October 1794, Drummond selling in November 1797 and Boyd in July 1798,[37] both at a loss. The firm had a comparatively small investment in stock of the United States, in the form of $55,422 of six per cent. deferred stock, which was bought from Henry Simons of Brussels and registered in Boyd's name in February 1796.[38] As described earlier, the firm's holding on the books of the Bank of England of Imperial annuities were at one time considerable, but they had been sold by September 1796.

Boyd's policy of investing heavily in the funds can be explained only by his incurably optimistic expectation of an early end to the war. There had indeed been signs from time to time that an accommodation might be possible. Early in 1795 the French had passed a decree restoring the property of British subjects, which had been confiscated in October 1793. At the end of January 1795 there had been a debate in the Lords on a

35. Information from Lloyds of London.
36. Theodore Cardwell Barker, *The Glassmakers Pilkington: 1826–1976*, London, Weidenfeld and Nicholson, 1977, pp. 15–22 and 488–490; Information from Mr. L.J. McDonald, Group Archivist Pilkington Brothers, Ltd; Boyd, Letter to the Creditors, op.cit., pp. 12 and 23.
37. East India Company Stock Ledgers.
38. Loan of 1790 six per cent. deferred stock, ledger 26, National Archives, Washington, D.C.

motion by the Duke of Bedford on peace with France. In September 1795, two representatives of the French Convention, Louis Monneron and Étienne François Senovert arrived at Dover, ostensibly to negotiate an exchange of prisoners.[39] Boyd knew both of them: Monneron had been a partner in the Paris banking house of Monneron Frères,[40] and had been concerned in Indian affairs. Shortly after their arrival, they wrote to Boyd, giving him a general account of the political situation in France.[41] Boyd, considering this correspondence of some interest, passed it to Pitt through John Fordyce.[42]

Pitt regarded the envoys with some suspicion, as he thought that their real mission might be to start peace negotiations,[43] and Monneron was refused permission to go to London. According to a French report Boyd accompanied Monneron to Canterbury, making frequent journeys from there to Walmer Castle, where he and Monneron saw Pitt almost daily. What passed at these meetings was not made public. The negotiations, whatever they were, were inconclusive, and after a week or so Monneron and Senovert returned to France, without either an agreement for the exchange of prisoners, or any understanding regarding peace negotiations.[44] On reaching France early in November, Monneron said that his real purpose had been to obtain an impression of the morale and resources of the country and the resoluteness of the British government to fight on.[45]

A month after Monneron left, there was an indication from the British side of a readiness to negotiate, in the form of the King's message of 8 December 1795, which was followed in February by instructions to Wickham, British Minister in Switzerland, as already mentioned, but this move did not lead anywhere, Some six months later, another attempt to negotiate was made from the French side. It appears that early in September, a French agent, referred to as Mr. I, was in England and in touch with Boyd, to whom he made certain proposals regarding peace negotiations. Boyd, through Fordyce, communicated with Grenville, who replied that 'some proof should be given that the proposal is really authorised by those in whose name it is made', but that 'on receiving such proof (whether it can now be furnished or after recurring to Paris for it) there would be a disposition to enter into the business on the footing proposed; . . .' Three days later, the proof was still lacking, and Grenville could only suggest that the intermediary, on his return to Paris, should report a willingness on the British side to enter into discussions.[46]

This cautious attitude, however reasonable, was little to the liking of Boyd and Benfield, for peace would mean a rise in the funds which would

39.   *Morning Chronicle*, 9 Oct. 1795.
40.   For Monneron Frères see Bouchary, op.cit., vol. III, pp. 181–247.
41.   Senovert to Boyd, 17 Oct. 1795, Monneron to Boyd, 17, 28 and 29 Oct. 1795, Chatham papers, PRO, 30/8/136.
42.   Fordyce to Pitt, 31 Oct. 1795, Chatham Papers, op.cit.
43.   Pitt to Addington, 4 Oct. 1795, *Life and Correspondence of the Rt. Hon. Henry Addington* . . . ed. Hon. George Pellew, 1847, vol. I, p. 156.
44.   *Morning Chronicle*, 22 Oct. and 5 Nov. 1795.
45.   Bouchary, op.cit., vol. III, pp. 225–7.
46.   Notes of Lord Grenville, 17 and 20 Sept. 1796, *Dropmore Papers*, vol. III, p. 562.

end their difficulties. Benfield, advised by Boyd of the Government's attitude, wrote back in disgust. 'the Truth is, the Minds of the Rulers are not equal to the Magnitude of the Objects, so that, instead of seizing the Moment when it offered, they have, on every Occasion, *delayed, withheld* and *repented*. This is the Instant when they should seize upon . . .'s Propositions, coute qui coute (sic), and place Confidence in some one, or some where, since, from the Nature of Things, it is not possible that great Objects and Points can be acquired without it'.[47] How serious these approaches were, it is impossible to say. At all events, in spite of the efforts made by Boyd, the Government was not prepared to follow them up, and hopes of peace faded.

The advance of £40,000 from the Government, while enabling Boyd, Benfield & Co. to pay the September instalment on the loan of 1795, brought no improvement in their general position. Until a rising market in the funds made it possible to sell their heavy holdings of scrip, they could only rely on temporary expedients. Every possibility of raising money was examined. In September, Boyd proposed to Benfield that some of his Indian securities should be realised. Benfield was inclined to agree, but suggested that as they were quoted at a considerable discount, it would be better not to sell outright, but to draw bills on India on the security of the assets he had there. He wrote to Boyd in September 1796: 'It is certainly extremely desirable for us to obtain Relief from India Funds, rather than look for it from the shifting Mode of Negotiation upon the Payments to the Emperor; and I think it possible to undertake almost any Payments in India, if that Time be given upon the Transaction'.[48]

Drawing on India was nothing new, and considerable amounts had already been remitted in this way. Between May 1795 and August 1796, Boyd, Benfield & Co. had drawn on Benfield's agents in Madras, Roebuck Abbott & Co., bills amounting to £84,510, most of which was from the sale of bonds of the Nawab of the Carnatic at a discount of twenty per cent. To avoid further losses of this sort, Benfield approached Fordyce in, or shortly after, October 1796, with a view to obtaining a loan. He declared to Fordyce that his property in India was worth eight lacs of star pagodas (£320,000), but Fordyce, with true Scottish caution, was unwilling to lend except against an assignment to him of specific bonds and other securities. This Benfield was not prepared to do, as 'such an Assignment would place him in India in the Light of a ruined Man'. The deal accordingly fell through, and only £16,400 was remitted in 1796.[49]

The year 1796 was one of increasing pressure for funds, and of unending search for escape from the predicament so plainly evident from Drummond's statement. On 4 October 1796, the day following its despatch, Boyd wrote a very personal and rather pathetic letter to Benfield, half defence of his own conduct, half apology for it. 'I had formed to

47. Benfield to Boyd, 25 Sept., 1796, Boyd, *Letter to the Creditors*, op.cit., App. 7.
48. Benfield to Boyd, 28 Sep., 1796, Boyd. op.cit., App. 8. The phrase 'shifting Mode of Negotiation' presumably referred to the circuitous remittance arrangements described in Chapter IX.
49. Boyd, op.cit., pp. 12/13, and App. 10.

myself', he wrote, 'the prospect of many, many years of happiness and comfort, with you and Mrs. Benfield. I was and am blest with the best of wives, and a charming family of children. My name stood high in this Country and in Europe: And all at once there burst upon me such a variety of disasters, that I was not equal to the shock'.[50] The days of triumph were over: from now on it would be a struggle to avoid defeat.

50.   Boyd to Benfield, 4 Oct. 1796, Forbes of Fettercairn Papers, NLS.

CHAPTER XI

Financial Schemes and New Loans

'. . . Mr. Pitt, standing between Mr. John Fordyce on the one hand and Mr. Walter Boyd on the other, may succeed for a time in the invention of stratagems, which, being calculated to make the fortunes of a dozen men in the City, will be pushed by them into temporary establishment, but every day must increase the evil until it arises above the power of quackery to heal.'

Morning Chronicle, 3 February 1797.

In the early autumn of 1796, less than six months after he had raised £7,500,000, Pitt was again in need of money, but conditions were most unfavourable for a new loan. The funds had fallen: three per cent. Consols were fifty-six, compared with sixty-eight in March, and there was a general credit stringency. Boyd was fully committed. He had been able to raise the funds required to meet the loan instalment due on September 9 only with the help of Dundas, and he was most reluctant to see another loan coming on the market. Pitt was of the same mind, for the terms of a new loan would be unfavourable. On September 8, Boyd and Pitt discussed the situation, without reaching any conclusion.[1]

Difficulties in the money market persisted, however, and a week later Sir John Sinclair, who, as already related, had earlier put to Pitt his ideas about remedying the shortage of money, addressed a letter to the Governor and Directors of the Bank of England on the same subject.[2] He proposed an increase of £10,000,000 in the Bank's capital, payable one-half in Bank notes and one-half in Exchequer Bills. While this would strengthen the Bank's position, it would increase the shortage of money. This, however, would be put right by his second and third suggestions, which were firstly, to allow the Bank to issue £2 and £3 notes, which would lessen the demand for specie from those who wanted it for small payments, and secondly, to give the Bank parliamentary authority to raise £1,000,000 in non-interest-bearing notes, payable twelve months from the date of issue. 'Such notes', he wrote, somewhat optimistically, 'would at once pass, by consent, without discount'. Thirdly, he proposed to deal with the external drain of gold by reducing the gold content of the guinea. This last proposal was amplified in a second letter sent on September 26.

The Committee of Merchants formed in the preceding April had been thinking on similar lines, although it is not clear whether they knew of

1. *Morning Chronicle*, 9 Sept. 1796.
2. **Sir John Sinclair, Letters written** to the Governor and Directors of the Bank of **England in September 1796** . . . &c. (1797).

Sinclair's proposals, which were not made public until later. For reasons which can only be surmised, the Committee was reconstituted. Lushington remained chairman, but Boyd dropped out, his place being taken by John Petrie. To launch their revised plan they called a meeting at the London Tavern on September 26. The idea of a parliamentary board of twenty-five members, which they had put up in April, was abandoned: instead, they proposed an increase in the capital of the Bank of England – a complete reversal of their previous policy.

Critics were not slow in pointing out the inconsistency. 'It is somewhat extraordinary,' wrote the *Morning Chronicle* on October 5, 'that this proposition should now come from a quarter where we used to hear only of the caprices of the Bank and of the injury which their abuse of power brought upon the public. We ought to look with an eye of jealousy to conversions so sudden'. Two days after the meeting in the London Tavern, *The Times* reported that during the previous few days the Bank had been liberal with their discounts.[3] This may or may not have been true; it is just possible that the Bank directors were trying to show that the complaints of the Committee were unjustified by discounting more freely — or at least spreading reports that they were more liberal.

By the middle of October, the Committee, still referred to as 'Mr. Boyd's Committee', had completed their work, and a few days later they met with the Chancellor and the Bank directors to submit four points. First, the Navy and Victualling Bills and other unfunded obligations should be funded. There was nothing particularly original in this idea, and there had been a funding about six months earlier. A large floating debt was clearly undesirable, and funding was the only practicable way of reducing it. Secondly, the Bank should increase its capital by £2,000,000. This, according to the Committee, would enable the Bank to increase its discounts by £6,000,000. Thirdly, they proposed that 'any person may mortgage to the Bank estates, public funds or other solid securities and during the existence of such mortgage, shall have fair mercantile bills to such amount discounted over and above the usual sum employed by the Bank in discounts.' Finally, they proposed 'that the Bankers of London, Westminster and parts adjacent shall be authorised by Parliament to form a company for a limited time and in consequence of each mortgaging to the body of Bankers solid property each shall issue notes of that firm to such amount in discounts of fair mercantile bills and that such notes shall for a limited time be deemed in law a good and proper payment of any kind or sort whatever'.[4] The proposals were ingeniously framed so as to appeal to each of the principal parties concerned. The Government was to fund its short-term debt. The Bank was to increase its capital. Private bankers of the metropolis were to be able to issue notes which would be legal tender. Merchants were to have greatly increased discounts. There was something for everybody.

What happened at the interview was not made public. It can only be assumed that the Governor convinced Pitt that the safety of the Bank and the maintenance of British credit demanded the rigours of credit restric-

3. *The Times*, 24 Sept. 1796.
4. *Morning Chronicle*, 21 Oct. 1796.

tion. Funding the floating debt, however, was another matter. On this most people were agreed, and a few days later holders of Navy and Exchequer Bills were invited to a meeting at the London Tavern with the Governor and Deputy Governor of the Bank to discuss proposals for funding.[5] The Governor elaborated the Treasury's plan, which gave holders of Navy and Exchequer Bills the right to exchange their holdings for three, four or five per cent. stocks. Although the terms provided the maximum income by an exchange into five per cent. stock, there was a general preference for the three per cent. stock, which was more marketable, and offered a better chance of capital appreciation after the war. Boyd, however, did not like the idea of creating a large amount of three per cent. stock. It infringed his 'monopoly'. He and the other contractors for the £18,000,000 loan therefore protested, claiming that no more three per cent. Consols should be created until the last payment of the loan – due on December 15 – had been made. They won their point. Pitt gave way, and postponed the exchange of Navy Bills for three per cent. Consols from October 18 to December 12.[6]

Meantime, the problem of alleviating the scarcity of money continued to attract attention. 'Every schemer', wrote the *Morning Chronicle* on December 1, 'has a plan for supplying the public with a circulating medium and for re-establishing a just proportion between the business done in the kingdom and the representative signs necessary for making payments'. At the end of November copies of a plan for an 'Original Security Bank' were being circulated, the idea being to form a bank which would issue small bills fully backed by Navy or Exchequer Bills or other government securities. The plan, almost certainly drawn up by William Playfair, inventor, company promoter and pamphleteer, was essentially the same as the one put forward by Boyd in the previous April, and it may be that he was responsible in some way for its revival.[7]

Pitt, at any rate, would have none of these ingenious plans, and turned to the task of borrowing £18,000,000 to help meet the £23,000,000 deficit for 1797. By the middle of November he had decided to raise money directly from the public, although warned by Henry Thornton that '. . . some compulsion or fear of compulsion might be necessary'.[8] On November 23 he addressed representatives of some of the leading monied houses, outlining a plan for a loan repayable within four years, or within a year from the conclusion of peace. On the same day he wrote to the Bank, saying that he contemplated proposing to Parliament that all persons having a certain income be required to lend a given proportion of it. He hoped, however, that compulsion would not be necessary, and that the Bank 'from their Zeal for the Public Service, and their Sense of the Importance of the present Crisis . . . will not be disinclined to take the lead

5. *Morning Chronicle*, 27 Oct. 1796.
6. *Morning Chronicle*, 28 and 31 Oct. 1796.
7. S.R. Cope, *The Original Security Bank, Economica*, Feb. 1946.
8. Henry Thornton to Pitt, 18 Nov. 1796, Chatham Papers, PRO, 30/8/183. Henry Thornton (1760–1815), philanthropist, banker and economist, was a brother of Samuel Thornton, a director of the Bank.

in a Measure, which must have the most beneficial effect on Public Credit. . . .'[9]

During the ensuing week Pitt produced to a series of meetings of monied men various plans for debentures carrying repayment options at rising prices, to discourage selling, which drew the *Morning Chronicle's* sarcastic reference on November 26 to the 'new-fangled sort of Subscription without a Loan and a Loan without a Subscription'. The bankers rejected these plans, and it was only on November 30 that Pitt produced and sent to the Bank one which seemed acceptable. At a meeting of the General Court of the Bank on the following day, the Governor announced that there was to be a public issue of five per cent. annuities, redeemable three years after the existing five per cent. annuities, holders to have the option of being repaid at par two years from the conclusion of peace, or of converting into three per cent. Consols at seventy-five. For each £100 subscribed, holders would receive £112. 10s. 0d of annuities.[10]

The *Morning Chronicle* remarked triumphantly: 'Mr Pitt has abandoned all his wild theories and has come back to the point from which he has so erroneously wandered, an open loan on a funded security.[11] Compulsion had been dropped. Instead, all the devices used by eighteenth century publicists were pressed into service to ensure the loan's success. The Lord Mayor received a letter from Pitt appealing for support. Prominent citizens gave the loan their blessing, Alderman Lushington declaring that 'Patriotism and Prudence went hand in hand'.[12] Privately, City houses expressed very different views. One banking firm wrote to their country correspondents: 'Mr Pitt expects the subscription will sell at some discount, but flatters himself, the Country will think as he does, that a large voluntary contribution may be the means of extricating them from their present difficulties'.[13]

Subscription lists were opened immediately after the terms had been announced, and subscribers by the hundred thronged the Court Room of the Bank, impelled by patriotism, by fear of being thought disloyal, or by a genuine belief that subscriptions to the loan would prove profitable. Newspapers reported the big subscriptions. the Bank of England took £1,000,000, the Bank directors and officers £500,000, and the East India Company £2,000,000. Leading mercantile and banking houses each subscribed £100,000, their number including Boyd Benfield & Co., Smith, Payne & Smiths, and Thellusson & Co.[14] By the evening of the first day, £18,000,000 had been reached when, as *The Times* put it, 'the lists were closed amidst scenes of the utmost confusion.'[15] Enthusiasm, however, soon evaporated. Dealings started at a premium of one and a half, but a

---

9. Pitt to the Governor and Deputy Governor of the Bank, 23 and 30 Nov. 1796, **Bank** of England Archives.
10. 37 Geo. III, c. 10.
11. *Morning Chronicle*, 2 Dec. 1796.
12. *Morning Chronicle*, 7 Dec. 1796.
13. Sir John Sinclair, *History of the Public Revenue of the British Empire*, 3rd ed., London, T. Cadell and W. Davies, 1803, vol. II, p. 202.
14. *Morning Chronicle*, 2 Dec. 1796; the Subscription List is in Accounts and Papers, 1796–7.
15. *The Times*, 2 and 6 Dec. 1796.

few days later the loan was at par, and by the end of December it was five discount. The result of the loan – the Loyalty Loan, as it came to be called – hardly supported Lushington's optimism.

Before Christmas 1796 it had become known in London that the French were preparing to invade England, and in the two succeeding months newspapers were full of invasion talk. There was a gradual withdrawal of guineas by nervous depositors. The sense of crisis was heightened by a local run on the banks in Newcastle on February 18, and when, a week later, news came that French ships had landed 1,200 men in Pembrokeshire, demands for gold in London threatened to exhaust the Bank of England's already depleted reserves. The critical situation naturally gave rise to considerable discussion both in the City and in political circles, and there were suggestions that drastic measures, such as making Bank of England notes legal tender, might be necessary.

Boyd, although realising that such a measure would probably ease the situation, and assist Boyd, Benfield & Co. in their difficulties, was strongly opposed to any action which would deprive Bank notes of their convertibility. His experience with French assignats had taught him to distrust an inconvertible currency. On Sunday, February 26, rumours were rife that some such action was contemplated. At two o'clock on Monday morning, Boyd wrote a long letter to his friend John Fordyce, with whom he had been discussing the situation earlier, urging the necessity of avoiding a suspension of cash payments, and begging Fordyce to get into touch with Pitt immediately. Fordyce tried to see Pitt on the following day, but failed, and could only hand Boyd's letter to the Speaker, Henry Addington.[16] It was too late. At noon on the Sunday, Pitt had obtained an Order of Council which relieved the Bank of its obligation to pay it notes in cash, and on the Monday, at the Mansion House, a large gathering of leading merchants and bankers unanimously declared that they would accept Bank notes in payment of any sum due to them, and would use their utmost endeavours to make all their payments in the same way.[17]

In Parliament, the opposition seized the opportunity to embarrass the Government by demanding a full enquiry. Pitt had to agree to the appointment of Committees in both Houses, but was able to arrange that his own supporters were well represented – so much so that the Duke of Bedford complained that the Lords Committee 'was composed not only of the zealous supporters of ministers, but of members of the very cabinet upon whose conduct they were appointed to decide.'[18] The Committees, instructed to enquire into the outstanding engagements of the Bank and the means they had of making good these engagements, examined a few carefully-chosen witnesses.

Boyd, selected because of his sympathies with Pitt as well as for his knowledge of banking and finance, gave evidence before both Committees on three topics: his firm's activities as agents for the Austrian Government; the foreign exchange and bullion market; and the Bank of England's

16. Boyd, Letter to Pitt, op.cit., pp. 72–3, and p. 103.
17. Sir Albert Edgar Feavearyear, *The Pound Sterling*, 2nd ed. Oxford, Clarendon Press, 1963, p. 138.
18. *Parliamentary History*, vol. 33, col. 517.

discount policy and its consequences. Regarding his transactions with the Austrian government, he said as little as possible. 'I do not conceive,' he told the Commons' Committee, 'that as the Agent for His Imperial Majesty, I am bound to enter into any Detail of the Situation of the Account of His Imperial Majesty with my House, further than as the same is connected with the Issues from this Government.'[19] He stated that no British coin had been sent abroad (export of British coin was prohibited), that nearly £1,200,000 had been sent in foreign coin and bullion, and that the balance of the loan remittances had been made in bills of exchange. He was examined at some length before the Lords Committee on the exchange with Hamburg, on which he gave a clear and detailed explanation. Before the Commons Committee he showed an equally extensive knowledge of bullion operations and movements since 1793.

Both Committees examined him at length on the Bank of England's discount policy, and to both he made quite clear his antagonism to the Bank. To the Commons Committee he said bluntly: 'I attribute the Drain chiefly to that Line of Conduct, which I believe the Directors of the Bank of England have pursued since the Month of December 1795, when they announced . . . certain Changes in the Quantity and Manner of conducting their Business of Discount', although to cover himself against the charge of being animated by personal bias, he added: 'I believe . . . that they must have conceived it to be proper and prudent in them to make the Changes which they then made'. Asked whether repayment of part of the Bank's advances to Government would remove the present difficulties (and it must be noted that the questions were framed in such a way as to suggest the answers) he replied emphatically, 'not in the least, it would only in my opinion tend to increase it unless . . . the Medium of Circulation were to be proportionately augmented. . . .' All this was just what Pitt wanted to hear, although it was hardly calculated to make Boyd popular with the Bank directors.

Early in March, the Commons Committee issued two reports; the first giving the outstanding demands on the Bank and the funds available to meet them; the second recommending that suspension should be continued. Shortly afterwards, the Bank Restriction bill to sanction the suspension was introduced in the Commons. Inconvertibility of Bank of England notes was still regarded by most people as a purely temporary departure from normality, a step which, however necessary in the circumstances, was one which should be retraced as soon as possible. Boyd was certainly of this opinion. Up to the eleventh hour, he had tried to prevent suspension of cash payments; under examination before the Committees of Secrecy he had put forward the view that suspension could have been avoided, and he was therefore entirely consistent in supporting provisions in the bill to enable the Bank to resume payments at an early date. At first he strongly favoured a scheme which apparently involved depositing cash with the Bank, either directly or through banking houses, a scheme which Pitt also favoured.

Various other schemes were discussed in circles close to the Government. Lord Auckland suggested that notes issued by the Bank

19. Commons Committee of Secrecy, 1797.

against specie or bullion deposited after the bill became law should bear an endorsement or distinctive mark, and be payable in gold on demand. In the course of time, he thought, many such notes would find their way back to the Bank, without gold being demanded for them, and in this way the bullion reserve of the Bank would gradually be increased. Further, he suggested, the Bank should be allowed at their discretion to issue notes payable in gold. Both these provisions, he said, would operate to prevent any depreciation of notes. Auckland canvassed this plan and gradually won his way. In discussion with Auckland, Boyd emphasised, 'with great clearness and force', that the material point was 'to show that the circulation of Notes payable on demand may forthwith be revived in the old form'. After two hours discussion, however, Boyd had to admit that the plan for depositing cash through bankers would not have this effect, and that Auckland's plan was the most promising.[20] This, with some modifications, finally gained acceptance, and when on March 31 Pitt introduced a clause providing that any person depositing cash (gold coin) at the Bank should be allowed to draw out three quarters of it in the same form, it was agreed to without a division.[21]

Within three months of the issue of the Loyalty Loan, Pitt was faced with the need to raise further funds, but with the Loyalty Loan at a discount, it was unlikely that another patriotic appeal would succeed. On the other hand, he seemed reluctant to revert to the old method of asking for bids. Possibly he was not satisfied that he would get the best terms if bids were asked for when the most powerful contractors were associated so closely together. Possibly, too, he felt it prudent to show some consideration to those whose loyalty in the previous December had proved somewhat costly. Whatever the reason, he announced to the Governor of the Bank of England in February 1797 that he wished to raise a loan 'in the same Funds, and if possible by the same Subscribers to whom Proposals would be made, with an Allowance for their Loss on the former Engagement; and that if he was disappointed in this Expectation, he must take other Measures as usual.'[22] It soon became clear that Pitt was to be disappointed; for although the subscribers to the Loyalty Loan were not averse to receiving 'an allowance for their loss', they were not anxious to take on further commitments.

By March, Loyalty Loan had fallen to nine and a half discount. Since only one instalment of ten per cent. had been paid, the scrip was practically worthless, and the Treasury were seriously considering what would happen if holders repudiated their liabilities and refused to make further payments. One suggestion put forward was that subscribers should receive compensation equivalent to four per cent. of their holdings, amounting, on the whole £18,000,000, to £720,000. In a minute dated 8 March 1797, the Treasury, while recognising the problem, considered that, at most, defaulters would not be more than one-third, which would make a deficiency of £600,000, so that to give compensation of £720,000 would be

20. Auckland to [?], Pitt Correspondence, CUL, Add. 6958/12.
21. *Parliamentary History*, vol. 33, col. 359–367; An Act for confirming and continuing . . . the Restriction . . . of Payments of Cash by the Bank, 37 Geo. III, c. 45.
22. Commons Committee of Secrecy, 1797, Appendix 9.

unjustifiable. Other measures considered were to make a small provisional loan of £1,500,000, to postpone payments on the Loyalty Loan for two or three weeks, or to form an association to take up at ninety per cent. such part of the loan as fell into default. 'Nothing can be done,' the writer concluded, 'except by personal discussions with intelligent Money'd people.'[23]

Four days later, Boyd wrote to Pitt on the same subject. He said that the second payment on the Loyalty Loan was unlikely to be forthcoming and that 'the approaching negotiation for a further sum cannot be carried thro' but upon terms that you would justly object to and be ashamed of'. Boyd's solution was the familiar one. 'If the Bank throws bank notes liberally into the circle *this week* I am sure that both these objects may be secured, and unless such liberality can be practised, I will venture to say they will not be secured. This is altogether independent of the necessity for liberality for the trade of the country, on which subject I am sure every Merchant whose opinion deserves consideration will cordially join me.'[24]

The bankers were less interested in the Bank's discount policy. They wanted a more tangible compensation for their losses than would accrue to them from a greater liberality in the part of the Bank of England. Represented by the influential Committee of Bankers, and headed by Lord Kinnaird, they told Pitt of the 'considerable hardships' they had suffered because of the fall in Loyalty Loan. Pitt expressed sympathy, but did not offer them anything, and took the same rather negative line in writing on April 7 to Sir George Prescott, of the banking house of Prescott, Grote, Culverden and Hollingsworth.[25] Prescott thereupon called a meeting of London bankers at the London Tavern, which resolved: '. . . that the Subscribers to the last Loan are entitled to relief and it is the general opinion that 15s. 0d. Long Annuity would be adequate compensation.'[26] Considering that this would be worth about ten-and-a-half per cent., the bankers' claims were on the generous side. Pitt's coolness to the idea of compensation mirrored feelings in the Commons, so that when a bill to allot subscribers 7s. 6d. Long Annuity for every £100 subscribed was brought in in June, it was passed by a majority of only one, and was dropped.[27]

In February, Pitt had said that he wanted to raise a new loan through the Loyalty Loan subscribers, but his negotiations with them had shown that they were not anxious to bid for a new loan. There seemed to be a general willingness among City houses to let Boyd's group have the loan without competition. Conditions in the market hardly favoured substantial borrowing. The Bank of England had just suspended payment of its notes in specie, and three per cent. Consols were fifty. News from abroad was bad. Napoleon had become master of Italy, and by the end of March his armies had outmatched and overpowered the Imperial forces to bring them

23. Minute dated 8 March 1797, Pitt Correspondence, CUL, Add 6958/11.
24. Boyd to Pitt, 12 March 1797, Pitt Correspondence, CUL, Add 6958/11.
25. Lord Kinnaird (d. 1805) was Chairman of the British Fire Office and was probably connected with the West End bankers, Ransom, Morland & Co., Pitt to Prescott, Pitt Correspondence, CUL., Add 6858/11.
26. *The Times*, 7 and 10 April 1797.
27. *Annual Register*, vol. 39 (1797) p. 143.

within striking distance of the Austrian capital. Pitt's borrowing problems were complicated by the still-unresolved negotiations with the Austrians for a further loan of £3,500,000, part of which would repay temporary advances. Towards the middle of April, the departure of George Hammond[28] for Vienna, with full powers to negotiate, caused a slight rise in the funds. The exchanges, too, were firmer, and Pitt decided not to delay any further.

On April 20 the contractors, Boyd, Robarts, Curtis, Goldsmid, E.P. Salomons and Thellusson attended a preliminary meeting at Downing Street, and four days later heard the terms for a loan of £14,500,000 for Great Britain and Ireland. For each £100 advanced, subscribers would receive £125 three per cent. Consols, £50 three per cent. Reduced, £20 four per cent. Consols, and 6s. 6d. of Long Annuity. In addition, they would be entitled to subscribe, pro-rata, to a British-guaranteed loan to Austria of not more than £3,500,000, with the proviso that if the amount of that loan were reduced, they would receive a smaller amount of Long Annuity. The Austrian loan would be in three per cent. Imperial Annuities, to be issued on the basis of £266 10s. 0d. of annuities for each £100 subscribed,[29] equivalent to a price of 44.15 per cent., giving a return of 6.80 per cent., without allowing for a one per cent. sinking fund.

The terms were based on prices only just below the market, and the news was depressing. On the very day the terms were fixed, newspapers carried reports of a naval mutiny. Foreign news was no better. Only a few days earlier, advices arrived from the Continent reporting the further military disasters suffered by the Austrian armies, the advance of the victorious French to within eighty miles of Vienna, the suspension of cash payments by the Bank of Vienna, and finally, a proclamation announcing peace overtures.[30] The contractors felt that the terms proposed did not take all these unfavourable developments into account, and expressed their dissatisfaction. Pitt, however, was not to be moved, and the contractors realised that they had no alternative but to accept.

Although on current prices the terms showed a profit to the contractors of nearly seven per cent., the actual results were much less favourable. Dealings in omnium started at four-and-a-half premium, closed at two-and-a-half premium, but when Solomon Salomons threw the whole of his participation on the market in two days, the price fell to par, an event which *The Times* termed 'unprecedented'.[31] 'The Contractors', Boyd wrote to Pitt, 'must be considerably soured with their bargain'.[32]

The signature of the Preliminaries of Leoben on April 18 meant that Austria was out of the war, and Pitt was obviously not prepared to make any further advances. The amount of the loan was therefore reduced so that it covered only the £1,620,000 already advanced, involving the issue of £3,669,300 three per cent. Imperial Annuities.[33] This reduction meant a reduction in the amount of Long annuity received by subscribers. Boyd's

28. George Hammond (1763–1815) was Under-Secretary of State at the Foreign Office.
29. *The Times*, 25 April 1797; 37 Geo. III, c. 57.
30. *Morning Chronicle*, 24 April and *The Times*, 24 April 1797.
31. *The Times*, 27 April 1797.
32. Boyd to Pitt, 25 April 1797, Chatham Papers, PRO, 30/8/115.
33. Grenville to Eden, 16 May, 1797, PRO, F.O. 7/49.

group was not particularly pleased by these changes. Peter Thelluson wrote to Pitt on behalf of himself and other contributors suggesting that an alteration should be made in the terms for the Austrian Loan, but Pitt was unsympathetic.[34] Four months later, Benjamin and Abraham Goldsmid protested against the reduction in the amount. Pitt made the obvious reply that it had been a condition of the agreement that the Austrian Loan might be less than £3,500,000, and that he had no intention of proposing a greater sum than was necessary to cover the advances already made.[35] To Boyd, the whole episode was an unwelcome demonstration of the fact that even a loan obtained without competition could prove unprofitable.

Although in the City, the terms of the Imperial Loan were not regarded with great favour, Pitt was able to get Parliament to act promptly, and the guarantee was approved on May 20 (37 Geo. III, c. 59). In Vienna, Thugut considered the terms onerous, and delayed ratification in the hope of obtaining an improvement. Six months later, the loan had still not been ratified and interest and amortisation on the 1795 loan was in default, the Emperor pleading Austria's financial difficulties, and complaining that the loan had been too late for it to be fully effective.[36] Pitt, however, was not prepared to give up, and Eden was instructed to press the matter in Vienna, but all he could get was a promise that someone would be sent to London to settle the matter. In March 1798 de Ransonet, a former councillor in the Finance Department of the Austrian Netherlands, arrived in London, with instructions to press certain financial claims on the British Government, which, if met, would provide money for debt service. If this failed, he was to offer payment in commodities, or, as a last resort, ask Boyd, Benfield & Co. for short-term accommodation. There ensued frustrating negotiations. Boyd was in no position to help without a Government guarantee. Ransonet, described unkindly as 'a talkative, indiscreet and boastful little man', was not authorised to promise ratification, and Pitt was adamant in refusing support without it.[37]

In the subsequent negotiations, Boyd was not involved. It was not until the end of 1799 that the Emperor agreed to ratify, and he did so then only on condition that the annual charge for three years from 1797, or until the end of the war, whichever was later, was borne by Great Britain. Formal ratification took place in February 1800, and three months later a further advance of £2,000,000 was agreed.[38] This agreement, also, was not honoured, and it was not until 1824, nearly a quarter of a century later, that the Austrian Government made any attempt to meet their obligations.

34. Pitt to Thellusson, 26 April, 1797, Pitt Correspondence, CUL, Add 6958/11. The Austrian loan gave a higher return than the British loan. Hence it would have been logical to *increase* the amount of Long Annuity if the Austrian loan were reduced, (as was done with the loan for 1795) not *reduce* it. Little wonder that the contractors were unhappy!
35. Pitt to Goldsmids 11 Aug. 1797, Pitt Correspondence, CUL. Add. 6958/11.
36. Eden to Grenville, 22 Oct and 1 Nov. 1797, Correspondence Relating to . . . the Loans raised for . . . Austria, Accounts & Papers, 1821, vol. 23; *The Times*, 4 Nov. 1797.
37. Helleiner, op.cit., pp. 107–112.
38. Minto to Grenville, 10 Dec. 1799; Grenville to Minto, 8 and 14 Feb. 1800, Correspondence relating to . . . the loans raised for . . . Austria. Accounts and Papers, 1821, vol. 23, p. 15.

Even then, Great Britain had to accept a mere £2,500,000 paid by Baring Bros, Reid, Irving & Co. and N.M. Rothschild in full settlement – an arrangement which drew from Henry Brougham, member for Winchelsea, a sarcastic reference to an Emperor who 'had the common honesty to pay us 2s. 6d in the pound upon the money he had borrowed of us so long ago.'[39] Until May, 1797, interest was provided out of funds in the hands of Boyd, Benfield & Co. or out of advances made by the Treasury to Austria for this purpose. Nothing was provided for the sinking fund, and the three per cent. annuities bought by Boyd for the sinking fund were sold.[40] From May 1797, interest and sinking fund were met out of the Consolidated Fund, and Imperial Annuities thus became a British Government security. The history of the Austrian loans provided no good augury for the stream of foreign loans which were to be marketed in London in the nineteenth and early twentieth centuries.

39. *Parliamentary Debates*, New Series, London, Hansard, vol. 10, col. 358.
40. Bank of England Stock Ledgers; Account respecting Imperial Stock. Accounts and Papers, 1797–8.

CHAPTER XII

Boyd Seeks Assistance

'I need not state the dreadful Consequences of any Calamity to my House at this time . . . I must in duty declare that it would shake the whole credit of the Country.'

Boyd to Dundas, 23 March 1797.

The outlook in the summer of 1797 was dark. Victory over the French seemed as far off as ever. The fleet was mutinous, and there was considerable unrest throughout the country. The money market, too, had its troubles. In February the Bank of England had been forced to take the unprecedented step of suspending payment of its notes in cash. Interest rates were high; Navy and Exchequer Bills were saleable only at heavy discounts, and three per cent. Consols were forty-eight-and-a-quarter in April, compared with sixty-eight a year earlier.

Under these conditions, the fortunes of Boyd, Benfield & Co. could hardly be expected to mend. In fact, from the beginning of the year, the firm had been increasingly pressed for money. It had still not been possible to obtain the additional Exchequer Bills for Houston & Co., for the Treasury would not sanction their issue until April. The situation was becoming critical, for Boyd was faced with the necessity of providing a large amount on March 24. His appeal to Pitt on March 12 for speedy action to relieve the shortage of funds had not met with a favourable response, and as the fateful day drew near Boyd became increasingly anxious. The general market situation had worsened meantime, with the failure on March 23 of the banking house of Thomas Harley, Cameron & Son.[1]

In these circumstances, Boyd decided to make an eleventh-hour appeal. In a letter written to Dundas on March 23 he explained that the failure of Harley, Cameron & Son had made it impossible to raise money on the certificates for £35,000 of Exchequer Bills for Houston & Co. 'Are there no means by which I may get the command of this Sum by tomorrow morning?' he asked. 'I have made incredible exertions — I have struggled with unparalleled difficulties and I had so far succeeded as to be within two or three days of ease and Comfort — I am now *really in danger of perishing in the very harbour.* . . . .' Towards midnight on the same day Boyd wrote to a friend, almost certainly Fordyce, whom he had tried to

---

1. *The Times*, 24 March 1797.

see earlier that day, without success. Fordyce was aware of Boyd, Benfield & Co's difficulties, for Benfield had tried to borrow from him in the previous October. The letter was full of disappointment at the failure to secure the relief so badly needed. 'I will not wring your friendly heart with any description of my present situation', he wrote. 'It is such as I have not merited, if direct and honourable views could have secured me against such an unparalleled Series of Calamities as have befallen me for the last Six months . . . I was touching the Goal which was to put an end to my Sufferings, but my evil Genius throws a fatal impediment in the way'.[2]

This letter was probably accompanied by a note by Boyd making suggestions for providing the sum he required; 'Could not an issue be made of the Amount of the £35,000? Either by way of Imprest to the Treasurer of the Navy, Paymaster of the Forces &c? Or could not an Issue be made to account of the £600,000 agreed to be lent to the Grenada planters &c? In fine, could not an Advance be made in some way or other so that we may have the use of this money which Govt. has actually to pay? If none of the above things can be done I trust that orders may be *accepted* payable at a particular period. – Perhaps we might get Acceptances of the Treasury to Bills drawn not by us, but by some name quite foreign to us, by which means the favour might be done to us without other people possessing similar orders having any pretense for making the same demand!' These frantic proposals, however, were of no avail.

There was only one course left: to make an appeal to Pitt. Boyd, confined to bed owing to a sprained leg, had to leave the matter to be handled by Benfield.[3] The approach was made through Lord Carrington, who represented to Pitt the importance of supporting Boyd, Benfield & Co. in view of the impending loan negotiations. Carrington had been a partner in Smith, Payne & Smiths, who were Boyd, Benfield & Co's bankers, and he may well have been acting as much to protect the family business as in the interest of Boyd.[4] The application was favourably received, and a large sum, apparently £100,000, was advanced by the Government to Boyd, Benfield & Co. for the import of silver. But to Boyd's bitter disappointment, the £18,000,000 loan did not bring the profits he expected, profits which he had hoped would enable him to repay the advance from the Government.

Worse still, the improvement in the firm's cash position as a result of the advance, was offset by Smith, Payne & Smiths' refusal to grant them further discounts. 'I did not imagine', wrote Boyd later, 'that it was to be followed by the forfeiture of all that confidence and all those acts of kindness and attention which Merchants usually experience from their Bankers . . . we found ourselves actually in much greater distress after receiving that assistance than before'.[5] To an increasing extent Boyd fell back on the devices used by merchants in distress – accommodation bills,

2. Boyd to Dundas, 23 March 1797, Boyd to [Fordyce] 23 March 1797, Note in Boyd's handwriting, unsigned and undated, ULL MS 898.
3. Boyd to [Fordyce] 23 March 1797, ULL, MS 898.
4. Robert Smith, first Baron Carrington (1752–1828) resigned from Smith Payne & Smiths in 1796 on his elevation to the peerage.
5. Boyd to Pitt, 7 Oct. 1799, Pitt Correspondence, CUL, Add. 6958/13.

foreign drafts and the like. Boyd admitted later that 'the Expedients resorted to by the House, for preventing its Fall, were various. Every one of them, while it put off the evil Day, only tended to insure the ultimate Arrival of that Day, with all the accumulated Consequences of the Disgrace, Discredit, Loss of Business and Sacrifices, which a State of unceasing Exertion of such a Nature necessarily occasioned. . . .'[6]

The decline in the firm's fortunes had been accompanied by a deterioration in the personal relationship between the two principal partners. A year earlier they had been on cordial terms, addressing each other in correspondence as 'My dearest Friend'. The two families exchanged visits, and Boyd's son Edward stayed for some time with the Benfields at Margate.[7] Now it was different. Boyd admitted later 'There was at that Time such a Misunderstanding between Mr. Benfield and me, that we never met nor had any direct Intercourse with each other. Mr. Benfield's Temper, Disposition, Habits and Pursuits, but above all, his Views for the House, I had discovered to be so different from mine, that there appeared no Possibility of our ever joining cordially, as Partners ought to do, in any Object of Business'.[8] In these unhappy circumstances, both wished to separate. Benfield had only a quarter-share in the business, and had played little part in its affairs; hence, negotiations were started for his retirement. Since the two principals were not on speaking terms, there had to be a go-between, a role assumed by John Petrie, who had done business with the firm for some years. At one stage in the negotiations the idea came up that Petrie take Benfield's place as partner in the firm. Petrie, however, was himself in great financial difficulties, and Boyd wrote afterwards 'it was not possible for our house to have stood a single week if such a change . . . had been made. The scheme was so completely absurd'.[9]

Another plan, no doubt Boyd's, was that Benfield should provide the firm with £120,000 in cash 'for the purpose of relieving us from the embarrassments which then weighed on us so heavily'. Considering that his original capital contribution was only £25,000, this was a stiff price to pay, and that he was willing even to consider it, showed his anxiety to cut his losses. To this proposal, he replied that he had no ready money, but that he would assign to the firm two lacs of pagodas of the East India Company consolidated fund (worth £80,000), which, he said, was all he possessed in India. Boyd was sceptical about this statement, and said afterwards that he thought that it was 'one of those usual Artifices to which some People think they may have Recourse, during a Negotiation, in order to obtain the best possible Terms'.[10] However, there was nothing to be done but to accept the statement, which he did with rather poor grace. He wrote to Benfield on 3 August 1797: 'SEEING there is actually no more than Two Lacks, to be sure no more can be assigned, *although it is difficult to com-*

6. Boyd, Letter to the Creditors, op.cit., p. 13.
7. Benfield to Boyd, 25 Sept. 1796, Boyd, op.cit. App. 7
8. Boyd, op.cit., pp. 17–18.
9. Boyd to Mary Frances Benfield, 9 Sep. 1797, Baring Archives. Petrie became bankrupt at the end of 1803, *London Gazette*, 31 Dec. 1803–3 Jan. 1804.
10. Boyd to Hoare, 16 Dec 1798, State of Facts, and Observations To the Gentlemen interested in the Mortgage of Shaftsbury and Woodhall for the service of Messrs Boyd Benfield & Co., Huskisson Papers, BL, Add. MS 38765 (hereafter cited as State of Facts), Appendix 7.

prehend how the Property, which last Year amounted to Eight or Nine Lacks, should now be reduced to Two: But as Two Lacks can only produce Two -thirds of the Sum necessary, the other Third must be found in some other Way'. In face of Boyd's insistance, Benfield agreed to put up three lacs[11]

Meanwhile, Boyd, unbeknown to Benfield, was negotiating with Laborde, then an émigré in London, for the acquisition of his share in Boyd, Ker et Cie. In the summer of 1797, the French government had provisionally restored Boyd, Ker et Cie's property, and a final restoration appeared likely. To assist in negotiations to this end, Ker and Boyd, Junior, were in France, and in touch with the French authorities. There was thus the prospect of Boyd, Ker et Cie proving a valuable asset. In August, Boyd agreed with Laborde to buy his share for £60,000, £23,482 to be set off against amounts advanced to Laborde's relations, and £36,518 payable in acceptances of Boyd, Ker et Cie. Laborde's relations were émigrés, and had been able to save only a small part of their property, and advances to them were of doubtful value. The acceptances of Boyd, Ker et Cie were good only if the firm recovered their French assets, in which event Laborde's share would also have some value. The terms, in fact, were ingeniously framed to fit the circumstances.

These moves by Boyd – for it is clear that he was the prime mover in both sets of negotiations – can be understood only in the context of the political situation. In June 1797, Pitt had sent Lord Malmesbury to Lille, to negotiate a basis for peace. Peace would undoubtedly cause a rise in the funds, which would solve the firm's difficulties. Benfield's share in the partnership, strengthened by a cash payment of £120,000, would be a most profitable acquisition. Furthermore, peace would in all probability mean the restoration of Boyd, Ker et Cie's assets, making possible the resumption of the profitable banking business in Paris. Not content with these glittering prospects, Boyd increased considerably the firm's holdings in the funds in order to benefit still more from the rise in prices on the Stock Exchange, which peace would bring. But his luck was out. The negotiations for Benfield's retirement, at one time promising, broke down on August 9. A few weeks later – on September 4 – the coup d'état in France made further Anglo-French conversations out of the question, and Malmesbury returned to England, his mission a failure. The new regime ordered the confiscation of Boyd, Ker et Cie's property, and forced Ker and Boyd, Junior, to flee the country. To add to Boyd's misfortunes, the funds, which had risen slightly in August, fell lower than before, on the news of the breakdown of the negotiations.

Boyd, gambling on an early peace with France, had lost. But gambler that he was, he continued to play to the end. It is probable that he had been kept informed of the course of the Lille negotiations by Walter Boyd, Junior. At any rate he was in touch with the French in October, when – according to his own account – he had hopes of being able to bring about peace[12] On Boyd's contacts with the French nothing can be said with any

11. Boyd to Benfield, 3 Aug. 1797, State of Facts, Appendix 8, Note in Benfield's hand-writing, undated, op.cit., Appendix 9.
12. Boyd to Pitt, 7 Oct 1799, Pitt Correspondence, CUL, Add. 6958/13.

certainty. He carried on an active correspondence in French in fictitious terms, and claimed that Boyd, Junior, was in touch with General Dumouriez.[13]

Dumouriez had always been averse to war with England, and in January 1793 his name had been mentioned in connection with possible peace talks. There was therefore nothing inherently improbable in the suggestion that he would act as intermediary between France and England. Pitt, however, was sceptical, and asked for proof of the authenticity of the arrangements proposed. On October 17, Boyd had an interview with Pitt, at which he submitted certain letters. Pitt was not satisfied, and when challenged, Boyd could only produce circumstantial evidence. All he could suggest was that Lord Malmesbury, without committing the British Government in any way, should give proof of the influence of Boyd's contact, and the sincerity of the French Government.[14] Pitt, still unconvinced, wrote Boyd a blunt note saying that further correspondence was 'wholly useless unless it contains, *in the very first Instance* the most unquestionable Proofs of Authenticity and the absolute Certainty that all we desire will be accomplished'.[15] This put an end to the negotiations, whatever they were, as no doubt Pitt intended it should.[16]

Boyd and Benfield were still at loggerheads, for a major dispute had arisen over the remittances from India. On September 4 1797, Benfield wrote formally to the firm claiming indemnification for the losses which he said he had incurred in realising the Nawab's bonds at a discount (which he put at fifteen per cent) and in remitting the proceeds of £84,510 to England at a time when the exchange was at a discount of sixteen per cent.[17] Boyd accepted the principle that Benfield should be indemnified for any loss which he had sustained by an operation undertaken 'for the sole Purpose of meeting the Wishes of the House', and offered to take the operation for the firm's account, so that instead of crediting Benfield with the proceeds, he would undertake to replace at a later date the bonds sold. Feeling that Benfield had not been very helpful, he concluded his letter with a strong protest: '. . . since the House has been in *great* and *alarming Distress*, you have constantly refused to give us any Assistance by means of your Funds in India, (except to a *very trifling amount*) and have uniformly preferred to this most natural and respectable Assistance, that the House should open its Situation to *others*: by which means the Credit of the House has been injured beyond Expression; and its Distresses, which *early* Assistance would have completely removed, are now arrived at that Extremity which must soon set *Remedy* at Defiance,. . . .'[18]. Benfield retorted: 'Mr. Boyd will doubtless recollect his solemn Assurances to me, that any Sacrifices of

13. For Charles-François Duperrier Dumouriez (1739–1823) see *Biographie Universelle (Michaud) ancienne et moderne*, reprint of ed. of 1854, vol. 11, pp. 543–561.
14. Boyd to Pitt, 17 Oct. 1797, Pitt Correspondence, CUL, Add. 6958/11.
15. Pitt to Boyd, 28 Oct. 1797, Chatham Papers, PRO, 30/8/102.
16. John Holland Rose, *William Pitt and the Great War,* London, G. Benn & Sons, 1911, pp. 325–6. Rose has suggested that the negotiations were only a device to assist Boyd's bull operations in the funds.
17. Benfield to Boyd, Benfield & Co., 4 Sept. 1797, Boyd, op.cit., App. 9 and 10.
18. Boyd, Benfield & Co. to Benfield, 6 Sept. 1797, Boyd, op.cit., App. 11.

the Sort, as well as the reasonable Exchange from India, according to the course there, should be made good to me. . . .'[19] The dispute gave rise to considerable correspondence between the two without any progress being made. Towards the end of September the deadlock seemed complete.

The summer had brought Boyd little except setbacks and disappointments. The Lille negotiations, as first so promising, failed to bring even the prospect of an early peace. The hope of recovering soon Boyd, Ker et Cie's assets had been shattered by the coup d'état in France on September 4. During the whole time, there had been the thought of the £100,000 obtained from Government, which still had to be dealt with. His relations with Benfield could hardly have been worse; negotiations for Benfield's retirement had broken down, and now there was the dispute over the remittances from India. Well might Boyd refer to his 'constant agony of mind' between March and October 1797.[20] The situation of the firm was so bad that he felt that the dispute with Benfield had to be settled at all costs. Accordingly, Libotton, no doubt on Boyd's instructions, conceded Benfield's claim for indemnification, and credited him with £28,632.

Boyd's concession seems to have healed the breach between the two, at least temporarily, for a few weeks later Benfield was working energetically with Boyd to save the firm. The urgent task was to find a way of repaying the £100,000 obtained from Government in the previous March. He accordingly wrote to Dundas on October 31, saying that he had considerable property in India, a part of which he wanted to remit to England, and asking whether Dundas would not use his good offices with the directors of the East India Company to persuade them to take £100,000 in Boyd, Benfield & Co's drafts on Benfield's agents in Madras, at the rate of 6s. 6d. for a star pagoda. Benfield did not fail to point out that, since the exchange at Madras was 8s. 6d. the offer was highly advantageous to the Company. Moreover, he was willing to take payment in the Company's five per cent. notes.[21]

This proposal never came before the Court of Directors, but further discussions resulted in a contract for the remittance of £100,000 to the Cape of Good Hope, ostensibly for army purposes. Accordingly, the Treasury instructed Boyd, Benfield & Co. on November 16 to remit £100,000 to the Cape, and asked them when they would be able to place that sum in the hands of the Deputy Paymaster there. Upon their providing security for the due payment of the money, the Treasury would issue them a warrant. The letter concluded by saying that they would be allowed 'the usual commission'.[22] The formal agreement was signed by Walter Boyd, Junior, and was guaranteed by Benfield and others.[23]

Possibly as a set-off to this amount, which Benfield was guaranteeing, the transfer to him of the Lambert Blair estate, in the colony of Berbice, Guiana, was discussed. The firm had acquired this estate from, or through,

19. Benfield to Boyd, Benfield & Co., 10 Sept. 1797, Boyd, op.cit. App. 12.
20. Boyd to Pitt, 7 Oct. 1799, Pitt Correspondence, CUL, Add 6958/13.
21. Benfield to Dundas, 31 Oct. 1797, State of Facts, Appendix 1.
22. Long to Boyd, Benfield & Co. 16 Nov. 1797, Treasury Out-Letters General, PRO, T. 27/49, p. 62.
23. State of Facts, p. 5.

Alexander Houston & Co. for £100,000, which had been applied in reduction of their debt to the firm. Boyd had hoped to sell the estate to improve the firm's cash position, but Benfield opposed a sale, as he saw in this estate a means of saving some of the capital he had put in to the firm, and he pressed for the sale to be made to him. This was eventually agreed, and the purchase price of £100,000 was debited to his account, off-setting the liability he had assumed for the payment at the Cape.[24]

The £100,000 received for the remittance to the Cape, although it enabled the earlier advance to be repaid, was not enough. In December, fresh negotiations were opened between the Navy Office and Boyd for a remittance of £100,000 to India. The Navy's need for money in India was no doubt genuine; it can hardly be doubted, however, that the initiation of negotiations with Boyd for an amount as large as £100,000 owed more than a little to the fact that Dundas was Treasurer of the Navy. Dundas, although willing to be helpful, had to act cautiously in view of his official position. He had made the earlier arrangement for the Cape remittance, without any direct evidence of Benfield's means. Now that an additional amount was to be contracted for, he wanted some assurance that Benfield had sufficient property in India to cover both transactions.

Instead of approaching Benfield direct, Dundas wrote to McDowall, asking him for a statement of Benfield's Indian property. McDowall passed the request to Boyd, who in turn passed it to Benfield. Benfield replied briefly in a note at the foot of Boyd's letter: 'My property in the Nabob's Debts at Madras and in Company's paper and including what my attornies have in hand and Monies they have to receive for me, amounts as nearly as I can state it to Seven Lacks and Forty Thousand Star Pagodas.'[25] This' Boyd forwarded to McDowall with a covering letter, in which he expressed the hope that it would be sufficient proof of there being ample means in India, and reminded him, as if to stimulate him to make the maximum efforts, that 'without this Facility, it will be utterly out of my Power to continue to your House [Alexander Houston & Co], that Support which is so necessary to its Salvation'.[26]

Dundas, although apparently satisfied with this declaration, still had to obtain Treasury sanction. For this purpose, resort was had to a slight subterfuge, for the last thing he wanted was for the transaction to appear artificial, or as one designed to assist Boyd, Benfield & Co. It was accordingly arranged that the Navy Board should write to the Treasury, setting out the difficulty they had experienced in providing cash at Madras and the Cape of Good Hope, and the 'enormous Discount' which was suffered in making remittances to these places. When they received this letter, the Treasury put the question back to the Navy Board, asking them to suggest 'the best mode of supplying specie for the Naval service so as to prevent similar inconvenience in future'.[27] The Board, thus prompted, approached

24. Boyd, op.cit., p. 3; Boyd to Pitt, 7 Oct. 1799, Pitt Correspondence, CUL. Add. 6958/13.
25. Boyd to Benfield, 16 Dec. 1797, State of Facts, Appendix 2; 7 lacs 40,000 star pagodas would be worth £296,000 at 8s. 0d. for a star pagoda.
26. Boyd to McDowall, 16 Dec. 1797, State of Facts, Appendix 3.
27. Long to Commissioners of the Navy, 12 Jan. 1798, Treasury Out-Letters-General, PRO, T. 27/49, p. 154.

Boyd, Benfield & Co., who immediately offered to supply sums totalling between £60,000 and £100,000 in instalments running from September 1798 to May 1799, payable at Madras, Bombay and the Cape. Boyd, Benfield & Co. would receive payment by drawing on the Navy Board bills bearing interest at five per cent. payable in fifteen months. This would give them paper they could discount immediately, even though they were not due to pay the first instalment for eight months.

The Navy Board's Committee of Accounts recommended accepting the offer in an amount of £50,000 for Madras and a like amount for Bombay, but asked for an improvement in the rates of exchange proposed by Boyd. At a conference which followed, the Treasury pressed for a reduction in the rate for Madras from 7s. 0d. for the star pagoda to 6s. 6d., and for Bombay from 2s. 4d. to 2s. 3d. Boyd was not in a strong position to bargain, and had to accept the Bombay rate of 2s. 3d., but managed to get the Madras rate to 6s. 10d. This was the basis eventually agreed, subject to Boyd, Benfield & Co. 'giving sufficient security of gentlemen of landed property in Great Britain'.[28] The terms, however, had a material point of difference from those originally proposed, for instead of Boyd, Benfield & Co. merely undertaking to pay in Madras and Bombay on various dates, they now had to draw bills.

Benfield immediately raised with Boyd strong objections to this alteration, saying that drawing bills was fraught with many dangers and difficulties. This development gave Boyd some concern, for he could not avoid the suspicion that perhaps, after all, Benfield's Indian assets were not all that they had been held out to be. Accordingly, on the following day, he wrote to Benfield, expressing his misgivings. 'The Fact is', he wrote, 'that in the whole of the Negotiation with Mr. Dundas, I have acted upon the belief, that you have Assets in India much more than adequate to the Discharge of the Engagements proposed to be entered into;. . . But now that, instead of an Undertaking to furnish Money (which, by your express Desire, was the Proposal we made) the Navy-Office *demand Bills*, I really do not see how we can proceed further in the Business. . . .'[29]

To this letter Boyd received a reply from Mrs. Benfield, who wrote; 'Mr. Benfield is so unwell, and his Mind so agitated, that he is unable to write'. Although agitated, he was not incapable of dictating a reasoned reply. '. . . it would be happy for the House, if it could obtain more accommodating Terms . . . for *the Assets in India, however adequate*, may be extremely difficult to convert into Specie. . . .' The letter continued by pointing out the difficulties in the way of making payments in Bombay, and suggested that the operation be confined to Madras.[30] This, at any rate, was a reasonable compromise, and since there was no suggestion in the letter that the Indian assets were not adequate, Boyd felt somewhat reassured. A day or so later, however, came like a bombshell a notification from the Board that they wished to turn down the transaction altogether, on the grounds that a vessel had just brought advices that considerable sums had been drawn upon them by their agents in India, which rendered

28.   Navy Board Minutes, 26 Jan. 1798, PRO, Adm 106/2661.
29.   Boyd to Benfield, 27 Jan. 1798, State of Facts, Appendix 4.
30.   Mary Frances Benfield to Boyd, 28 Jan. 1798, State of Facts, Appendix 5.

it unnecessary to arrange any remittances from London.[31] Boyd replied that any alteration 'would be atended with great inconvenience', but he promised to consult his partner.[32]

Benfield, apprised of the news by Boyd, was insistent that at least the arrangements for the remittance to Madras should stand. Late that night he wrote to Boyd: 'The Half must be taken on *Madras* since it is reduced to *that*: perhaps *that* once done, more may be settled for, at the Cape. But it cannot be true, that the Agents have drawn for Money for the Periods of time it was proposed we should pay it. . . . Perhaps you will see Sir Andrew Hamond,[33] upon the subject of the Cape, quitting the Bombay Ground, in preference to any Thing else. – The Fifty Thousand Pounds once done, I doubt not we may get farther'.[34] Boyd accordingly pressed the Navy Board to agree to the £50,000 for Madras, which they did on February 5.

A few days later, Walter Boyd, Junior, signed an undertaking to make the remittance, and Boyd, senior, Benfield and three partners of Alexander Houston & Co., who still owed Boyd, Benfield & Co. well over £100,000, signed as sureties.[35] By so doing, the three Houston partners, if all went well, would be helping to save Boyd, Benfield & Co. If, however, the remittance to Madras were not made, and they were called upon to pay under the bond, any payments they made would reduce their indebtedness to Boyd, Benfield & Co. Thus, after months of difficult negotiations, Boyd had secured a breathing space. The total amount of £150,000 obtained from the Government now appeared as payment under legitimate contracts with public departments, and for a few months, the fulfilment of these contracts was unlikely to be questioned.

The growing difficulties which threatened Boyd, Benfield & Co. were suspected, if not known, by some of those who were accustomed to bid for loans. In October 1797, while Boyd was away from town at Margate, tentative steps were taken to form a list to replace Boyd's, on the assumption that his financial position would not allow of his contracting. Boyd sensed a conspiracy to oust him from his position as the leading loan contractor, and he believed, rightly or wrongly, that Daniel Giles was behind it.[36] 'When I consider the *quarter* from whence these insinuations came', he wrote, 'no wonder I have been injured'.[37] For one reason or another, nothing came of this move, and he maintained his position.

In February 1798 came Pitt's much-publicised – and much-criticised – voluntary contribution. The Lord Mayor of London, John William Anderson, called a meeting at the Royal Exchange, and a committee consisting of over one hundred merchants and bankers was formed to back an appeal for gifts to help to meet the cost of the war. A temporary office was

31. State of Facts, p. 6.
32. Navy Board Minutes, 3 Feb 1798, PRO, Adm. 106/2661.
33. Sir Andrews Snape Hamond (1738–1828) was Conptroller of the Navy.
34. Benfield to Boyd, 3rd Feb. 1798, State of Facts, Appendix 10.
35. Navy Board Minutes, 31 Jan, and 5 Feb., 1798, PRO, Adm. 106/2661; Select Committee on the Tenth Naval Report, Appendix B, p. 112.
36. Giles' term of office as Governor of the Bank was over, and, although still a director, he was free to contract for loans.
37. Boyd to Fordyce, 24 April 1798, Pitt Correspondence, CUL, Add. 6958/12.

opened on the Royal Exchange, which, when the subscription list was opened, was filled with hundreds of traders, merchants, and others, who crowded in to subscribe sums ranging from one guinea upwards. For a firm such as Boyd, Benfield & Co., the contribution was voluntary only in name, for a house which claimed to be counted among the leading merchants in the City could hardly stand aside without giving rise to doubts about its loyalty and financial position. Boyd accordingly joined the committee, and subscribed £3,000 in the name of the firm, promising to repeat the subscription every year during the war.[38]

In April 1798, Pitt invited bids for a loan of £17,000,000, and when the lists of contractors were examined it was seen that, in spite of everything, Boyd once more headed a strong group. His leadership, however, was no longer undisputed, a fact which became evident when, before the bidding, the members met at Boyd's house to discuss the terms on which the group's bid would be made. Bidding was to be in Long Annuity, and discussion took place on the amount which should be offered. 'Their first idea', Boyd related to Fordyce afterwards, 'was 6s. 6d. – I brought them down to 5s. 9d. and there they stuck for a long time. I got them down to 5s. 4½d. and after a very long discussion and strong remonstrances, I got Mr. Robarts and myself authorised to go if it should appear necessary as low as 4s. 11d'. Boyd was evidently afraid that one of the other groups would bid under him, for when forms were filled in at Downing Street on April 23, Boyd insisted on going to the lowest figure authorised.

For once, Boyd's judgement failed him, for although he secured the loan, the nearest bid to his was that of the bankers, whose bid of 6s. 10d. was higher even than the 6s. 6d. which had been proposed initially by his colleagues.[39] Pitt, greatly pleased with the result, announced in the Commons that the loan had been concluded 'with a competition of four parties of unquestionable solidarity and character' – this was surely a thrust at Boyd's detractors – and said that the bargain was 'more favourable to the public than any, even the most sanguine, could hope for'.[40] Boyd, on the other hand, came in for criticism when his colleagues learned by how much their bid was below the others, but he expressed himself as fully satisfied at having counteracted what he felt to be a conspiracy to bring him down.

He had now to see that the omnium did not fall to a discount. On the day following the bidding he sent an urgent appeal to Fordyce, in which he said that the object of the conspirators was not merely to eliminate the House of Boyd, but also to bring down the price of the funds so that they could secure 'an exorbitant bargain' for themselves. 'For God's sake, my dear Fordyce', he wrote, 'do what may happen to be in your power to impress Mr. Pitt with a due sense of the importance of the *success* of our Loan. If he *can* do any thing to counteract the unwarrantable manoeuvres that I know will be practised by the disappointed and above all by the Giles party, I am sure he ought to do it. The Splendor of his admini-

38. *Morning Chronicle*, 10 Feb. 1798; Macpherson, *Annals of Commerce*, op.cit., vol. IV, p. 440.
39. *The Times*, 24 April 1798.
40. *Morning Chronicle*, 24 April 1798.

stration demands it. I don't want to get great profits'.[41] Boyd's modesty was no doubt due to a realisation that he had cut the price so fine that great profits were out of the question. Omnium opened at one-and-a-quarter to one-and-three-quarters premium, and remained steady at this level, a result which, in the circumstances, must have been regarded by the contractors with satisfaction, if not with enthusiasm.

Yet the end was near. In June 1798 the Treasury, becoming uneasy, asked Boyd, Benfield & Co. how much of the £100,000 had been sent to the Cape. Boyd did not reply.[42] What point was there in replying? It was too late for further subterfuges. In the same month came a blow which finally destroyed Boyd, Benfield & Co's credit. One of their bills, tendered to Smith, Payne & Smiths, for discount, was rejected. The amount was small – a mere £600 – and this action, as Boyd put it, 'gave a blow to our credit which no act nor address nor assistance could ever get the better of'.[43] Worse was in store, for the bills for £50,000 drawn on Madras were shortly to be returned unpaid.

With these misfortunes crowding in on him, Boyd made a final desperate effort to avert failure. He decided to pocket pride, and ask for help from the Bank of England, the institution he had opposed, criticised and attacked so bitterly during the previous three years. On 28 June 1798 there was submitted to the Court of Directors of the Bank a letter from Boyd, Benfield & Co. asking for accommodation. The Court considered that the letter raised issues of some importance, and referred the matter to an open Committee of the whole Court.[44]

During the next few days Boyd had several interviews with the directors, two of whom were shown a statement of Boyd, Benfield & Co's affairs. The proposal was that merchants and others who were connected with the house should each guarantee a certain amount, the money to be advanced by the Bank. There was evidently some difficulty in finding the required number of guarantors. Jasper Atkinson, junior, a partner in Smith & Atkinson, who was one of those organising the assistance, wrote to William Huskisson on July 1, asking whether he would allow his name to be added to the list of guarantors which was to be submitted to the Bank on the following day. Huskisson expressed sympathy, but declined, saying that he was not in business, was not known to the Bank and would be undertaking a commitment which he could not discharge.[45]

At the same time, Fordyce was working with Atkinson on another plan. It appears that the Treasury were to be asked to obtain an advance from the Bank on the strength of Atkinson's guarantee. Difficulties arose at once. On July 2, Benfield, having obtained Atkinson's consent, found that the Treasury refused to proceed any further. Atkinson, not unnaturally, felt aggrieved, and his confidence in Boyd, Benfield & Co. was consider-

41. Boyd to Fordyce, 24 April 1798, Pitt Correspondence, CUL, Add. 6958/12.
42. Long to Boyd, Benfield & Co., 13 June and 15 Aug. 1798. Treasury Out-Letters, General, PRO, T. 27/49, p. 58, T. 27/50, p. 18.
43. Boyd to Pitt, 7 Oct. 1799, Pitt Correspondence, CUL, Add. 6958/13.
44. Bank of England Court Minutes, 28 June 1798.
45. Atkinson to Huskisson, 1 July 1798; Huskisson to Atkinson (draft, undated) Huskisson Papers, BL, Add. MS 38735, ff. 86–89. Huskisson (1770–1830) was Under-Secretary of State for War.

ably shaken, for he could only conclude that the Treasury were aware of facts which were not known to him. Boyd therefore felt that any further approach to Atkinson would do more harm than good, and he asked Fordyce not to see Pitt, as had been arranged. The best plan, he thought, would be to postpone any further application to the Bank until July 5, for the fleet from the West Indies had just arrived, and would no doubt bring some remittances which would improve his position.[46] Fordyce, in spite of Boyd's preference for waiting, felt that contact should be made with the Government, which he did on July 4, but without success.

While these steps were under way, Charles Wall, of Barings, had been working out the technical details of a plan to borrow £80,000 from the Bank. There were to be sixteen 'guarantors', each of whom would furnish a note, payable at two months, and these notes were to be discounted by the Bank, and renewed succesively over a period of eight months, possibly over twelve, Boyd, Benfield & Co. undertaking to pay them off when the operation ended, or in any event not later than 4 March 1799.[47] The notes were to be secured by a mortgage on Benfield's property at Woodhall, which, yielding an annual income of £6,500 was valued at £182,000. This, after deducting prior charges, would give adequate, although not generous cover for the £80,000 advanced. The Bank, with Boyd's permission, communicated the statement of the firm's affairs to the sixteen who would be guarantors, and they said they were satisfied.

In the Bank, the Court discussed the matter early in July, when they resolved to provide the accommodation until the end of February, if necessary.[48] The sixteen guarantors included the brokers, Cole, Godwin & Coles, Kymer, McTaggart & Co., Arthur & Larken, and J.J. Angerstein; and the merchants, Turnbull, Forbes & Co., J.H. Schneider & Co. and William Lushington. There were two jobbers, Meyer Cohen and Mark Sprott. Robarts, Curtis & Co., and Benjamin and Abraham Goldsmid leading members of Boyd's group of loan contractors, were also among the sixteen.[49] Boyd said nothing to the guarantors about the £150,000 he had previously obtained from the Government, explaining later that 'it was deemed highly expedient to withhold from the Lenders and indeed from every Body, the knowledge of the Assistance received from Government, (seeing that it was the Secret of Government fully as much as of Boyd, Benfield & Co.)'. In addition to the £80,000, Boyd obtained £50,000 on Benfield's Shaftsbury property.[50]

In spite of the firm's almost hopeless position, Boyd was determined to retain his position as a loan contractor, if he could. At the end of October 1798, Pitt let it be known that, although no loan was required immeditely, 'monied men' should be prepared with lists, in case a small loan were necessary before the end of the year. The other members of Boyd's group were aware of the general state of his affairs, although the full story was not yet known, and they felt that he might no longer be acceptable to the

---

46. Fordyce to Dundas, 3 July 1798, Melville Papers, NLS, MS 1041, f. 49.
47. Hope & Co. to Charles Wall, 2 July 1798; Henry Smith to Baring & Co., 20 July 1798, Baring Archives.
48. Bank of England, Court Minutes, 6 July 1798; Baring Archives.
49. Above named to assignees, 2 May 1801; Treasury In-Letters, PRO, T1/860/1963.
50. Boyd, op.cit., p. 14.

Treasury as a contractor. Even if he were, they would have some hesitation in signing a contract with him. Accordingly, on October 29, a meeting was called, probably by Robarts, to consider what action should be taken, and to this meeting all the members of the group, except Boyd, were invited. At the last minute, Boyd, hearing of the meeting, decided to attend, even though uninvited.

The meeting had apparently started when he entered the room. It was impossible for Robarts and the others to conceal their purpose, and they had no alternative but to explain to Boyd that, in spite of the high regard which they had for him personally, his financial position was such that they would have to ask him not to attempt to bid at the head of their group. To soften the blow, they offered to reserve £500,000 of the loan for him as a token of their respect for him personally, and as an expression of confidence in his firm. Boyd was not one to give up without a fight. Acceptance of their offer would mean abdication, and he brought all the arguments he could to justify his maintaining his position. According to one report, he convinced them 'that they were not yet sufficiently strong to kick down the ladder by which they had risen'. Opinion, however, seems to have been divided, and at the end of the meeting the formation of a separate list seemed likely.

The issue of the loan was delayed for a month. In the interval a good deal of activity took place among contractors, and several lists were formed in readiness for the loan, which was expected to be between £17,000,000 and £18,000,000, although by December 7, when Pitt invited contractors to Downing Street to bid, he had reduced the amount to £3,000,000. There were five groups interested. The group formerly headed by Boyd had been reconstituted, and now comprised Robarts, Curtis & Co., Thellusson Brothers & Co., the Goldsmids, and Salomons. Daniel Giles had a list. A group of twenty-one banking houses formed another, while a fourth consisted of a number of stock exchange firms. Finally, Boyd submitted a list in conjunction with Angerstein and the old-established banking house of Devaynes & Co., of 39, Pall Mall. Boyd had been defeated, but not decisively. He no longer headed the group which for four years had dominated the money market, yet that group itself had lost ground. There were now powerful competitors in the field. Moreover Boyd was still at the head of a list, and his associates, Angerstein and Devaynes, were both men of substance, although neither had contracted for loans for some years. As events turned out, neither Robarts' nor Boyd's group was successful, the loan being secured by the bankers.[51]

The firm's difficulties were aggravated by the still considerable extent to which their funds were tied up in advances to Alexander Houston & Co., who had only just been able to keep going, even with the substantial aid from Government in Exchequer Bills. While Boyd could press Houstons to reduce their indebtedness, to press them so hard as to force them into bankruptcy would have been counter-productive. Houstons, for their part,

---

51. *The Times*, 24 Nov. 4 Dec. and 8 Dec. 1798. Boyd was accepted as a bidder, even though Samuel Thornton, Deputy Governor of the Bank, had warned Pitt that he thought that Boyd, Benfield & Co. could not be saved. Select Committee on the Tenth Naval Report, Evidence of Thornton, p. 60.

did not want Boyd, Benfield & Co. to fail, as they could hardly find another firm to finance their current business and keep them afloat. Each had an interest in the other's survival. Boyd, Benfield & Co's. partners had no more real estate which could provide a basis for further borrowing, but Houston's partners did. The problem was to find lenders. In this situation an ingenious but somewhat complicated plan was worked out in the autumn of 1798. Its authorship is not apparent from the surviving documents, but it is not difficult to imagine that it came from Boyd's fertile mind. It was unveiled at a meeting in Glasgow, attended by 'friends and supporters' of Alexander Houston & Co. It provided that Walter Boyd, Junior, would draw bills on Boyd, Benfield and Co. in favour of Houston & Co., who would endorse them to one or other of the thirty or so subscribers to the plan, most of whom were Galsgow or Paisley merchants. These bills would be discounted or used as collateral for advances.[52]

A large amount, apparently about £100,000 was raised in this way, Details have been found of eighty-five bills, totalling £60,000, drawn in September and October 1798 in amounts ranging from £250 to £1400. Some subscribers sold their bills, which found their way to London, the buyers including well-known firms such as the bankers, Smith, Payne and Smiths, the merchant bankers Reid, Irving and Co., and John Julius Angerstein. One was even bought by the Bank of England. As security, some of Houston Rae's real property was conveyed to the Glasgow banker, Archibald Graham, as trustee on behalf of the subscribers.[53] The direct beneficiary of this strange arrangement was presumably Alexander Houston & Co., but some benefit might have accrued to Boyd, Benfield & Co., as Houston's bankers. Perhaps they did not deserve to benefit, for they paid none of the bills as they matured and the whole episode ended in a tangle of legal actions which went on for several years. For both firms it represented a final desperate attempt to avoid failure.

52. Minutes of Meeting of Friends and Supporters of Messrs A. Houstoun and Company, SRO, GD 237/BX 134/BD1.
53. Alexander Houston & Co., 1st, 2nd, 3rd and 4th Summons, 1798, SRO, GD 134, bundle 2.

CHAPTER XIII

Failure

'That the downfall of the House was the act and deed of *Boyd* is palpable to every man of business at all connected in its affairs'.

Benfield, January 1803.

'. . . if the Truth were known . . . I shall appear, if not an innocent Man, unjustly accused, and cruelly treated, at least 'A Man more sinned against than sinning''.

Boyd to Turnbull, 21 April 1799.

Although Boyd, Benfield & Co. were able to maintain their position as loan contractors, their general situation showed no improvement, and, towards the end of 1798, the creditors, becoming anxious, pressed for the appointment of trustees to conserve the assets and make possible an orderly liquidation. The breach between the two principal partners had widened, so that when it came to appointing trustees, they acted independently, Boyd making Jonathan Hoare trustee of his property, and Benfield giving irrevocable powers to John Henry Schneider. The differences between the two soon developed into an open quarrel. Returning from a visit to Benfield at Woodhall Park late in November or early in December, Schneider called on Boyd to discuss the firm's affairs and in course of conversation remarked that Benfield's Indian property had been dissipated in supporting Boyd, Benfield & Co. This Boyd denied flatly, but took the matter no further.[1]

Some two weeks later his hand was forced. On December 13, at the close of a discussion at which McDowall, Bogle, Hoare, Boyd, Boyd Junior, and Schneider were present, Schneider openly accused Boyd of having drawn the bills on India against Benfield's inclination, and in spite of the entreaties of Mrs. Benfield, and said that Benfield had repeatedly told Boyd that only a small part of his (Benfield's) fortune was in India. To this Boyd replied that Benfield had declared his Indian property to be seven lacs 40,000 star pagodas. Schneider thought that this was impossible, and referred darkly to a letter which Benfield had signed, but which in fact had been written by Boyd.

Boyd resented bitterly these accusations, and on the following day wrote to Hoare, his trustee, giving an account of the negotiation of the remittances to the Cape and to India and enclosing copies of the correspondence, which, he said, he would place before Pitt and Dundas.[2] Friends

---

1. Schneider to Pitt, 1 Jan. 1799, Chatham Papers,, PRO, 30/8/176. Schneider was the senior partner in J.H. Schneider & Co., merchants; Jonathan Hoare was a partner in Harman, Hoare & Co.
2. Boyd to Hoare, 14 Dec. 1798, State of Facts, Appendix 6.

intervened and dissuaded him from this latter step, and instead, Boyd arranged a meeting at which those who had been at the earlier meeting, and in addition Benfield and Fordyce, were present. The meeting had an inauspicious start, for Benfield insisted at the outset on the withdrawal of Walter Boyd, Junior, saying that he would not open his mouth as long as Boyd, Junior was there. This demand having been met, Boyd's letter to Hoare was read. To the case made by Boyd, Benfield replied that the declaration that his Indian assets were worth seven lacs 40,000 star pagodas, had been extorted from him by Boyd, 'by threats to blow up the House', and produced the declaration in Boyd's handwriting, which he admitted he had signed, although knew at the time that he did not have property in India to that value. To support the thesis that Boyd, too, knew of the real value of this property, Benfield produce a memorandum written by Boyd in August 1797, in which Boyd had accepted a figure of two lacs given by Benfield. Boyd countered by asserting that every word of the declaration of December 1797 had been dictated by Benfield in the presence of Walter Boyd, Junior.[3] When eventually the meeting broke up the breach between the two was wider than ever. Among so many accusations and counter-accusations it is hard to find the truth. It is clear that Benfield signed two statements, one of which he must have known to be false, and his insistence on the withdrawal of Boyd, Junior, who had been present when Boyd had written the declaration at Benfield's dictation, tells against him. On balance, Boyd's story seems to be the more plausible of the two.

Schneider, as holder of Benfield's power of attorney, knew of the firm's liabilities to the Government, and as the year drew to a close he realised that there was a real danger that the Government might step in ahead of the other creditors. Early in 1799, therefore, he asked to see Pitt to explain the position and discuss means of liquidating the firm's affairs and those of Alexander Houston & Co.[4] Pitt, however, seemed disinclined to do anything beyond demanding payment of the £50,000 bills which had been returned unpaid. It now became generally known that the firm were heavily indebted to the Government, and there were rumours that the Government would issue a writ of extent.[5]

The guarantors of the £80,000 loan from the Bank, headed by Schneider, called a meeting at the London Tavern on February 5 to consider their position. Both Boyd and Benfield were present, and Boyd came in for considerable criticism. He was accused of having dissipated Benfield's fortune of £500,000 in speculations undertaken without Benfield's knowledge, and of having induced the Government to advance £150,000 on the strength of a false declaration of Benfield's Indian property. Towards the close of the meeting, after Boyd and Benfield had withdrawn, there were some bitter comments from the guarantors, who felt that when Boyd, Benfield & Co. accepted assistance, they should have disclosed that they had given a bond for £100,000 for the fulfilment of the contract for the remittance to the Cape. Boyd, learning afterwards of what had been said, felt that the criticisms made, although directed at Boyd,

3. Boyd to Hoare, 16 Dec. 1798, State of Facts, Appendix 7.
4. Schneider to Pitt, 1 Jan 1799, Chatham Papers, PRO, 30/8/176.
5. Turnbull, Forbes & Co. to Boyd, Benfield & Co., 5 April 1799, Boyd, op.cit., App. 20.

157

Benfield & co., constituted an attack on his character, to which he had to give some answer. He accordingly prepared 'A State of Facts, and Observations'[6] in which he gave his version of the negotiations of August and December 1797, supported by copies of some of his correspondence with Benfield and others. This, printed in pamphlet form, was circulated by Boyd to the creditors. By accident or design, copies reached the press, and by the middle of February excerpts from the acrimonious correspondence had been published for all the world to read.

Pressed by their creditors, with the threat of an extent of the Crown hanging over them, and at loggerheads with each other, Boyd and Benfield had only one course open – to liquidate. Drummond had withdrawn from the partnership already, having given notice, early in 1798, of retiring at the end of the year.[7] The situation was most involved, not merely on account of the complexity of the firm's own affairs, but also because of their relations with Boyd, Ker et Cie. Furthermore, Boyd and Benfield had claims on each other for large amounts. It was accordingly proposed that the liquidation should take place under the supervision of inspectors appointed by the creditors. There ensued a short struggle between Boyd and Benfield as to who should be liquidator. Much to Boyd's annoyance, Benfield succeeded in persuading the inspectors that he should be appointed the sole liquidator, on the understanding that the settlement of the claims which the partners might have on each other should be postponed until all the creditors were satisfied, and that the matter should then be submitted to arbitration.

Boyd protested vigorously: 'The Person who professes the most complete Ignorance of the Affairs of the House, has been selected for the Liquidation of its Affairs, while to me, who had the chief Direction of the House, is assigned the humble Office of communicating such Information as my Situation naturally enabled me to acquire'.[8] There was point in Boyd's objection, and it is difficult to see why a neutral liquidator was not chosen. On 8 March 1799, almost exactly six years after their formation, Boyd, Benfield & Co. were dissolved, and the liquidation placed in the hands of Benfield.[9]

Early in 1799, trustees of Benfield's property were appointed, Schneider surrendered the power of attorney given him by Benfield, and became trustee jointly with Francis Henry Christin, Thomas Reid and Thomas Smith, with Sir Francis Baring as umpire.[10] During February and March, the trustees met almost daily, to prepare for the Treasury proposals for an orderly liquidation. They were faced with many difficulties. The firm's affairs were extremely involved: Boyd refused to co-operate, or even to give them a list of his separate property. According to Schneider, Boyd had made over his property to Hoare. Benfield, however, alleged that Boyd had refused to assign, and had merely declared that he would apply

6.   Huskisson papers, BL Add. MS 38765, ff. 1–14.
7.   Select Committee on the Tenth Naval Report, Evidence of Drummond, p. 69; *London Gazette*, 5–9 March 1799.
8.   Boyd to John Turnbull, 21 April 1799, Boyd, Letter to the Creditors, op.cit., App. 21.
9.   *London Gazette*, 5–9 March 1799; *The Times*, 11 March 1799.
10.   Benfield, *Case of Paul Benfield*, op.cit., p. 2.

for the benefit of the firm any balance which remained after his personal liabilities had been discharged. In any case, the amount of his property was small.

The inspectors soon had reason to regret their decision to make Benfield sole liquidator, for they met with nothing but resistance and constant disputes. Benfield's English property was estimated to be worth £282,000, after discharging the mortgages of £70,000 on the Hertfordshire estate, and the house in Grosvenor Square,[11] and immediately the trustees were appointed they instructed agents to sell. Benfield, however, put every obstacle in the way; he refused to give the agents any information, directed a continuous stream of protests to the creditors at the 'rash and precipitous proceedings', and tried to convince the Treasury that the delay was due to procrastination on the part of the trustees.

These disputes led to an open break, when he took it upon himself to discharge every clerk employed by the firm, and to take on new clerks who were unfamiliar with the complicated affairs they were expected to liquidate. He also engaged two lawyers, Forster of Lincoln's Inn and Harrison of the Temple, to assist him in the strife which arose between himself, the inspectors and the trustees. Thus reinforced, he called a meeting of creditors, from whom he sought to obtain an extension of his powers. But the creditors had learnt their lesson: so far from giving him what he wanted, they accused him of acting fraudulently, and of concealing assets of the firm. This he strongly denied, although the effectiveness of his protests was somwhat weakened, when, two days after the meeting, he sent to the inspectors bills of exchange amounting to £7,000.[12]

In March 1799, the Treasury took formal steps to protect their claim, and an inquisition was made under Exchequer Commission, the Commission finding that the three partners were indebted to the Crown for £100,000, which had been paid to Boyd, Benfield & Co. in December 1797.[13] Since, however, the debt was amply covered, the creditors asked that the sale of the property should not be forced, and obtained an assurance from Pitt, confirmed by the Treasury, that if the trustees undertook that repayment of the debt would have priority, he would allow them reasonable time.[14]

Still refusing to admit defeat, Boyd made what was to be his final attempt to retain his position as a loan contractor. Early in June 1799, Pitt invited bids for a £15,500,000 loan, and the preliminary meeting disclosed that six groups were prepared to bid. Among these was a group represented by Stirling of the banking firm of Hodsoll, Stirling and Co., John William Anderson, of the merchant house of Anderson and Co., and Agnew, of Walwyn, Strange, Dashwood and Co., the Bond Street bankers. In submitting their list, the group explained that 'they wished to bid on Mr. Boyd's behalf as well as on their own.' This move could hardly

11. Baring to Long, 23 March 1799, Treasury In-Letters, PRO, T. 1/818/999.
12. Baring to Long 28 March 1800 (Printed) Chatham Papers, PRO, 30/8/111.
13. Writ of non omittas copias ad satisfaciendum and extent, 23 Jan. 1800, PRO, E. 144/40.
14. Turnbull, Forbes and Co. to Boyd, Benfield and Co., 5 April 1799, Boyd op.cit., Appendix 20; Long to Baring and others, 30 March 1799, Treasury Out-Letters-General, PRO, T. 27/50, p. 371.

have come as a surprise, since, a short while before, Boyd had sent a circular letter to those on his list, informing them that Walwyn, Strange, Dashwood and Co's bidding 'was to be considered as a continuation of his lists for the Loan.' Boyd had two links with this group. One was with Anderson, who had been a member of his Committee of Merchants in April 1796, and the other was with one of the partners of Walwyn, Strange, Dashwood and Co., James Charles Stuart Strange, who was Dundas' son-in-law. Pitt consulted Samuel Thornton, the Governor of the Bank, and Job Mathew, the Deputy Governor. Both said that Boyd, Benfield and Co. were insolvent, and that the addition of Hodsoll, Stirling and Co, and Anderson and Co, 'did not give sufficient solidarity to the list'.[15]

On the day of the bidding, June 5, the representatives of all six groups met in the Chancellor's house in Downing Street. Before the proceedings started, Pitt called Stirling, Anderson and Agnew into an adjoining room, and explained tactfully that 'in their list there was a difficulty which they would easily comprehend, which to him was insurmountable. He was bound in an affair of such interest to the public, and of such delicacy, to consult persons whose situation gave them the best means of informtion and without the remotest disrespect to the gentlemen present, he submitted to them the feeling that pressed on him mind about their entering into the compeition with a list so formed.' In the long discussion which followed, Pitt made it clear that the decision was not directed against them. 'Nothing would give him more pleasure than to see them on future occasions at the head of lists.'[16] Although Pitt spoke guardedly, his meaning was clear. The name of Boyd, whose house a few years before had had 'a lease of the money market', was no longer acceptable. After that, said Samuel Thornton, '. . . no mercantile house would have given them credit to any extent.'[17]

Now, it was just a matter of time. In December 1799, the creditors met, and passed a resolution requiring the partners to submit sworn statements of their separate property. Boyd made two affidavits. In the first, he declared his personal property at £9,441, most of this amount being accounted for by his house in Putney Lane, Putney, which was subject to a charge of £5,067. His personal debts were £3,940, so that his net personal assets amounted to only £434.[18] In the second affidavit, Boyd declared that the only acting partners in Boyd, Ker et Cie were himself, Ker and Boyd, Junior, and that the only commandite partners were Walckiers and Laborde. Boyd also declared that Boyd, Ker et Cie were interested under his name in Boyd, Benfield and Co. This latest statement did not suit Boyd, Junior, who had no desire to see amounts recovered by Boyd, Ker et Cie distributed to Boyd, Benfield and Co's creditors. He accordingly replied by a declaration on oath, denying that the Paris house was interested in the London house.[19] These controversies were of no great

---

15. Select Committee on the Tenth Naval Report, Evidence of Samuel Thornton. p. 5. and p. 60.
16. *Morning Chronicle*, 6 June 1799.
17. Select Committee on the Tenth Naval Report, p. 61.
18. Boyd, op.cit. p. 16.
19. Benfield, op.cit. p. 1.

interest to the secured creditors, and the Treasury decided that enforcement of the claim of the Crown ought not to be further postponed. On January 23 a writ of extent was issued by the Crown, under which the sheriffs were to seize the property which had been owned by the partners on 4 December 1798.[20]

In March 1800 came the long-expected announcement that a commission of bankruptcy had been awarded against Walter Boyd, Paul Benfield and James Drummond, who were required to appear before the Commissioners at Guildhall.[21] The news attracted little comment in the press, for the firm's position had been generally known for some time, and the partners' bankuptcy would not have serious repercussions in the market, as it might have done two or three years earlier. The prevailing opinion (which proved to be erroneous) was that Benfield's Indian assets would cover the deficiency.[22] Under the commission of bankuptcy, Thomas Reid, George Ward and William Mainwaring were named as assignees, to whom the partners assigned all their real property.

The usual steps were taken to block the firm's assets, and orders to this effect were issued to the East India Company[23] and the Bank of England. In fact, the firm's drawing account at the Bank showed a credit balance of only £28, and it had not been operated since October 1798. The account had been opened in January 1794, and showed a turnover in the first year of £1,488,000. In 1795, owing largely to the payment in and out of approximately £4,000,000 on account of the Imperial Loan, the turnover was £9,207,000. The following year saw a sharp fall to £427,000; there was a recovery to £839,000 in 1797, but a further fall to £392,000 in 1798. The balances maintained declined correspondingly: whereas in the early years they were in thousands, in 1797 they were in hundreds.[24] The rise and fall of the firm's fortunes could not have been illustrated better.

The bankruptcy proceedings precipitated a pamphlet war between Boyd and Benfield. On 7 April 1800, Benfield sent a circular letter to the creditors, giving his version of events. He said that he had no knowledge of the firm's losses in the spring of 1796, nor of the disorder in the firm's books, and he complained that he had been obliged to provide funds and mortgage his property for the firm's benefit. Boyd's rejoinder came in a letter to Sir Francis Baring, in which he denied that Benfield had been ignorant of the firm's losses, and accused Benfield of drawing out more than he had put in. He did not deny the 'disorder in the firm's books', for which he could hardly escape responsibility. Benfield then sent another letter to the creditors, dated April 26, stating that while he had put close to £400,000 into the firm, over £300,000 had been advanced to 'certain persons', meaning the other partners and associates of the two firms. He asserted that the bona fide creditors were comparatively few, and their demands comparatively trifling, and demanded that a new commission be

20. Writ . . . of extent, 23 Jan. 1800, PRO, E. 144/40. The date of 4 December 1798 was exactly one year after the issue of the warrant for £100,000 by the Treasury.
21. *London Gazette*, 22–25 March 1800. They appeared at Guildhall on 1 and 8 April and 6 May.
22. See, for example, *Glasgow Courier*, 29 March 1800.
23. East India Company Court Minute Book, 18 April 1800.
24. Bank of England Drawing Account.

appointed with wider powers. Boyd's reply, in the form of a letter to the creditors dated May 5, constituted a detailed, and on the whole convincing refutation of Benfield's accusations.[25] The Letter in printed form covered twenty-three pages, in addition to which there were twenty-three appendices, consisting of accounts, memoranda and letters bearing on the matters in dispute.

Boyd's final examination before the bankruptcy Commissioners came on 24 June 1800 at Guildhall, where, in accordance with the usual practice, he laid on the table his and his wife's personal effects: two gold watches, a picture snuffbox, a box of trinkets (his wife's) and £51.2s. 0d. in money, all of which were returned to him.[26] In September Drummond was granted a discharge, and Boyd one two months later[27], Benfield, the only partner with any appreciable assets, remaining undischarged.

Proceedings under the Crown's extent were more protracted. Varous inquisitions were held and a schedule of what purported to be the assets of the firm was prepared.[28] It totalled over £7,300,000 and was little more than a list of debit balances in the firm's books, which, in any case, had not been kept up to date. Taking it at its face value, it revealed a deplorable situation. Eliminating purely nominal accounts, debtors and other assets amounted to £1,333,000. Nearly one half of this sum was due by the partners and their associates. Boyd was shown as owing £294,000 and Drummond £22,000. Boyd, Ket et Cie owed £110,000 and Boyd, Junior, Ker, de Kessel and Laborde a total of nearly £89,000. Benfield's accounts showed a net amount due to him of £47,000.

The greater part of the other assets of the firm, totalling £711,000, was accounted for by domestic advances of £553,000. Charles Herries & Co., bankrupt in 1798, owed £188,000; Alexander Houston & Co., £148,000 (which was eventually repaid in full) and E.P. Salomons, nearly £17,000. There were also advances to Count Starhemberg of £19,000 and to Viscount de Sandrouin of £9,000, which help to explain the close collaboration between the Austrian representatives and the Imperial agents during the loan negotiations. Of debts due from abroad at least two were unrealisable: Walckiers, who had failed in 1796, owed nearly £66,000, and Veuve Nettine et Fils, £33,000. The schedule showed little in the way of readily realisable assets, a situation which should not have surprised anyone. The jury appointed to inquire into the position were not greatly helped by the schedule, and they could produce only a somewhat inconclusive report.

For nearly a year, Benfield tried hard to persuade the Treasury to have recourse to the partnership assets before selling his own property. The Treasury, however, had no intention of becoming involved in the complications of Boyd, Benfield and Co's liquidation when their debt could be recovered in full by a straightforward sale of property, charged to them for

25. Boyd to Sir Francis Baring, 12 April 1800, Baring Archives; Letter to the Creditors of the House of Boyd, Benfield and Co., from Walter Boyd, Esq., 5 May 1800. Benfield's letters have not been found, and the above summary of their contents has been based on quotations from them in Boyd's replies.
26. Session Papers, 16 Nov. 1802, vol. 662/7, p. 4, Signet Library.
27. *London Gazette*, 16–20 Sept. 25–29 Nov. 1800.
28. Inquisition, 15 Aug. 1800, Schedule A, PRO, E 144/40. Amounts have been rounded to the nearest thousand.

this very purpose. Accordingly, in June 1801, the Woodhall estates were sold, realising over £180,000, and the Shaftsbury property, owned jointly with William Bryant, was sold for £35,000 and half the arrears of rent.[29] Even then Benfield repeatedly pressed the Treasury to appoint an inspector, feeling that Boyd might want to conceal certain assets, or delay their realisation. The Treasury, however, paid little attention to these pleas, and, in any case, political developments were soon to change the entire course of the affair.

29. Mainwaring and Reid to Treasury, 23 June 1801, Treasury In-Letters, PRO, T1/884.

CHAPTER XIV

Recovery

'. . . there is nothing which could afford me so much real pleasure as to see *all* my Creditors completely satisfied. I *know* and *have* always known that there is more than enough to pay every just demand'.
Boyd to Huskisson, 23 November, 1801.

In March 1801 Pitt resigned, and an administration was formed by Addington. Lord Hawkesbury,[1] the new foreign secretary, lost no time in bringing the war to an end, and on March 21, Otto, the French agent in London for the exchange of prisoners, was informed that the British Government was disposed to enter into peace negotiations. For the creditors of Boyd, Benfield and Co., as well as for the partners, this had special significance. Once it became possible to recover the assets of Boyd, Ker et Cie, estimated by Boyd to be worth £600,000,[2] the whole situation assumed a different complexion. No news of the progress of negotiations was made public for several months, and Boyd found the waiting period very trying. 'My mind', he wrote in June 1801, 'is sinking fast under my present life of inactivity, and the galling sense of being engaged in no pursuit by which my numerous family may be supported & properly introduced into life.'[3]

His financial embarrassments weighed heavily upon him. He had given up his town house in Sackville Street, and was now living in Bury Street, St. James's. He hoped to be able to live in his old house in Putney, the lease of which had been bought for him by the West-end bankers, Adey, McGeorge and Co., but interest on the purchase-money and taxes were so heavy that he doubted whether this would be possible. Ever since his bankruptcy, he had been entirely dependent upon the kindness of friends. In February 1801, the houses which had formerly been associated with him in contracting for loans took the £28,000,000 loan for 1801, and gave him a share in it, which yielded a profit of between £4,000 and £5,000, enabling

---

1. Henry Addington (1757–1844) was Chancellor of the Exchequer and First Lord of the Treasury from March 1801 to April 1804; Robert Banks Jenkinson (1770–1828) who had the courtesy title of Lord Hawkesbury from 1796, was Foreign Secretary from March 1801 to May 1804.
2. Benfield, Circular to the Creditors of the late House of Boyd, Benfield & Co. Paris, 4 April 1803, p. 1, Huskisson Papers, BL. Add. MS 38236, ff. 254–5.
3. Boyd to Huskisson, 30 June 1801, Huskisson Papers, BL. Add. MS 38736, f. 317.

him to repay debts he had incurred to maintain himself and his family. Much as he appreciated it, their assistance made him realise the extent of his fall. He wrote somewhat pathetically to Huskisson. 'I think it has made me more sensible than I was before of the dreadful reverse I have sustained and the cruelty of being literally without any revenue whatsoever.'[4]

It was characteristic that, even with all his financial worries, Boyd was able to bend his mind to writing and publishing in 1801 a 112-page pamphlet on currency matters. Entitled *A Letter to the Right Honourable William Pitt on the Influences of the Stoppage of Issues in Specie at the Bank of England. . . .,* it attracted attention immediately with the simple theme, forcefully presented, that the rise in prices was due to an excessive issue of Bank notes following the suspension of cash payments by the Bank. The arguments were oversimplified, but they played a useful part in the development of monetary theory during the period.

Soon after the signature of the peace preliminaries in London on October 1, holders of French securities met at the London Tavern to consider what should be done to recover what was due to them. A committee was formed, including Boyd, and a meeting with Lord Hawkesbury took place in November. At the meeting Hawkesbury asked the committee to submit to him proposals for the liquidation of the claims of security holders 'on such moderate principles as might be reconcilable to the arrangements which have been made in France with the creditors residing in that country, without altogether putting outselves on the same footing with them.'[5]

In the following month, negotiations for a definitive treaty were opened in Amiens between the French representative, Joseph Bonaparte, and Lord Cornwallis.[6] Article twelve of the preliminaries had provided that all sequestration of property should cease on the signature of a definitive treaty, and that claims of both countries should be submitted to competent tribunals. Within a week or so, however, the French representatives were proposing that English claimants should not receive better treatment than French. News of this move became known in the City early in December. British holders of rentes had no intention of allowing their case to go by default, and immediately despatched Walter Boyd, Junior, to Amiens, armed with memorials for Cornwallis, urging that provision for the payment of British claims in full should be made in the definitive treaty.[7] Fortunately for the British claimants, Cornwallis would have nothing to do with the French proposals. He pointed out that the British Government had not touched the funds or property of French citizens, whereas the French Government had seized everything owned by British subjects, and had made only nominal repayments. Whatever the law applicable to French citizens, said Cornwallis, France could not apply an unjust law to foreigners. The French amendment was accordingly withdrawn, and the

4. Idem.
5. Boyd to Huskisson, 23 Nov. 1801, Huskisson Papers, Supplement, Vol. 1, BL., Add. MS 39948, f. 15.
6. Charles Cornwallis, 1st Marquis and 2nd Earl Cornwallis (1738–1805).
7. *The Times*, 9 Dec. 1801.

definitive treaty, signed at Amiens on 27 March 1802, repeated the provision of the preliminaries with regard to the settlement of claims.[8]

Progress towards a settlement, however, was slow, and by the middle of the year little had been done. Boyd was still without any income, and was relying on the assistance of Huskisson, Anderson and other friends. He had decided to sell the lease of his Putney house, which, after repaying the mortgage on it, would give him enough to pay his current debts. He was anxious to get to Paris, in order to see what could be recovered of Boyd, Ker et Cie's property, but lack of funds delayed him,[9] and it was not until later in the year that he crossed the Channel.

Benfield, too, went abroad towards the end of 1802, but for different reasons. Pursued by his creditors, and feeling that as long as he remained in England, he was in danger of being imprisoned for debt, he fled to France, where at least he had some property which had not been attached by his creditors – his holdings of life annuities, which he had bought through Boyd, Ker et Cie in 1793. He soon discovered that Ker and Boyd, Junior, were also in Paris, and that they had filed a claim for the books, securities and money of Boyd, Ker et Cie, and had claimed possession of 9 rue de Grammont. It appeared to Benfield, that the advances made by Boyd, Benfield and Co. to the Paris firm and their partners had been the chief cause of his ruin, and he was determined that anything recovered from them, should go to Boyd, Benfield and Co. He had therefore lodged a formal objection to the release of the Paris firm's property, until his personal debts, and those of the London firm, had been settled, and this objection had been upheld. But if Boyd could not get anything, neither could Benfield.

This was the situation when Boyd, through his legal adviser in Paris, Perrignon, indicated to Benfield his desire for an amicable arrangement. A meeting was accordingly arranged at which Boyd and Perrignon on the one hand, and Wild, representing Benfield, and his lawyers, Jaubert and Armey, on the other, were present. But the rift between the two was now so great that reconciliation was impossible, and, according to Benfield, the only result of the meeting was a declaration by Boyd that he would never enter into any arrangement. Thereupon, Benfield set out his case in two printed circulars, addressed to the creditors, one in January and the other in April 1803.[10] The decision to block Boyd, Ker et Cie's assets left Boyd with no alternative but to appeal, which he did early in 1803. For the appeal, he had to submit extracts from Boyd, Benfield and Co's books, which he was able to obtain only after repeated requests throughout most of 1803. In December, however, the Appeals Tribunal ruled in his favour,[11] and much relieved, Boyd was able to turn his mind to the recovery of Boyd, Ker et Cie's assets.

Meantime, however, war between France and England had broken out again. Relations had become increasingly bad from August 1802, and

8. Christopher Guillaume Koch and F. Scholl, *Histoire Abeégée des Traités de Paix* . . ., Paris, Gide Fils, 1817, vol. 6, p. 131, vol. 10, p. 520.
9. Boyd to Huskisson, 10 June 1802, Huskisson Papers, BL. Add. MS. 38737, f. 5.
10. Benfield, Case of Paul Benfield. . ., 1803,; Benfield Circular to the Creditors . . . 1803, op.cit., p. 2.
11. Boyd to Labouchère, 1 Dec. 1803, Hope Archives.

agreement on certain provisions of the Treaty of Amiens could not be reached. On 26 April 1803, Whitworth, British Ambassador in Paris, delivered an ultimatum, and within a month the two countries were again at war. In common with other British subjects in France, Boyd, Benfield, and Boyd, Junior, were interned as hostages. They were not harshly treated, and enjoyed valuable privileges. Nevertheless, the lack of real freedom, the absence of useful occupation, the separation from relations and friends in Britain, and for many, financial distress, made their lot unenviable.[12]

Boyd, too, was short of money, but he was fortunate in having friends who could help. John Williams Hope and Pierre César Labouchère, both of whom he had known before the Revolution, were now re-established in Amsterdam, as Hope and Co., and constituted a channel through which Boyd could correspond with friends in England and receive financial assistance. In Scotland, Sir William Erskine raised a fund for him, to which Sir Walter Scott, among others, subscribed. Huskisson, too, gave generously.[13] Through Hope and Co., funds could be remitted from England to France without much difficulty. The amounts were small, usually only £100 or £200 at a time, but Boyd greatly appreciated them. In November 1803, came through this channel the welcome news that a Mrs Greene of Norwich, presumably a relative, had left his wife a legacy of £1,000. 'Nothing as pleasant as this had happened to us for years', he wrote to Labouchère.[14] One great consolation was his happiness with his wife. 'Her love for her children and her attachment to me', he wrote, 'has given her always so to say supernatural strength, which has sustained us all!'[15] Almost as difficult to bear as the lack of money, was the lack of occupation. At least as early as 1802, when the Sinking Fund bill was under discussion, Boyd had been interested in the redemption of the national debt. In 1804, as much to occupy his mind as for any other reason, he wrote a paper to prove that Britain's national debt was much nearer its final extinction than it was in 1786.[16]

In 1805, reports of the proceedings against Henry Dundas, now Lord Melville, reached Boyd through newspapers and correspondence. The tenth report of the newly-appointed Commissioners of Naval Enquiry, had revealed that Alexander Trotter, Paymaster of the Navy, had speculated with public money. The matter was investigated by the Select Committee on the Tenth Naval Report, whose report set out the full story of the advance of £40,000 made to Boyd, Benfield & Co. in 1796.[17] Melville had been Treasurer of the Navy at the time, and could not escape responsibility. In Parliament the report gave the opposition plenty of ammunition for attacking Pitt and Melville, but after a bitter debate, a resolution was

12. For a general account of conditions, see John G. Alger, *Englishmen in the French Revolution*, Sampson, Low & Co., London, 1889; John G. Alger, *Napoleon's British Visitors and Captives*, 1801–1815, A. Constable & Co., Westminster, 1904.
13. *Journal of Sir Walter Scott*, ed. John G. Tait, London, Oliver & Boyd, 1950, p. 528.
14. Boyd to Labouchère, 7 Nov. 1803, Hope Archives.
15. Boyd to Labouchère, 19 Sept. 1803., Hope Archives.
16. Boyd to Jn Hooke Greene, 12 Aug. 1805, Huskisson Papers, BL Add MS 38737 f. 95. The paper has not been found.
17. *Cobbett's Parliamentary Debates*, vol. 5, Appendix, cols. I–CXXXI.

carried to the effect that the transaction, 'although not conformable to law, appeared at the time to be called for by the peculiar exingencies of public affairs', and an Act was passed (45 Geo. III, c. 78), indemnifying all those concerned. Boyd resented particularly the attack on Melville. 'I persist in my opinion', he wrote to his brother-in-law, J.H. Greene, 'that Lord Melville is the worst used man that ever existed. I hope he will still live to triumph over all those dirty fellows who have been plotting his ruin'.[18] Boyd's hope was fulfilled. A motion of impeachment in the following year ended in Melville's acquittal.[19]

In the same year, 1805, an opportunity came for Boyd to participate once more in international negotiations. A year earlier, Gabriel Julien Ouvrard, the French contractor, financier and speculator, embarked on a series of complicated financial operations to facilitate the payment of the subsidies which Spain was obliged to make to France. For this purpose, Ouvrard undertook to arrange a ten-million guilder loan for Spain, which would be sold by Hope & Co. in Amsterdam. Ouvrard considered that Boyd, in Paris, would be useful as an intermediary. It was a role very different from the one he was accustomed to play, but he accepted it, perhaps because he felt he needed some occupation, perhaps because it brought in a little income.

It was not altogether easy. On several important points he found himself supporting views of the Spanish government or of Ouvrard which proved unacceptable to Labouchère. He proposed at one point that the bonds should be made out in the names of a Dutch firm, Van de Hoeven, and Ouvrard, whereas Labouchère had to insist on their being in the name of Hope & Co. On a question of the issue-price of the bonds, he took the side of the Spanish government, when he should have realised that the last word rested with Hope & Co. On another occasion, at a time when money in Paris was tight, he wrote to Hope & Co. suggesting the payment of one million guilders in advance of the delivery of the royal warrants in Amsterdam. Labouchère, understandably, was not prepared to advance any money until complete agreement with the Spanish government had been reached and the warrants delivered. Altogether, his re-entry into the world of international finance, limited as it was, was not an unqualified success.[20]

The years went by. Benfield died in Paris in the spring of 1810, so poor that his funeral had to be paid for by English residents in Paris.[21] Boyd's hostility to his former partner, whom he had once addressed as 'My dearest Friend', was apparently maintained to the end. His feelings towards Mrs Benfield, however, were anything but hostile. He had, it seems, been on friendly terms with her for some years. In 1797, a letter to her complaining about her husband's attitude to the firm, closed with the words 'I am in all vicissitudes of fortune . . . Most affectionately your's, Walter Boyd'.[22] Now, thirteen years later, his affections were apparently

18. Boyd to Green, 12 Aug. 1805, Huskisson Papers, BL Add MS 38737 f. 96.
19. Holden Furber, *Henry Dundas, First Viscount Melville, 1742–1811*, London, Oxford University Press, 1931, pp. 148–172.
20. For these negotiations, see Buist, op.cit., chapter 10.
21. Wraxall, op.cit., vol. IV, p. 94.
22. Boyd to Mary Frances Benfield, 9 Sept 1797, Baring Archives.

unchanged, for he was writing to Huskisson at the end of 1810: 'Mrs Benfield is a person for whom I have a most sincere respect and the most unbounded devotion and friendship'.[23] He was still fretting at the enforced inactivity of his life, all the more difficult to bear, because of the discussions then going on in England on the report of the Committee on the High Price of Bullion. Situated as he was, there was little that he could contribute: all that was possible was to arrange for the republication of his *Letter to the Rt. Hon. Wm. Pitt,* which he had first published in 1801.

At this time, he had high hopes of being released. In April 1810 a British commissioner, Colin Alexander Mackenzie, arrived in Morlaix with the object of concluding a convention for the exchange of prisoners, and, after prolonged negotiations, it was agreed in principle that hostages interned in 1803, as well as prisoners of war, were to be exchanged. At the last moment, however, negotiations broke down.[24] He was still dependent for the support and education of his family on the 'bounty and generous confidence of a few old and faithful friends'.[25] Huskisson and Melville and his son, Robert Dundas, busied themselves to find a post for Boyd's only surviving son, Robert, now fourteen years old.[26] Boyd hoped that he could obtain permission to send Robert to England. The first attempt failed, but the second was successful, and in March 1811, Boyd was able to send his wife and son to England, his wife returning to France two months later.[27]

In the summer of 1812, Napoleon was carrying all before him in Russia, and an allied victory seemed remote. To Boyd, then in the tenth year of his detention, and living in straitened circumstances, the outlook was depressing. He found some relief in drawing up a plan for modifying the sinking fund. As might be expected, the pamphlet reveals him as a staunch supporter of the principle of a sinking fund, but concerned that its cumulative effect would place too heavy a burden on the budget. He accordingly proposed a reduction in the annual sinking fund contributions. The war prevented his sending his plan to England at that time, and it was published only after his return.[28]

In March 1814, the victorious Allies entered Paris, and on May 30, the first Peace of Paris was signed. The treaty of commerce of 1786 between Great Britain and France had provided that in the event of war, the subjects of each, resident in the territory of the other, should be allowed to stay during peaceable behaviour, and that if their removal was deemed necessary, they should be allowed twelve months in which to remove their property. In spite of this, as has been seen, the French had arrested British subjects and sequestrated their property. Under the Peace of Paris it was agreed that sequestration of property should cease, and that damages should be paid on award by a joint commission.

Boyd was back in London before the end of 1814, and turned immed-

23. Boyd to Huskisson, 29 Dec. 1810, Huskisson Papers, BL. Add MS 38738, f. 48.
24. Alger, *Englishmen in the French Revolution* op.cit., pp. 272–3.
25. Boyd to Huskisson, 1 Feb., 1810, Huskisson Papers, BL. Add. MS 38738, f. 14.
26. Boyd had at least three sons living in 1796, but all but one, Robert, died before 1810. Benfield to Boyd, 25 Sept. 1796; Boyd, op.cit., Appendix 7.
27. Boyd to Huskisson, 29 Dec. 1810, 20 March 1811 and 14 June 1811, Huskisson Papers, BL Add. MS 38738.
28. Walter Boyd, *Reflections on the Financial System of Great Britain and particularly on the Sinking Fund* . . . J. Hatchard, London, 1815.

iately, despite broken health, to the daunting task of preparing claims on the French Government. He was still without means, so that although he had gained his freedom, and could look forward to recovering his property in France, his financial position was now worse than it was during his internment. Advances made by personal friends had ceased, and despite all the care exercised by his wife and Boyd, Junior, their outgoings were heavy. The records of Boyd, Ker et Cie, having been released in August, premises were rented and clerks engaged to deal with the work involved in preparing and presenting claims.[29] 'The expenses of our liquidation are necessarily considerable. . . .', he wrote to Huskisson at the end of 1814, 'and if no settlement takes place soon of any of our claims, we shall find ourselves shipwrecked in the harbour.'[30] He continued: 'Do you think there is no way whatever by which some assistance might be procured to me from Government not a *Gift* for that I have no title to but merely an advance which might be reclaimed out of, or at least reimbursed from the first payment made to us by the French Government? . . .'[31] On Huskisson's advice, he applied to the Commissioners,[32] but, not surprisingly, they were unable to help.[33]

To add to Boyd's embarrassments, some of his French creditors, imagining that his claims had been liquidated, commenced legal proceedings against him, and obtained writs for considerable sums. Boyd, Ker et Cie, accordingly appealed to the Board for their protection early in December. It was not in British interests that French creditors should get priority in this way, and the Board readily agreed to give Boyd, Ker et Cie. the protection they required.[34]

There was much detailed work to be done. Claims had to be supported by documents, a matter of no little difficulty, considering that the transactions on which they were based had taken place nearly twenty-five years previously. Some of those whose evidence would have been useful had died. Geneste had fallen a victim to the Revolution in 1794: François Laborde had died in exile in London in 1802; and Benfield was dead. By October 1817, Boyd had lodged thirty-five claims, of which twenty-four were for Boyd, Ker et Cie, four for the assignees of Benfield, one for Boyd, Junior, and six for himself.[35] The Commissioners dealt with claims fairly promptly, for by the middle of 1816, the first payments in rentes were being received.

Boyd, however, was not yet out of his difficulties, for certain creditors endeavoured to attach the rentes, as they were transferred to him by the Commissioners. The Foreign Secretary, Lord Castlereagh, to whom Boyd appealed for protection, submitted the case to legal officers of the Crown. The lawyers replied cautiously that they thought it was reasonable that

29. Commissioners for French Claims Minute Book, 19 Jan. 1815, PRO, T. 78/267, p. 797; Bouchary, op.cit., vol.II. p. 138–39.
30. This metaphor recurs in Boyd's letters.
31. Boyd to Huskisson, 16 Dec. 1814, Huskisson Papers, BL. Add. MS 38739, f. 316.
32. Boyd to Huskisson 28 Dec. 1814, Huskisson Papers, BL. Add. MS 38739, f. 325.
33. Commissioners for French Claims Minute Book, 19 Jan. 1815, PRO, T. 78/267, p. 797.
34. Commissioners for French Claims Minute Book, 5 Dec. 1814, PRO, T. 78/267. p. 677.
35. Lists of British Claims, PRO, T. 78/268.

some 'collateral expedient' should be resorted to, if the fulfilment of the treaty resulted in the just claims of the creditors being defeated. Boyd's answer was that to deny the creditors the right to attach rentes would not enable him to defeat the just claims of the creditors. 'It would only prevent rapacious and ungenerous creditors from being paid sooner than others of a different description.' The attachments were soon taken off.[36]

By the autumn of 1821, the rentes received by Boyd on behalf of the assignees of Boyd, Benfield & Co. had been sufficient to pay in full all the debts proved against the partners, and leave a surplus. This amounted to no less than £53,329, of which £20,264 arose from Benfield's separate estate and £33,065 from the joint estate of Boyd and Benfield. Most of this was earmarked to meet interest and certain claims made by the trustees of Anthony Gileducki and Houston & Co. Drummond had formally declared that he was not entitled to any share in the partnership assets, since he had retired from the firm as from 31 December 1798. Boyd and Mrs Benfield and her children accordingly entered into a number of deeds, dividing up the remaining partnership property. Shortly afterwards a renewed commission of bankruptcy was issued against Boyd, Benfield and Drummond, and the firm's affairs finally wound up.[37]

Certain claims, which had been rejected by the Commissioners, were still outstanding, and Boyd had appealed to the Privy Council, which had not yet given a decision. There was, however, little point in delaying further the winding up of Boyd, Ker et Cie. Walter Boyd, Junior, had died in Paris on 20 January 1820, and Ker, now sixty-five, wished to retire. He accordingly transferred to Boyd his share of the firm, and authorised him to liquidate their affairs. Boyd, Ker et Cie were accordingly dissolved as from 31 August, 1822.

The creditors of Boyd, Benfield & Co. had had their claims met in full, and they had every reason to be satisfied. Sir Walter Scott, not always the most reliable of reporters, gives in his Journal a highly coloured account of what happened. Boyd, accordingly to Scott, told the creditors 'that he was pennyless unless they consented to allow him a moderate sum in name of percentage'. Scott then records that 'a muck worm was base enough to refuse', but was 'over powered', and that £40,000 to £50,000 was given to Boyd as an ex gratia allowance for his labours over seven years.[38] Certain it is that they made him an allowance, and it is probable that it was close to £50,000. About £33,000 of it he invested in £40,000 three per cent. Consols in April 1823.[39] At a cost of £17,000, he bought Plaistow Lodge, a handsome house built by the merchant banker, Peter Thellusson, in 1780, standing in extensive grounds near Bromley, Kent. He was able to maintain the estate in good order, and he entertained lavishly. In the servants' quarters, he kept open house to tradesmen and others, and it was not

36. Boyd to Huskisson, 8 July, 1816, Huskisson Papers, BL. Add. MS 38741, f. 85.
37. Claims on France, PRO, T. 78/5, award 56.
38. *Journal of Sir Walter Scott*, ed. John G. Tait, Edinburgh, Oliver and Boyd, 1950 pp. 528–9.
39. Bank of England, Stock Ledgers.

uncommon, so it was said, to hear three or four violins being played of an evening.[40]

In April 1823, he re-entered Parliament as member for the ancient borough of Lymington, whose eighty or so constituents he represented until 1830. No trace has been found of his activities as a legislator, and none of his speeches is recorded in the official reports. Sir Walter Scott dined with him in April 1828, and recorded his impressions: 'He is good lookin(g), but old and infirm. Bright dark eyes and eyebrows contrast with his snowy hair, and all his features mark vigour of principle and resolution'.[41]

Vigour of principle and resolution Boyd still had, and even at the age of seventy-five, he had not lost his interest in financial questions. In the same year in which he dined with Scott, he discovered that Lord Grenville, now sixty-nine and retired from public life, had published a pamphlet making the point that the advantages of a sinking fund were illusory if it were not covered by a revenue surplus. This was too much for Boyd, who immediately published a sixteen-page rejoinder: *Observations on Lord Grenville's Essay*. Boyd admitted that in time of war, there would be new borrowings in excess of the amount of debt redeemed by the sinking fund, but believed that, even in these circumstances, sinking fund clauses in loan contracts should be observed in order to keep faith with investors.[42] He had a valid point.

His refusal to accept the rejection by the Commissioners of certain of his claims was justified, for the Privy Council ruled on several of them in his favour. On two major claims, one on the Duché de Valois and the other on the Duché de Luxembourg, he was awarded nearly one million francs[43] (£39,000); and although legal costs were no doubt heavy, he must have regarded the result with some satisfaction. By the time he came to make what was to be his last will, his assets were considerably more than the amount he had been allowed by his creditors. His wife died on 10 January 1833, aged seventy two[44] and, a few weeks later, he made a will, appointing as his executors Alexander Baring, Pierre César Labouchère, William Key, Robert Dundas Boyd (a nephew), and Edward Richardson, his lawyer. Three years later he made a codicil. He left his son, Robert, a life interest in his real property, with reversion to his (Robert's) sons. To each of his four daughters, he left the income on £14,000, which was to pass on their deaths to their respective husbands, with reversions to their children. An eminently sensible arrangement for a family man.[45]

He died at Plaistow Lodge on 16 September, 1837, aged eighty-three, and was buried, with his wife, in the catacombs of Bromley Parish Church.[46] The grant of probate indicated that his net personalty within the

40.   E.L.S. Horsburgh, *Bromley, Kent, from the Earliest Times to the Present Century*, [London] Hodder & Stoughton, 1929, pp. 181–3. The house is now used as a school.
41.   Scott, idem.
42.   *On the supposed Advantages of a Sinking Fund*, London T. Bensley, 1828; Walter Boyd, *Observations on Lord Grenville's Essay on the Sinking Fund*, London, John Hatchard and Son, 1828.
43.   PRO, Privy Council Register, Jan. 1823–June 1824.
44.   Holworthy, op.cit., p. 16.
45.   PRO, Prob. 11 1884, will dated 21 Feb. 1833 and codicil dated 6 Oct. 1836.
46.   The church was almost totally destroyed in an air raid in April 1941.

ecclesiastical province of Canterbury was £180,000[47], to which has to be added the value of Plaistow Lodge and assets in other jurisdictions. The total of his estate must have been more than £200,000. Considering that twenty-five years earlier he had been dependent on the charity of friends, this represented a remarkable recovery, and a happy ending to a chequered life.

47. PRO, Probate Register, Oct. 1837.

CHAPTER XV

Retrospect

'and who was this Boyd? He was doubtless a man of great talent and enterprise; perhaps an honest man; of powerful imagination, great vigour of mind and body, plausible in conversation, skilful in drawing up a project, and perpetually teeming with financial schemes'.

Samuel Whitbread in the House of Commons, 14 June 1805.

Boyd's dramatic career in international finance began in Brussels, with a brief association with Veuve Nettine et Fils, bankers to the Emperor of Austria. Brussels soon proved to be only a jumping-off ground for the larger and more developed financial markets of Paris. There, within only a few years, he built up an active and apparently prosperous banking business. Too few records have been preserved to make possible a full description and balanced appraisal of his activities in this period. That he showed initiative and technical ability is apparent from his operations in securities, foreign exchange and bullion.

The verdict on his judgement on more basic issues is less clear. With hindsight, it is only too easy to fault him for his apparent blindness to the political trends in France after 1789. Few people, however, then saw how the Revolution would develop, and in this respect Boyd was no worse, and no better, than most of his contemporaries. As events turned out, he was right in holding on to the Paris business as long as he could, for in the end it proved to be his salvation. If, in 1789, he had foreseen coming events and liquidated Boyd, Ker et Cie, or sold out, and brought the proceeds to England, they might well have been swallowed up in the bankruptcy of the London firm a decade later.

In 1793 he joined with Paul Benfield, a nabob of dubious reputation, to form a merchant banking firm in London. He might have preferred to have as partner an experienced banker who knew the London market and had a good reputation in it, and who would bring in the capital required. Perhaps he tried, and failed, to find someone with these qualifications. In the end, the need for capital overrode all other considerations. The result was that the business, based on Benfield's capital and reputed wealth, was run by Boyd virtually single-handed, and the outcome might have been different had he had a partner who could have participated in the firm's major decisions, and exercised a restraining influence.

That Boyd had business ability is clear. His evidence before the Lords and Commons Committees of Secrecy in 1797, his correspondence, and his many financial schemes, all bear the mark of a man who was master of his trade. He could set out a closely-reasoned argument; he wrote in a forceful and compelling style, in French as well as in English. In discussions and negotiations, he displayed great skill, whether it was a matter of maintaining the rights of loan contractors, or of bringing his associates to his way of thinking.

There was an engaging boldness and freshness in his outlook. Austria needed £3,000,000 to equip her armies? Boyd, barely established in London, would raise a loan for the Emperor, even if foreign loans were unpopular, and the well-entrenched mercantile houses in London looked unfavourably on a newcomer. Pitt required money on the Continent? Boyd's foreign correspondents would furnish it. Was temporary accommodation needed for an empty Treasury? The house of Boyd could provide it, even if the Bank of England would not. He was tenacious. When, for a year and more, the firm were repeatedly on the brink of failure, there were his unorthodox, desperate, slightly dishonest, but always ingenious expedients to postpone the day of reckoning. Even after the decision to liquidate had been taken, he never renounced his leadership of the market, and still fought to retain control, and it was only the Chancellor's veto in 1799 that ended his career as a loan contractor. In exile, in Paris, after 1801, his eager, restless spirit was continually chafing at inaction and fretting at the discomforts of poverty — and continually planning for the recovery in his fortunes, which he was convinced must come in the end.

These qualities, however, would have had limited scope without good connections. Success depended on knowing the right people. It is uncertain when and how Boyd first came to know Pitt. Possibly the introduction came through Benfield. At all events, from the beginning of 1794, the two were in frequent touch. Pitt consulted him on questions on which he might be expected to be well-informed, listened to his schemes, even if he did not adopt them, and availed himself of the services, which, for a consideration, the firm of Boyd, Benfield and Co. were always prepared to render to the Government. Next in importance to his connection with Pitt, was that with Dundas, a fellow-countryman for whom Boyd clearly had a great respect, and whose influential position enabled him to be of great service.

Friends in the City of London could be hardly less valuable than those at Westminster. Entry into the higher circles in the City was not gained easily. His alliance with the Thellussons, with the bankers, Robarts, Curtis and Co., and the group of merchants and jobbers headed by Benjamin and Abraham Goldsmid was a shrewd move, yet it was a marriage of convenience, rather than a love match. For the purpose of contracting for loans, the alliance suited everyone, but it did not lead to co-operation in other fields. Boyd was always somewhat of an outsider. He was Pitt's man, and was never accepted by the Whig merchants – Sir Francis Baring, the Thorntons, the Harmans and the Mellishes, who were close to the Bank of England, and formed part of the establishment. Boyd seemed to find his closest friends among his fellow countrymen: John Forbes, Edward MacCulloch, John Petrie, John Fordyce and William MacDowall.

The firm's agency for the Imperial Austrian Government was the pivot on which many of their other activities turned. The business came to them through Walckiers, who provided the link between Boyd, Ker et Cie in Paris, and Veuve Nettine et Fils in Brussels. Within a year of the formation of Boyd, Benfield and Co., a loan of £1,000,000 was under discussion, and within two years a contract had been made for a loan of £6,000,000.

This was big business, even though the amount eventually issued turned out to be only £4,600,000; and it yielded a handsome profit of nearly a quarter of a million pounds. It was not obtained without difficulties and dangers, and had Pitt been unwilling to provide a British guarantee, there would have been no Austrian loan, and Boyd, Benfield and Co. might have remained insignificant, instead of soaring, and eventually crashing. The Imperial loan brought Boyd, Benfield and Co. valuable, if indirect, benefits. It gave them the use of substantial cash balances, which were awaiting remittance, and which could be employed profitably in London or elsewhere. It was only unfortunate that they did not use these opportunities wisely.

The Imperial agency also brought with it business in the foreign exchanges. It was a business in which Boyd had been active in Paris as well as in London, and which he knew thoroughly – as his testimony before the Committees of 1797 shows. Individual transactions brought only moderate profits, but there were ways of making the business yield more than the bare third or half per cent. which was the usual commission charged by merchants for arranging remittances. At all events, it was remunerative enough to make Boyd anxious to carry out large operations for the Government – which he did. There were risks, of course. Correspondents might become insolvent, and bills might come back protested. But this, after all, was a risk run by any merchant with an active foreign business.

The foreign exchanges served as a means of obtaining or granting credit, as well as making remittances. Hence to handle large remittances, whether on account of the Austrian loan or for the British Government, was to control funds which could be profitably employed, either in London or places abroad, and to be able to undertake other operations which, by themselves, would have been unprofitable. Furthermore, if the name of Boyd, Benfield and Co. were seen frequently in mercantile transactions, little comment would be excited if similar bills were negotiated for the firm's own needs. Altogether it would have been difficult, in the circumstances, to have discovered a better foundation for an international merchant banking business.

Closely connected with the business of raising loans for Austria was that of contracting for loans for Great Britain. If Boyd, Benfield and Co.'s widespread network of correspondents abroad enabled them to send abroad the proceeds of Austrian loans, it was only their connections in the City which enabled them in the first place to find subscribers for those loans. That Boyd, a newcomer to the City, could so quickly assume the leadership of a powerful group, and contract for a loan of £18,000,000 for Great Britain, as well as for a loan for Austria, was a tribute to his negotiating skill, as well as to his boldness and imagination. Having gained 'a lease of the market', Boyd was determined to keep it. In establishing the principle that no new loan could be issued before the preceding one was fully paid, he gained a notable victory, and it is doubtful whether, in addition, he needed to hold substantial amounts of stock for his own account. Did his fellow-contractors do so, or did they let him assume the whole burden? Press reports suggest that some of the other members of the group were involved, but such reports cannot altogether be relied upon.

What seems clear is that his sanguine temperament blinded him to the forces which would weaken the market: the financial strain of the war, which would necessitate heavy Government borrowing in the market at rising interest rates; remittances abroad for military expenditures and subsidies, which would cause pressure on the exchanges and a loss of gold; and the efforts of the Bank to protect its position, which would mean a restriction of credit. Ignoring danger signals, he was carried away by the prospect of peace with France, which would bring about a rise in the funds. Once started on this path, he had to continue, at increasing cost, until nemesis overtook him. In addition to speculations by the firm, all three partners operated in the funds for their own account – Boyd, Junior, without his cousin's knowledge. Not for the first time in the history of a business, nor for the last, the unsuccessful private speculations of the partners greatly weakened the firm to which they belonged.

What part did the Bank of England play in all this? What substance was there in Boyd's accusation that the Bank had been hostile to him since the autumn of 1795? Outwardly, the Bank were correct in all their relations with his firm. They gave them considerable discount facilities. Yet it is evident that, beneath the surface, there was ill-feeling on both sides. Boyd's attitude was hostile from early in 1796. That the Bank, for their part, were displeased with Boyd's transactions with the Government, is beyond doubt. Daniel Giles, who was Governor at the critical period, seems to have been more against him than the others, possibly because he was a loan contractor himself, and resented the quick success of a rival. It is, however, doubtful whether the Bank's attitude played a significant part in Boyd's downfall. At the end, nothing the Bank could have done would have saved him.

There remains to be considered the firm's mercantile business. They had adequate capital and good connections abroad, yet in the six years of their existence they ran into serious difficulties in this field. Of their consignment business and their transactions in merchandise, little is known. As part of their mercantile business, they made advances to other merchants at home and abroad, and it was unfortunate that two of the largest borrowers, Alexander Houston and Co. and Charles Herries and Co., found themselves in difficulties. Alexander Houston and Co. had a first-class reputation, but even before Boyd started to finance them, they were over-extended on the basis of short-term credit on the London market. Thus when the slave insurrection broke out in Grenada and St. Vincent in 1795, they were vulnerable, and only survived thanks to the wealth of their partners and government aid. Charles Herries and Co. lost heavily as a result of the French Revolution, and, lacking the capital resources and governmental support which sustained Houstons, they failed in 1798. It is difficult to escape the impression that Boyd's continued advances to Herries and Co. were based more on a long-established connection with a compatriot, than on an objective appraisal of the risks involved. However sound these firms might have been, there was slight justification for Boyd's advancing £400,000 to Houstons and nearly £200,000 to Herries, when his firm's own capital was only £85,000. Some of their smaller loans, too, became illiquid. Veuve Nettine et Fils were allowed to draw £33,000, even though the Austrian Netherlands were first threatened, and then occupied, by the French. It was a generous, but rash, gesture to Boyd's former partner, Walckiers. Generous, too, were Boyd's advances to Laborde's relations, in exile in England and without means. As in other affairs, his optimism led him into trouble.

Boyd lived in a world which was changing, politically and economically, under the pressures of revolution and war. Markets, not least the London money market, were uncertain and unstable. In this environment some entrepreneurs flourished, while others stagnated, or failed. The pressure of competition and the fear of failure were always in the background, and the temptation to step just a little over the thin line which separates honesty from dishonesty was sometimes irresistible. As has been seen, there were several occasions on which Boyd's conduct was open to criticism, but he has to be judged in the light of contemporary mores.

That here and there, corruption and sharp practices could be found in the City, even within the Bank of England, is undeniable. For instance, it had long been the practice for the head of the Bank's Discount Office to receive from firms discounting bills, money and presents 'to a very considerable amount', and it was discovered, and stopped, only in 1804.[1] Another case came up in 1810, when Abraham Goldsmid attempted to gain a preference in the funding of Exchequer Bills, and had to admit publicly to having given £5,000 of stock to the clerks of the Exchequer Bill Office.[2] On the Stock Exchange there were 'many cases of ingenious deception', of which the fabrication by Charles Random de Beranger of the news of the death of Napoleon in 1814 was the most notorious.[3] Although few instances of this sort came into the open, there were no doubt others which lay beneath the surface. In political life corruption and bribery were rife, and evoked few protests. Boyd's partner, Benfield, despite his reprehensible conduct in India, obtained, thanks to his wealth, a seat in Parliament and a partnership in the City and he was by no means the only one. On the other hand, there were many, like Henry Thornton, whose rectitude could not be doubted.

Boyd had many of the qualities of a successful entrepreneur. He was ambitious, bold and tenacious; he had an inventive mind, a persuasive tongue and more than a little taste for speculation. Thanks to Benfield, he started with adequate capital. What he often lacked was sound judgement, and this was his undoing. In the eighteenth century, as today, success or failure in merchant banking depended on that elusive quality of judgement.

1. Clapham, *Bank of England*, op.cit., vol. II, p. 13.
2. Cope, Goldsmids, op.cit., pp. 188–9.
3. Edward Victor Morgan and Wm. A. Thomas, *The Stock Exchange*, . . , London, Elek Books, [2nd. ed., 1969] pp. 50–1.

Sources

The following abbreviations are used in the list of sources below and in the text:

Adm   Admiralty
AN   Archives Nationales, Paris
BL   British Library
CUL   Cambridge University Library
HMSO   HM Stationery Office
IO   India Office Library and Records, BL
NLS   National Library of Scotland, Edingburgh
PMG   Paymaster-General
PRO   Public Record Office
SRO   Scottish Record Office, Edinburgh
ULL   University of London Library

Manuscripts

Admiralty — Navy Board Minutes, PRO. Adm. 106.
         — Transport Board, PRO, Adm. 108.
Archives Nationales, Paris, AN Series T and T*.
Bank of England, Committee of Treasury Minutes
         — Court Minutes
         — Drawing Accounts Ledgers.
         — Stock Ledgers
Baring Archives
Benfield, Paul, Papers, IO
Boyd-Dundas Letters, ULL, MS. 898
Calonne, Charles Alexandre de, Papers, 1785–1800, PRO

Chancery, Judicial Proceedings (Equity Side), PRO
Chatham Papers, PRO
Dundas, Henry, Papers of, Kress Library, Harvard University
East India Company, Court Minutes, IO
        — Stock Ledgers, IO
Exchequer, Extents and Inquisitions relating to Crown Debtors, PRO.
Forbes of Fettercairn Papers, NLS
Foreign Office, Austria, General Correspondence, PRO
        — Switzerland, General Correspondence, PRO
Hope Archives, Gemeentelijke Archiefdienst, Amsterdam.
Houston, Alexander & Co., Papers relating to, NLS
        — Ledger K, NLS
Huskisson Papers, BL
Liverpool Papers, BL
Lloyds Register of Shipping
McDowall of Garthland Papers, SRO
Melville Papers, NLS
Paymaster-General, Ledgers, PRO
Pitt Correspondence, CUL
Probate Register, PRO
St. George's, Hanover Square, Register of Marriages
Short, William, Papers of, Library of Congress, Washington, D.C.
Stuart Stevenson Papers, NLS
Treasury Board Minutes, PRO
Treasury, Commissioners for French Claims, Papers, PRO
        — In-Letters, PRO
        — Out-Letters, General, PRO
U.S. Stock Ledgers, National Archives, Washington, D.C.

Official Reports and Publications

House of Lords

Report of Secret Committee. . to enquire into the Order of Council of . . .
   1797.

House of Commons

Accounts and Papers, 1796–7.
   Account of . . . Sums . . . remitted for . . . the Loan of 1795.
   Account of the Sum of £2,500,000 to defray Extraordinary Expenses for
     1796.
   Account of the Advances made . . . for His Imperial Majesty.
   Account of the Dates of the several Bills drawn . . . for His Imperial
     Majesty.
   List . . . of the subscribers to the loan of £18,000,000 for . . . 1797.
   Reports from the Commitee of Secrecy . . . [on] . . . the outstanding
     Demands on the Bank, 1797.

Resolutions &c relating to the Imperial Loans.
Accounts and Papers, 1797–8. Account of . . . Mortgage Actions of the
  Bank of Vienna.
Reports from the Select Committee upon the Tenth Naval Report, 1805.
Accounts and Papers, 1821, vol., 23.
    Convention between His Majesty and the Emperor of 4th May, 1795.
    Correspondence Relating to . . . the Loans raised for Austria.
    Claims on France . . . Papers relating thereto.

Parliamentary Proceedings

Cobbett's Parliamentary Debates, vol. 5
Commons Journals, vol. 51
Debrett's Parliamentary Register, vol. XLIV
Parliamentary Debates, new series (Hansard), vol. 10
Parliamentary History, vols, 31, 32 and 33

Statutes

35 Geo III, c.15, c.50, and c.80.
35 Geo III, c.6 (Ireland).
36 Geo III, c.74.
37 Geo III, c.27, c.45 and c.57.

Newspapers and other Periodicals

Annual Register, 1795 and 1797
London Gazette, 1799 and 1800
London Newspapers: Evening Mail, London Chronicle, Morning Chronicle,
    Morning Post, Oracle, St. James' Chronicle, The Times, True Briton
Other Newspapers: Glasgow Courier, Saunder's News Letter (Dublin)
Lowndes, W. London Directories, 1794 and 1795
Sessions Papers (Scotland)
Réimpression de l'ancien Moniteur (Paris), vols. XVI and XXII

Contemporary Books and Pamphlets (to 1837)

Bank — the Stock Exchange — the Bankers . . . London, E. Wilson, 1821.

Baring, Sir Francis, Observations on the Publication of Walter Boyd, Esq., M.P., London, J. Sewell, J. Debrett, 1801.

Benfield, Paul, Case of Paul Benfield, Esq., . . . [London, 1803]
— Circular to the Creditors of the late House of Boyd, Benfield & Co., 1803

Boyd, Walter, Letter to the Creditors of the House of Boyd, Benfield & Co. . . London, Henry Reynell, 1800.
— Letter to the Rt. Hon. William Pitt. . . London, J. Wright, 1801.
— 2nd ed., London, J. Wright, J. Mawman, 1801.
— Observations on Lord Grenville's Essay on the Sinking Fund, London, J. Hatchard, 1828.
— Reflections on the Financial System of Great Britain . . . London, J. Hatchard, 1815.

British Merchant, Guildhall broadside 6.161,1795.

Encyclopaedia Britannica, 3rd ed., vol. VIII, Edinburgh, A. Bell and C. MacFarquhar, 1797.

Grellier, John J., Terms of all the Loans . . . London, John Richardson and J.M. Richardson, 1812.

Grenville, William Wyndham, baron, On the supposed advantages of a Sinking Fund, London, J. Murray, 1828.

Macpherson, David, Annals of Commerce, Manufactures, Fisheries, and Navigation . . . London, Edinburgh, 1805.

Morgan, William, Facts addressed to the Serious Attention of the People of Great Britain . . ., London, 1796

Riquetti, Honoré Gabriel, Comte de Mirabeau, De la Caisse d'Escompte, [Paris?] 1785.

Scottish Corporation: An Account of the Institution, Progress and Present State of the Scottish Corporation in London . . . London, 1806–12.

Sinclair, Sir John, Letters written to the Governor and Directors of the Bank of England, in September, 1796, . . London, 1797.
— History of the Public Revenue of the British Empire, 3rd ed. London, T. Cadell and W. Davies, 1803–4.

Thornton, Henry, An Enquiry into the Nature and Effects of the Paper Credit of Great Britain, ed. with an introduction by F.A. von Hayek, London, G. Allen & Unwin, 1939.

Correspondence and Documents Published After 1837

Auckland, Journal and Correspondence of William, Lord Auckland, vol. III, London, Richard Bentley, 1862.

Historical Manuscripts Commission, 14th Report, Appendix, Part V (Dropmore Papers), vol. II, 1894, vol. III, 1899.

Jefferson, Thomas, Papers of, ed. Julian P. Boyd, vol. 16, Princeton, Princeton University Press, 1961.

Parrel, Christian de, Les Papiers de Calonne, Paris, Cavaillon Mistral, 1932

Thürheim, A. Graf, Briefe des Grafen Mercy-Argenteau . . . an den Grafen Louis Starhemberg . ., Innsbruck, Verlag der Wagnerschen Universitäts-Buchhandlung, 1884.

Vivenot, Alfred von, Quellen zur Geschichte der Politik Oesterreichs während der französischen Revolutionskriege, vols. IV and V, Vienna, Wilhelm Braumüller, 1885 and 1890.

— Vertrauliche Briefe des Freiherrn von Thugut, Vienna, Wilhelm Braumüller, 1872.

— Thugut, Clerfayt, und Wurmser, Original-Documente, Vienna, Wilhelm Braumüller, 1869.

Scott, Sir Walter, Journal of, ed. John G. Tait and W.M. Parker, London, Oliver and Boyd, 1950.

Wraxall, Sir Nathaniel William, Historical and Posthumous Memoirs of, 1772–1784, ed. Henry B. Wheatley, London, Bickers & Son, 1884, vol. IV.

Books and Pamphlets Published After 1837

Acres, Wilfrid Marston, The Bank of England from Within, 1694–1900, London, Oxford University Press, 1931.

Addington, Rt. Hon. Henry, first Viscount Sidmouth, Life and Correspondence of, ed. Hon. George Pellew, London, J. Murray, 1847.

Alger, John Goldworth, Englishmen in the French Revolution, London, S. Low, Marston, Searle & Rivington, 1889.

— Napoleon's British Visitors and Captives, 1801–1815, Westminster, A. Constable & Co., 1904.

Antonetti, Guy, Une Maison de Banque à Paris au XVIIIe siècle: Greffulhe Montz et Cie, 1789–1793, Paris, Editions Cujas, 1963.

Barker, Theodore Cardwell, The Glassmakers Pilkington: 1826–1976, London, Weidenfeld and Nicholson, 1977.

Bigo, Robert, La Caisse d'Escompte (1776–1793), Paris, Les Presses Universitaires de France, 1927.

Biograhie Nationale. . . de Belgique, Brussels, Establissements Émile Bruylant, vol. 13, 1894–5, vol. 26, 1936–8.

Biographie Universelle (Michaud) Ancienne et Moderne, reprint of ed. of 1854, vols. 11 and 22.

Bouchary, Jean, Le Marché des changes de Paris à la fin du XVIIIe siècle, Paris, P. Hartmann, 1937.

— Les Manieurs d'Argent à Paris à la fin du XVIIIe siècle, Paris, M. Rivière et Cie, 1939–43.

Brooke, John, see Namier.

Buist, Marten G., At Spes non Fracta, Hope & Co., 1770–1815, The Hague, Nijhoff, 1974.

Checkland, Sydney George, Two Scottish West India Liquidations after 1793, Scottish Journal of Political Economy, June, 1957.

Clapham, Sir John Harold, The Private Business of the Bank of England, 1744–1800, Economic History Review, vol. XI, 1941.
— The Bank of England, a History, Cambridge University Press, 1944.

Collyer, James Nicolson and Pocock, John Innes, Historical Record of the Light Horse Volunteers of London and Westminster . . ., London, Wright, 1843.

Cope, Sydney Raymond, The Goldsmids and the Development of the London Money Market. . ., Economica, May, 1942.
—The Original Security Bank, Economica, February, 1946.
— The Stock-Brokers find a home: Guildhall Studies in London History, April, 1977.
— The Stock Exchange Revisited: A New Look at the Market in Securities in London. . ., Economica, February, 1978.

Courtois, Alph., et fils, Histoire de la Banque de France. . ., Paris, Librairie de Guillaumon et Cie, 1875.

Cussans, John Edwin, History of Hertfordshire. . ., London, Chatto & Windus, 1870–81.

Devine, T.M. An eighteenth century business élite: Glasgow West India Merchants, c. 1750–1815, Scottish Historical Review, April, 1978.

Ehrenberg, Richard, Grosse Vermögen . . . Das Haus Parish in Hamburg, Jena, Verlag von Gustav Fischer, 1925, vol. II.

Feavearyear, Sir Albert Edgar, revised by E. Victor Morgan, The Pound Sterling. . ., Oxford, Clarendon Press, 1963.

Furber, Holden, Henry Dundas, First Viscount Melville, 1742–1811. . ., London, Oxford University Press, 1931.
— John Company at Work. . ., Cambridge, Mass., Harvard University Press, 1948.

Hawtrey, Sir Ralph G., Currency and Credit, 4th ed., London, Longmans, Green & Co., 1950.

Hayek, F.A., von, see Thornton.

H.E.B., Flight of Capital from Revolutionary France, American Historical Review, vol. XLI, July, 1936.

Helleiner, Karl F., The Imperial Loans, Oxford, Clarendon Press, 1965.

Holworthy, Richard, The Monumental Inscriptions in the Church and Churchyard of Bromley, Co. Kent, London, Mitchel Hughes and Clarke, 1922.

Horsburgh, E.L.S., Bromley, Kent, from the Earliest Times to the Present Century, [London] Hodder & Stoughton, 1929.

Jenks, Leland Hamilton, The Migration of British Capital to 1875, New York, Alfred A. Knopf, 1927.

Koch, Christophe Guillaumede, and F. Schöl, Histoire Abregee des Traités de Paix. . . vol. II, Paris, Gide fils, 1817–18.

Lüthy, Herbert, La Banque protestante en France. . . vol. II, Paris, S.E.V.P.E.N., 1961.

Mathiez, Albert, Robespierre Terroriste, Paris, La Renaissance du Livre, 1921.

Morgan, Edward Victor and W.A. Thomas, The Stock Exchange. . ., London, Elek Books, [1969].

Namier, Sir Lewis and John Brooke, The House of Commons 1754–1790, vol. II, HMSO, 1964.

Olivier—Martin, François Jean Marie, L'Organisation Corporative de la France d'ancien régime, Paris, Recueil Sirey, 1938.

Pimodan, Comte de, Le comte F-C de Merci-Argenteau, Paris, Librairie Plon, 1911.

Pirenne, Henri, Histoire de Belgique, vol. V, Brussels, Maurice Lamertin, 1926.

Pocock, see Collyer, J.N.

Pressnell, Leslie S., Country Banking in the Industrial Revolution, Oxford, Clarendon Press, 1956.

Price, Frederick George Hilton, A handbook of London Bankers. . . London, Leadenhall Press, 1890–1.

Price, Jacob M, France and the Chesapeake. . . Ann Arbor, University of Michigan Press, 1973.

Riley, James C., International Government Finance and the Amsterdam Capital Market, 1740–1815, Cambridge University Press, 1980.

Rose, John Holland, William Pitt and the Great War, London, G. Bell & Sons, 1911.

Sherwig, John M., Guineas and Gunpowder: British Foreign Aid in the Wars with France 1793–1815, Harvard University Press, Cambridge, Mass., [1969].

Silberling, Norman John, Financial and monetary policy of Great Britain during the Napoleonic wars, Quarterly Journal of Economics, Cambridge, Mass, vol. 38, 1924.

Taylor, George V., The Paris Bourse on the Eve of the Revolution, 1781–1789, American Historical Review, July, 1962.

Toulmin, Joshua, History of Taunton, new edition by James Savage, Taunton, John Poole, 1822.

Wheeler, James Talboys, A short history of India. . ., London, Macmillan & Co., 1880.

GLOSSARY

ACCOMMODATION BILLS (or accommodation paper): bills not drawn in connection with commercial transactions, but to raise money on credit.

ANNUITIES: stock on which regular payments of interest are made, usually half yearly. Perpetual annuities, such as 3 per cent. Consols, are annuities on which no date for the repayment of principal has been fixed. There are also annuities, payments on which cease after the period of year specified in the contract, without any repayment of principal as such. If the period is based on the life of a person or persons, they are termed life annuities.

ASSIGNEES IN BANKRUPTCY: persons who are elected by the creditors, or appointed with their approval, to whom the debtor's estate is assigned.

BEAR: a person who sells stock for delivery at a future date, in the expectation that meanwhile prices will fall, so that he can buy in at a lower price than the price at which he sold.

BILL OF EXCHANGE: an order in writing by one person (the drawer) to another (the drawee) requiring him to pay at a fixed or determinable future time or on sight or on demand, a certain sum to a third person (the payee) or to his order or to bearer. A bill payable at sight or on demand must be paid on presentation to the drawee. When a bill payable at so many days after sight is presented to the drawee he must note on it the date of sighting, so as to establish the date on which it becomes payable. Bills of exchange are sometimes called drafts.

BOND: a deed whereby a person (the obligor) obliges himself, his heirs, executors and administrators, to pay a certan sum of money to another at a certain time. There is often a condition added that if the obliger does some particular act, the obligation shall be void, but will otherwise remain in full force. A bond to secure the repayment of money is generally twice the amount of the principal to be repaid.

BOND (goods in bond): goods liable to customs duties are stored in special warehouses known as bonded warehouses under charge of customs officers until the importer pays the duties and takes possession of the goods.

BULL: a person who buys stock in the expectation of being able later to sell at a higher price.

CALL MONEY: money deposited by banks with brokers, repayable on demand.

CERTIFICATE (in bankruptcy): a certificate granted by not less than four-fifths of the creditors, signed by the commissioners and authenticated by the lord chancellor, entitling the bankrupt to a decent and resonable allowance out of his effects, for his support.

CHECK (or cheque): a written order by a person (the drawer) to a bank or banker to pay a specified sum to a person (the payee) or to bearer.

COMMISSION OF BANKRUPT: an award made on the application of one or more creditors to persons, known as commissioners, who, if they have proof that the debtor has committed an act of bankruptcy, declare him bankrupt.

CONTINUATION: the carrying over of the settlement of a Stock Exchange transaction from one settlement date to the next.

DEBENTURE: a certificate certifying that a certan sum of money is owing to the person named in it, and frequently stating the rate of interest and repayment terms.

DEMURRAGE: detention of a vessel beyong the time agreed upon; the payment made for such detention.

DISCOUNTING: the purchase of a bill of exchange or promissory note at its face value, less simple interest from the date of purchase to the due date. Although discounting a bill or note at 5 per cent. gave the discounter a return of slightly more than 5 per cent., this was not regarded as usury (q.v.).

DRAFT: see bill of exchange.

EXCHEQUER BILL: a bill bearing interest, often at 3 pence or 3½ pence a day for every £100 principal, issued under authority of Parliament at the Exchequer Bill Office.

EXPORT POINT: the rate of exchange at which it pays to export gold or silver coin, or bullion, after allowing for the cost of shipment and insurance and loss of interest during transit.

EXTENT: a process by which the body, lands and goods of a debtor who has defaulted may be taken to compel payment of the debt. The sheriff has to cause the lands and goods to be appraised before he delivers them to the creditor.

EXTENT OF THE CROWN: all obligations to the Crown are preferred before those to any other creditor who has not obtained judgement before the Crown commenced the action.

FLOATING DEBT: short-term debt.

FUNDED DEBT: long-term or perpetual debt.

FUNDING: the process of converting floating debt into funded debt.

FUNDS: a general term applied to the annuities and other government obligations forming part of the national debt, particularly to that part of the debt which is quoted on the Stock Exchange.

JOBBER: originally a speculator who deals in stocks for time (q.v.); later a middle-man between buyers and sellers, called on the Stock Exchange a dealer.

LAC, LACK, LAKH: one hundred thousand.

MONEY, A TRANSACTION FOR: a Stock Exchange transaction which has to be settled within three days.

OCTROI: a privilege, right, or concession granted by a government.

OMNIUM: the aggregate of the different stocks given to subscribers to a government loan.

PENNY (pl. PENCE): a coin worth one two-hundred-and-fortieth of a pound.

PROMISSORY NOTE: a plain and direct engagement in writing by a person (the maker) to pay a specified sum to another person (the payee), or to his order or to bearer.

PROTEST: action by a notary on behalf of the payee or an indorsee of a bill which the drawee refuses to accept, or having accepted it refuses to pay it at maturity.

REMITTANCE: money sent from one place, or person, to another. Foreign remittances were usually made by sending bills of exchange, coin or bullion, and sometimes by sending securities or goods.

SCRIP (an abbreviation of SUBSCRIPTION RECEIPT): a receipt issued for a portion of a loan subsribed, usually on payment of the first instalment.

SURRENDER: a voluntary act by a debtor which protects him from arrest until his final examination has been made.

TIME, A TRANSACTION FOR: a Stock Exchange transaction for future settlement, usually at the next settlement or account day.

USANCE: the period fixed by mercantile custom or usage, between the date a bill of exchange is drawn and the date on which it becomes payable. Originally this period was in many places a month, but when in course of time the period became longer, it was frequently expressed as so many usances. For example, a bill payable at two months was expressed as payable at two usances.

USURY: interest charged at a rate higher than the maximum rate of 5 per cent. allowed under 12 Anne, st.2, c.16.

Index